Praise f

THE DEVIL'S TRICK a

T0017462

"In his trademark style, Boyko delivers anot.   ...arrative, exploring Canada's contentious and contested involvement in the Vietnam War. . . . In this revealing book, Boyko lays bare the lies and lessons of a foreign war that bled into Canadian society, and which still remain relevant." —Tim Cook, author of *The Fight for History*

"Among the wealth of Vietnam War analysis, John Boyko's *The Devil's Trick: How Canada Fought the Vietnam War* deserves a respected place. . . . This book has many strengths. And, if a Canadian historian, reporter, Asia watcher, or diplomat in training ever needed a primer on placing the war in its time, Boyko's first thousand words do the trick." —*Canada's History*

"[A] compelling study. . . . John Boyko is an impressive historian with seven [other] well-received books to his credit. . . . [A]mbitious and far-reaching . . . [*The Devil's Trick*] skillfully unfolds a complex narrative. . . . I came away not only impressed by the power of the narratives he creates but by his sensitive handling of issues that continue to affect us. . . . [A] powerful, thought-provoking book." —*The Peterborough Examiner*

"Historian John Boyko is a good researcher and an even better writer." —*The Tyee*

"Boyko embraces his story's complexity, and with engaging prose he focuses on those who navigated the maelstrom—cursed, like all of us, with their own circumstances, preconceived notions, and imperfect information. . . . *The Devil's Trick* is also remarkable in its balanced treatment of perhaps the most politicized conflict since the Second World War. Too many books on the Vietnam War are mere polemics, with just enough history to make them seem credible. Boyko's telling, aided by his interviews with four of his six subjects, lets the characters help drive things through their own words and memories. Boyko asks his reader not to view the Vietnam War as just or unjust but to see that war is hell, with flawed human beings on all sides and caught in the middle." —*Literary Review of Canada*

"Boyko [is] a gifted storyteller. . . . Boyko draws lessons from each story of this war—how it affected our diplomacy, our economic interests, our emerging identity as a separate nation, our humanitarian policy and our international reputation. His eloquent summary is tinged with hope and warning." —*Diplomat and International Canada*

ALSO BY JOHN BOYKO

Sir John's Echo: The Voice for a Stronger Canada

Cold Fire: Kennedy's Northern Front

*Blood and Daring: How Canada Fought the
American Civil War and Forged a Nation*

Bennett: The Rebel Who Challenged and Changed a Nation

Into the Hurricane: Attacking Socialism and the CCF

Last Steps to Freedom: The Evolution of Canadian Racism

Politics: Conflict and Compromise

JOHN BOYKO

THE DEVIL'S TRICK

HOW CANADA FOUGHT THE VIETNAM WAR

Vintage Canada

VINTAGE CANADA EDITION, 2022

Copyright © 2021 John Boyko

Published by Vintage Canada, a division of Penguin Random House Canada Limited, Toronto, in 2022. Originally published in hardcover by Alfred A. Knopf Canada, a division of Penguin Random House Canada Limited, Toronto, in 2021. Distributed by Penguin Random House Canada Limited, Toronto.

Vintage Canada and colophon are registered trademarks.

www.penguinrandomhouse.ca

Library and Archives Canada Cataloguing in Publication
Title: The devil's trick : how Canada fought the Vietnam War / John Boyko.
Names: Boyko, John, 1957- author.
Identifiers: Canadiana 20190158697 | ISBN 9780735278028 (softcover)
Subjects: LCSH: Vietnam War, 1961-1975—Participation, Canadian. | LCSH: Vietnam War, 1961-1975—Diplomatic history.
Classification: LCC DS558.6.C3 B69 2022 | DDC 959.704/3371—dc23

Cover and interior design: Andrew Roberts
Image credits: Cover: (helmet) © GBlakeley, iStock/Getty Images; p. 9, courtesy UBC Archives Photograph Collection; p. 37, courtesy Blair Seaborn; p. 67, Mike Slaughter/*Toronto Star* via Getty Images; p. 101, courtesy Joe Erickson; p. 131, courtesy Doug Carey; p. 161, courtesy Rebecca Trinh

Printed in United States of America

2 4 6 8 9 7 5 3 1

Penguin
Random House
VINTAGE CANADA

This book is dedicated to
Sue, Jennifer, Kenzie, and Anna,
and all their stories yet to be told.

CONTENTS

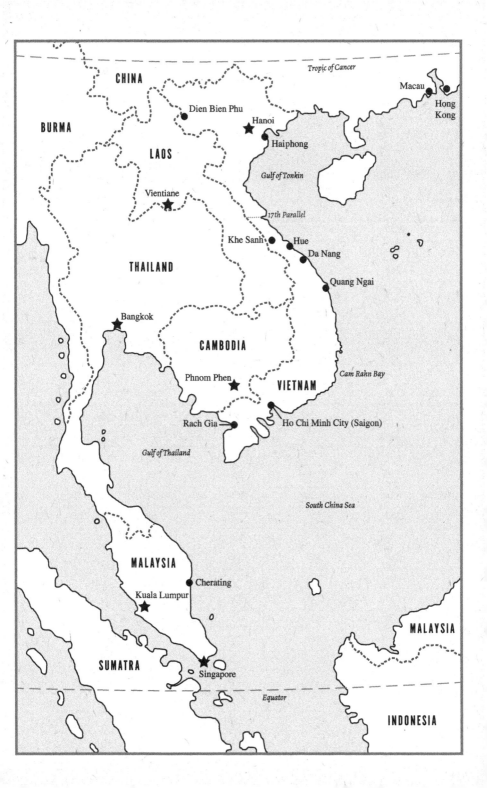

STORIES THAT MATTER

War is about sending our children to kill theirs. The devil's trick is convincing leaders that war is desirable, the rest of us that it's acceptable, and combatants that everything they are doing and seeing is normal or, at least, necessary.

Canada has always been a warrior state. It has fought or involved itself in war proudly, often reluctantly, and sometimes covertly. Some wars were noble pursuits and others just good business. Sometimes forgotten, and even at the time widely denied, is that among Canada's wars was the Vietnam War, the slow-motion tragedy that revealed the devil's trick at its wiliest.

There were Canadians in Vietnam fighting and dying in American uniforms; others were working in Canadian-run hospitals; and there were Canadian diplomats in Vietnam who tried to stop the war before it began, and then monitored its carnage. There were Canadian weapons in Vietnamese cities, villages, and jungles and falling from the sky. Back home, young Americans flooded north to escape the war, while Canadians were taking to the streets to urge lawmakers to stop it, or at least end Canada's involvement. When the guns finally fell silent, if only for a while, more Canadian diplomats headed to Vietnam. Soon, thousands of desperate refugees fled postwar madness, many finding sanctuary in Canada. The war changed everything and everyone it touched. The war changed Canadians. It changed Canada.

One cannot fully comprehend the Vietnam War without understanding Canada's role in it. One cannot fully understand Canada or the United States without considering the war's lies and lessons. We deserve the truth, and we need the lessons, because the Vietnam War still echoes in the stories we tell ourselves about who we are, who we are not, and who we aspire to be.

We must begin by placing the war in its time. First, the war's American phase and Canada's involvement, from the mid-1950s to the late 1970s, occurred during a period of sweeping changes in Canada and the United States that challenged all that had been considered certain. A generation that had suffered the Depression and fought the Second World War and were finally enjoying peace and prosperity, were being confronted by attacks on unspoken rules. Those in defiance of all that was thought proper presented discomforting questions about who should be in charge and who should know their place; whether more people should share the benefits of good times; and even the relevance of material comfort. The Civil Rights and burgeoning Indigenous Rights movements were forcing re-evaluations of original sins. Quebec's Quiet Revolution saw bombs killing innocents amid demands for Canada's splintering or, at a minimum, a fundamental redefinition of nationhood. A youth quake, reflected in music, fashion, art, and attitude, and fuelled by the raw clout of baby-boom numbers was redefining social norms. The Women's Movement's Second Wave and the licence afforded by the newly invented birth control pill were slowly spurring changes from bedrooms to boardrooms.

As the war progressed through the sixties, its brutality was seen every night on the widely watched Canadian and American television evening news programs—along with police dogs ripping flesh, night sticks cracking heads, radicals throwing rocks at the prime minister, fires consuming buildings, the public murders of progressive leaders, protests in universities, and young men burning draft cards.

Within the broad context of so much challenge and change, the war united some families and divided others. It unified the movements and linked individuals in the streets with those privately hoping for change. In Canada and the United States, Vietnam became a symbol for all that was wrong and needed to be fixed or torn down. Until late in the war, Canadian and American political leaders and the business and media elites who supported it seemed wedded to the status quo. The power structures they represented became the ramparts to be breached by those wanting to replace the old with the new. Communities split as the elites drew support from those who felt that anti-war beliefs, the various movements, and all those long-haired kids were unpatriotic and dangerous.

Second, we must contextualize the war by recalling that it was part of the larger Cold War. In the Second World War the liberal West joined the communist Soviet Union to defeat the fascist Nazis. Even before Hitler shot out what was left of his brains, however, the alliance was crumbling. At the February 1945 Yalta Conference, Britain, the United States, and the Soviet Union planned a postwar world with Soviets and Americans struggling for global dominance. With the war's end, guns and money were sent to the competing sides in every nationalist movement, civil war, and crooked election. In August 1949 the Soviet Union successfully tested its first nuclear weapon. The West appeared to be no longer safe. Just two months later, a decades-long revolution ended with the formation of a communist government in China. The West appeared to be no longer winning.

In 1945 Igor Gouzenko, a young clerk working in Ottawa's Soviet embassy, had defected and revealed there were communist spies operating in Western countries. In February 1950, American senator Joseph McCarthy began insisting that communists had infiltrated unions, the government, the military, and Hollywood. People were encouraged to see "reds" under every bed and to choose to be dead rather than red. Four months later, communist North Korea invaded the non-communist South, and Canada joined the American-led coalition to push it back. Meanwhile, books, comics, and movies told of alien invasions as tremendously popular cowboy movies and television shows spoke of taming frontiers—but they were all really about battling communists. Three strings of radar lines across Canada's north watched for incoming Soviet bombers. Communities practised air raid drills, families built fallout shelters, and teachers taught children to hide under their desks in the faint hope that the thin bit of plywood would protect them from a nuclear onslaught.

The "Red Scare" led most Americans and Canadians to support more of their tax money being diverted to defence and more of their personal freedoms being ignored to weed out subversives. For a while, it also led a majority of Canadians and Americans to support the fighting of communists in Vietnam as parents tucked their children into bed each night knowing that either by design or accident, nuclear annihilation could be visited upon them before breakfast.

Finally, we must also consider the war from the Vietnamese perspective. The war's roots can be traced back to 111 BCE, when an ethnic group called the Viet was conquered by China, leading to a centuries-long struggle for independence. In the 1600s Portuguese and then French missionaries began converting the region's people to Christianity. In 1857 French ships arrived to support priests who were being mistreated by locals. Attacks on those ships led to an invasion and by 1897 the creation of French Indochina, composed of what later became Vietnam, Laos, and Cambodia. Vietnamese nationalists attacked the French colonizers as they had the Chinese.

Ho Chi Minh was among a group of outspoken nationalists deported by the French in 1911. Ho's thirty-year exile took him around the world, even to the United States, where he lived for a while in Boston and New York City. Ho was in Paris when world leaders assembled at Versailles to settle the recently ended First World War. American president

Woodrow Wilson was promoting self-determination as a guiding principle of the postwar world, and Ho wrote to him asking that it be applied to Vietnam by having the French leave and his people granted self-rule. Wilson either did not see or ignored the plea. With America's blessing, the French kept their colony. Ho travelled to the Soviet Union and China, where he studied, spoke, and wrote of the yoke of colonialism—and communism as a means to end it.[1]

In September 1940, with France distracted by its defeat by Hitler, Japan took Vietnam as part of its territorial expansion. Four months later, by then in his mid-fifties, malarial, and frightfully thin, Ho returned home, with five comrades. It was at this time that he adopted the latest of several aliases—Ho Chi Minh, meaning "He Who Enlightens." In May 1941 his small group merged with other nationalists to become the League for the Independence of Vietnam, the Vietminh. It was soon carrying out guerrilla actions against the Japanese. Ho contacted agents of America's Office of Strategic Services, the precursor to the CIA, which supplied him with weapons and support. He worked briefly with OSS officer Lieutenant Colonel Paul Dewey, who in September 1945 was killed in an ambush, America's first Vietnam casualty.

With the dropping of atomic bombs on Japan, Ho seized the moment, oversaw the abdication and exile of the puppet emperor Bao Dai and, on September 2, 1945, declared Vietnam a unified, independent state with himself as president. Before a cheering crowd at Hanoi's Ba Dinh Square, he began his speech by quoting Thomas Jefferson in espousing the idea that he pledged would guide Vietnam's new government: "All men are created equal; they are endowed by their Creator with certain unalienable rights; and among these are life, liberty, and the pursuit of happiness."[2]

Weeks later, with the support of British troops and the tacit backing of American president Harry Truman, France overthrew Ho's government and re-established its Indochinese colony.[3] Ho negotiated with the French and some agreements were signed but, when it became clear that France would never allow genuine self-rule, Ho ignited a new guerilla war to win back his country. Understanding the power of Cold War alliances, he declared himself a communist and won Chinese and Soviet support.

In 1946 the United States gave $160 million to help the French in Indochina.[4] In 1950, while also fighting in Korea, Truman declared that the United States would not allow the Vietminh to take Vietnam, arguing that its fall would eventually result in the entire region becoming communist. The first American Military Assistance and Advisory Group (MAAG) arrived in Vietnam in September with money, advisors, and weapons to augment French forces.

The conflict had thereby become a Vietnamese civil war, a nationalist war of liberation, a European colonial war, and a Cold War proxy war. By the end of 1952 the United States had sent $1 billion to support French efforts.[5] Its funding rose annually, so that by 1953 it was paying 80 percent of the war's escalating cost. Meanwhile, with 100,000 French troops in Vietnam and already having suffered over 50,000 casualties, the French peoples' patience for the war was evaporating.[6] And then came the turning point.

French general Henri Navarre had created a French fortress in a long, narrow valley in northwest Vietnam. Fifteen thousand young men dug in. The brilliant Vietminh general Vo Nguyen Giap, one of the handful of exiled nationalists who had returned to Vietnam with Ho back in 1941, moved fifty thousand troops to the surrounding hills. On March 13, 1954, his artillery began pounding the French at Dien Bien Phu.

The battle captured the world's attention and certainly that of American president Dwight Eisenhower, who had publicly spoken of the danger of Vietnam becoming communist lest surrounding countries fell like dominos.[7] Eisenhower was urged by the French and his own advisors to send help. His generals asked him to consider a nuclear strike. The president said no.[8]

The nations involved in the recently suspended Korean War and the ongoing Indochinese War had agreed to meet in Geneva to settle both. On May 8, 1954, just as delegates were taking their places at the first plenary session, they received the startling news that the French had surrendered at Dien Bien Phu. The Geneva Conference, focused by the French defeat, led directly to Canada's involvement in what became the war's next phase.

In the pages that follow, six Canadians will act as our guides with their experiences leading us through the story of Canada's Vietnam War. First is Canadian brigadier general Sherwood Lett, a decorated veteran of two world wars, who led the Canadian delegation that arrived in Vietnam shortly after the Geneva Conference, a decade before the landing of American troops. Lett and the Canadians risked their lives enforcing an unstable peace while wondering if they were stopping a war or merely acting as American lackeys and midwives to a new one.

With American battleships steaming across the Pacific, respected Canadian diplomat Blair Seaborn spirited himself to Hanoi for a clandestine meeting with North Vietnam's prime minister. His top-secret reports presented Washington with a road map to peace with honour. If Seaborn could convince the Americans to see the vision of the future he was so clearly providing, those ships could turn around and the war could be stopped before it began.

Claire Culhane worked in a Canadian hospital in Vietnam. But, enraged by what she was seeing, she returned home ahead of schedule. Culhane confronted Canadians with the lies they were being told and all they were choosing to ignore about complicity with the CIA and arms sales to the Americans. She implored Canadians and their leaders to consider the morality of supporting what she declared an immoral war.

Joe Erickson was among the thirty thousand young Americans who evaded the war by heading north. Many Canadians welcomed or

ignored the war resisters, while others smeared them as cowards, traitors, or part of the youth rebellion that threatened values they held
dear. Canada commemorated its 100th birthday in 1967 with a world's
fair and a fresh wave of patriotism, while debates about immigration
and the invasion of the un-American Americans such as Erickson
forced them to consider exactly what they were celebrating.

Doug Carey was among the twenty thousand Canadians who
headed the other way to fight in the war that so many his age were pro-
testing against or fleeing. Carey and his fellow Canadians suffered the
horrors of jungle warfare. Many died. Those who survived endured the
long and dreadful struggles of emotional and physical recovery.

Rebecca Trinh and her family lived in a comfortable Saigon neighbourhood but, when the Americans left Vietnam and the communists
took power, the family ran out of choices. They needed to run and risk
their lives to save their lives. The Canadian government partnered with
faith-based groups, grass-roots organizations, and passionate individuals in welcoming waves of desperate Indochinese refugees—even as
some Canadians called for the door to be locked shut.

The stories of our six guides are not biographies but invitations.
They urge us to consider the stories of many others who, together, tell
us how Canada fought the Vietnam War and was changed by it. They
remind us that as lives are shaped in great swirls of historical change,
a nation's grand story is written.

CHAPTER 1

SHERWOOD LETT AND THE
THREE HUNDRED DAYS

Sherwood Lett learned Vietnam's first lesson when he stepped from the plane: the heat's a beast. The jet-lagged fifty-nine-year-old Canadian steeled himself against the blazing sun and stifling humidity and shook hands with those welcoming him to Saigon. After touring the bustling city, he met his International Control Commission staff and then was briefed by officials from India, Poland, Vietnam, Britain, and the United States. He asked polite but probing questions and, as was his custom, listened more than he spoke.

Two days later, on October 29, 1954, Lett landed at Hanoi's smaller, less chaotic, but equally steamy airport and was surprised by a far grander reception. The streets along his route to the Metropole Hotel fluttered with red banners, bunting, and flags. From the back seat of a long white car, Lett smiled and waved at crowds standing three-deep, cheering, clapping, and singing. He laughed and waved off his colleagues' embarrassment when, at the hotel's reception desk, he learned that the crowds had confused him with the Russian ambassador, who was due to arrive on the next plane. The incident presented Vietnam's second lesson: nothing is as it seems.

More briefings helped him understand that the challenges before him were even greater than he had anticipated. Lett was to lead the Canadian effort to persuade sworn enemies to behave as friends and Cold War belligerents to remain at bay, all while preserving a brittle peace that, with any luck, would end one war and avoid another. Lett's experience, intellect, positive disposition, and self-deprecating sense of humour rendered him the best possible choice for the impossible job.

Sherwood Lett was born in Iroquois, Ontario, but, since his father was a minister and his mother a supportive spouse, he and his six siblings were always moving. His broad range of interests and insatiable curiosity were evident at Vancouver's McGill College (later the University of British Columbia), where he played the flute in the orchestra, served on the executive of the Literary Debating Society, was the lacrosse team's goalie, and coached the women's hockey team. Lett enlisted to serve in the First World War and survived the muddy calamity of Passchendaele. He was promoted to adjutant, his battalion's chief administrative officer, and earned a Military Cross for his gallantry and courage in leading men into battle at Amiens.

After the war, he resumed his studies, earning a Rhodes Scholarship and completing his law degree at Oxford University. It was there that he met another promising Canadian student, future prime minister Lester B. Pearson. Lett was called to the bar in 1922 and five years later was a partner at Vancouver's Davis, Pugh, Davis, Hossie, Ralston, and Lett. He enjoyed a wide circle of friends and memberships in prestigious clubs, served on the University of British Columbia Board of Governors and Senate, and for six years was chancellor.

Lett had remained active in the local militia, and with Hitler's invasion of Poland he returned to military service. He was appointed brigade major with the 2nd Canadian Infantry Division and then with the 6th Canadian Infantry Brigade in England. He was eventually promoted to brigadier and was in command of a regiment at the ill-fated Dieppe Raid when shrapnel shattered his upper right arm. After two operations, and with his arm still in a sling, he became deputy chief of the General Staff in Ottawa but soon returned to England to command the 4th Canadian Infantry Brigade. Lett received a telegram from Canada's minister of justice and then a personal visit from Prime Minister William Lyon Mackenzie King offering an appointment to the Supreme Court of Canada, but he declined in order to continue his service. Five months later, he led the 2nd Canadian Division's post-D-Day drive into France, where, in an attack at a village on the Orne River, shrapnel tore into his right leg. Lett was dispatched back to Canada, where he was made a Commander of the Order of the British Empire and then medically discharged.

Lett returned to his successful law firm, which became E.P. Davis and Company. His military reputation, connections, and legal acumen led to a number of federal government appointments. For instance, he chaired the Committee to Study the Provision of Officers for Canada's Post-War Army and was instrumental in saving and redesigning Kingston's Royal Military College. In 1947 his old friend Pearson, who had become deputy minister of external affairs, asked Lett to join a commission to investigate developing trade and diplomatic relations with Japan. Six years later, Lett served as an advisor in West German hearings regarding former Nazi soldiers still being held as prisoners.

In the summer of 1954 Lett was happily married to Evelyn, the proud father of two adult daughters, Mary and Frances, and enjoying life as the senior partner in a thriving law firm, where he specialized in corporate law. He then received a message from Secretary of State for External Affairs Pearson about a new challenge abroad. The heart can't learn what the head knows for sure, and so, while Evelyn supported her husband's being away for a year, there were tears. Lett accepted the appointment. Effective August 24, he became Canada's commissioner to the International Control Commission (ICC), with the rank of ambassador. Two months later, he was sweltering at Saigon's airport.

Sherwood Lett was in Saigon because of what had happened three months earlier in Geneva. On May 8, 1954, delegates from the United States, Britain, the Soviet Union, France, China, and North and South Korea had gathered around long tables arranged in a big square in a massive and ornately decorated green and bronze conference room. They were to bring a conclusion to the Korean War, which had paused with an uneasy truce. Behind them, jammed to the tall frescoed walls, were delegations from all the countries that had been involved in the war. Canadians John Holmes, Chester Ronning, and Lester Pearson were present because Canada had sent 22,000 troops to Korea, and 516 had died. The Big Five powers also planned to settle the ongoing Indochina War. For those separate sessions, delegates from the regions of Cambodia, Laos, and North and South Vietnam were invited to observe from the back tables as their fates were determined by others.

Delegates had begun gathering in late April and were well settled into private villas outside the city for a conference expected to last perhaps three months. The British and Soviet co-chairs gavelled the first plenary session to order and prepared speeches were read. Everyone knew, however, that the real work and deal making was already happening in anterooms and hallway conversations. As a result, while not formally part of the Indochina meetings, the Canadian delegates offered help where they could. Holmes later described the Canadians as acting like an "unobtrusive oil can."[1]

All the attendees understood that, after Josef Stalin's death in March

1953, the Soviet Union was seeking ways to refocus on domestic economic issues rather than expensive and dangerous foreign entanglements, while China had just embarked on a five-year plan to bolster its
economy and so was similarly preoccupied. Everyone also knew that
America's Eisenhower administration wished to no longer just con-
tain communism but to push it into retreat, including in the Far East.
Britain was still finding its way in a new world order in which it was a
shadow of its former self and cared mostly about holding together the
fragile Western alliance. Meanwhile, besides suffering the humiliating
Dien Bien Phu defeat, just six weeks after the conference began, the
French government fell. Newly elected prime minister Pierre Mendès-
France promised to resign if an Indochina ceasefire was not in place
within a month of his taking office. The major powers at the table were,
therefore, somewhat like poker players who'd all shown their cards
before placing the first bet.

Due to distrust amid a plethora of ulterior motives and Cold War
concerns, the Korea talks quickly broke down.[2] Negotiations continued
for weeks but those assuming that nothing would come of them were
proved right when a June 15 adjournment left the embattled peninsula
doomed to decades of a ceasefire without permanent peace.

The Indochina talks appeared to be headed toward a similar fate.
The good intentions of Canadian delegates were often stymied by the
Americans, who made no secret of the fact that the United States
thought the Indochina talks should not be taking place at all, believing
them to be a sham, dominated by communists.[3] While they had been
committed to the Korean negotiations, American delegates failed to
appear for days on end at the Indochina talks and were often blatantly
aggressive in their anti-communist belligerence. Holmes blamed the
Americans for the Western power discord over Indochina and for
intentionally sabotaging the proceedings.[4] In a cable to a worried Prime
Minister Louis St. Laurent, Pearson stated that the Indochina talks
appeared to be going nowhere. But, he added: "I would repeat that it has

been made clear to all concerned that we have not, and do not expect to have, any obligation in respect to Indochina."[5]

The Canadians nonetheless persevered and, in so doing, enhanced their reputation as helpful fixers. Chester Ronning, for instance, who had learned Mandarin when his father led the Canadian mission in Beijing, met with Chinese premier Zhou Enlai. Ronning emphasized that the Western nations were more unified than they appeared, especially in their desire to ensure a lasting peace in Indochina. Unfortunately, when American secretary of state John Foster Dulles happened upon Zhou and Ronning chatting during a coffee break and Zhou offered his hand, Dulles scowled and theatrically stormed away.

With the Korean talks ended and Pearson already back in Ottawa, Holmes and Ronning headed home. Pearson told the House of Commons of the Korean stalemate and expressed hope that the ongoing Geneva talks might yet bring peace to Indochina. He added, though, that given the already stretched external affairs budget, Canada would be unable to assist with policing that peace.[6]

On the morning of the Geneva Conference's last scheduled day, July 20, 1954, the Indochina War's two primary belligerents, France and the Vietminh, signed the Agreement on the Cessation of Hostilities in Vietnam. It almost didn't happen because arguments had raged over membership in the proposed three-nation commission that would be responsible for implementing and overseeing the agreement. Debate was finally settled when Zhou Enlai suggested, and all agreed, that the commission should be headed by India, as a non-aligned state, with Poland representing the communist alliance and Canada representing the democratic West.[7] The International Commission for Supervision and Control was immediately dubbed the International Control Commission, or ICC. Its headquarters would be in Vietnam, with stations in Laos and Cambodia.

Prime Minister St. Laurent learned that Canada had been named to serve on the ICC not through official diplomatic channels but from news reports.[8] In deciding whether the country should agree to serve, he considered a number of factors. Superseding them all was that Canada was in what would later be called its Golden Age of diplomacy. It had emerged from the Second World War with a powerful military and booming economy. Its external affairs department brimmed with young, talented diplomats and bureaucrats, all eager to have Canada punch above its weight in the creation of an enduring postwar peace. Canada's new foreign policy direction had been publicly outlined by then secretary of state for external affairs St. Laurent in a January 13, 1947, lecture at the University of Toronto. Canada's international efforts, he said, would be guided by five principles: national unity, promoting the Western concept of liberty, respect for the rule of law, promoting the Christian concept of human values, and accepting responsibility for international progress commensurate with Canada's role in the world. Pearson agreed with the principles and later added: "Canada could not escape the effects of international storms by burying [its] head in the sand. [Canada] should play a part in trying to prevent the storms by accepting international commitments to that purpose."[9] Pearson was a realist who knew that acting through organizations such as the United Nations and the North Atlantic Treaty Organization (NATO) would not allow Canada to overtly influence superpower policies. But, he explained, "I hoped we could influence the environment in which they were pursued."[10]

Never to be forgotten in the pursuit of these lofty principles and the realpolitik consequences of living up to them was Canada's complex and indispensable relationship with the United States. Pearson believed that the increasing integration of economic and defence strategies of Canada and the United States was the price to be paid for safety, prosperity, and the advancement of Canada's interests on the world stage.[11] To that end, Canadian leaders and diplomats employed what they called quiet diplomacy, where criticism and advice were spoken in private as others shouted in public.[12]

Also influencing Canada's ICC decision was the legitimacy of Cold War fears. St. Laurent left no space between the Canadian and American interpretations of the global communist menace when, in 1948, he said: "Totalitarian communist aggression constitutes a direct and immediate threat to every democratic country, including Canada."[13] Similarly, on February 2, 1951, Pearson stated in the House that the government believed in the domino theory and made specific reference to stopping communism in Indochina lest the entire region fall one country at a time and, in so doing, bring the world closer to a nuclear confrontation.[14]

Canada's involvement in Indochina began in December 1952, when NATO's North Atlantic Council decided to allocate funds and weapons for France's Indochinese colonial war. St. Laurent had been reluctant to sign the agreement. Pearson and other cabinet members convinced him to do so due to domino theory fears, a desire to be a good NATO partner and a reliable American and French ally, and the economic imperative of protecting the supply of rubber and tin from the region. From 1950 to 1954, Canada sent $61.2 million worth of arms, aircraft, and other military supplies to France, knowing full well that it probably all found its way to Indochina.[15]

This tangle of considerations was expressed around the big oval cabinet table when St. Laurent devoted a week to considering whether to accept Canada's ICC appointment. The United States had originally wanted Belgium to be the ICC's Western representative, but its colonial past had rendered that choice problematic. A message from the American State Department indicated that Eisenhower now supported Canada's being on the ICC.[16]

Cabinet finally agreed that if Canada refused to participate, it could irritate the Americans and possibly lead to the collapse of the Geneva Agreement, a renewal of the war, and a dangerous Cold War chain reaction. The Vietnam assignment was the price Canada needed to pay for its bold principles, Cold War declarations, American alliance, and Golden Age arrogance. The invoice had arrived. Canada stepped into Vietnam.

St. Laurent did not announce the decision so much as whisper it. On July 28 a short and unceremonious press release stated that Canada would serve on the ICC. Almost predicting failure, the carefully chosen words noted that the success of the venture would ultimately be up to the people of Laos, Cambodia, and Vietnam.

Things then moved quickly. The scramble to get people in place forced external affairs officials to make things up on the fly. Military leaders made no secret of the fact that they saw Vietnam as an irritant, a dangerous distraction from the more important priority of addressing the Soviet threat in Europe, but they cooperated admirably in establishing the new mission.[17] Pearson appointed skilled and experienced diplomat, and current high commissioner to New Delhi, Escott Reid, to the delegation, and diplomat R.M. MacDonnell as Canada's acting ICC commissioner. Just two weeks after learning that Canada had been chosen to be a part of the ICC, the Canadian team was in New Delhi meeting with its Indian and Polish counterparts. On August 11, the Polish, Indian, and Canadian teams arrived at the ICC headquarters in Hanoi.

While MacDonnell got things started, Pearson had only one man in mind to take over and command Canada's ICC delegation. He needed someone with the personality and patience to deal with the ICC's competing parties and those entering the bitter truce. That person also needed war zone experience and a sharp legal mind to manoeuvre through the intricacies of the Geneva Agreement and its complex implementation. Pearson needed Sherwood Lett.

John Holmes wrote: "[Lett] was not only a soldier but also judicial by training and temperament. No one could have been more fair-minded."[18] The American consul in Vancouver observed, "The Canadian government could not have selected a finer man for this difficult position."[19]

In his home in Vancouver, Lett began preparing for his mission by carefully reviewing the Agreement on the Cessation of Hostilities in

Vietnam. It divided Vietnam at the 17th parallel with a three-mile demilitarized zone on both sides. Within three hundred days, the Vietminh were to move their troops and materiel north of the line and the French were to remove theirs from all of Indochina. Prisoners were to be exchanged. All civilians who wished to relocate to one side of the line or the other would be helped to do so. Ho Chi Minh's government would rule the Democratic Republic of Vietnam (DRVN) north of the 17th parallel. Emperor Bao Dai, through his newly appointed prime minister Ngo Dinh Diem, would govern the Republic of Vietnam (RVN), south of the line. Neither government was to join military alliances or import new military hardware.

The ICC was to establish fixed teams at specified cities and mobile teams in Cambodia, Laos, and Vietnam, which would move where needed to supervise, observe, inspect, and investigate the application of the agreement's provisions. The teams would be directed by and report to the Canadian-Polish-Indian ICC commissioners, who would submit reports and recommendations to the Joint Commission. The Joint Commission, composed of French and Vietminh representatives, would then order disobedient parties to straighten up and obey the rules. The ICC would also submit reports to the British and Russian representatives of the Geneva Conference, who would meet when necessary. The arrangement ensured that Canada, India, and Poland would be not be acting as peacekeepers, or even cops, but as crossing guards.

Lett also read the Final Declaration, which had been approved in Geneva the day after the signing of the Agreement on the Cessation of Hostilities in Vietnam. Its thirteen parts reiterated much of what the Agreement said but offered specific details. Of special significance was paragraph six, which said Vietnam's 17th parallel was temporary. Paragraph seven stated that Vietnam would be reunited under one government, to be chosen in a July 1956 election to be held in the North and South.

In establishing the election date, the Final Declaration seemed to determine an end to the ICC mission, for by July 1956 Vietnam would hopefully be at peace, united, and free of colonial rule. By that time, Cambodia and Laos would also have become independent states. But Lett understood the shadow that lay over the Final Declaration. The Americans had agreed with ending the fighting in Indochina but didn't like the idea of allowing a communist government to remain in North Vietnam with an army to defend a delineated territory.[20] American and South Vietnamese delegates in Geneva also believed the communist North would rig the election in its favour, and so neither would sign the Final Declaration. To mask the refusal of the two parties to sign, it was decided that all the participating countries would be listed at the beginning of the document—but then none would be asked to sign.

The day after the Geneva Conference issued its Final Declaration, President Eisenhower had disingenuously stated at a news conference that while he was happy a settlement had been reached, the United States had not been a belligerent in the fighting and had not been involved in negotiating the agreement. "Accordingly," he continued, "the United States has not itself been a party to or bound by the decisions taken by the conference, but it is our hope that it will lead to the establishment of peace consistent with the rights and needs of the countries concerned."[21]

With none of the major powers other than France having signed the Agreement on the Cessation of Hostilities in Vietnam and none having signed the Final Declaration, Lett and Pearson worried that the non-signatories were free to sabotage both in pursuit of their Cold War goals in the region. Pearson was particularly afraid that actions by the United States, China, and the Soviet Union could escalate to a nuclear holocaust.[22] In letters to British prime minister Robert Anthony Eden and Indian prime minister Jawaharlal Nehru, Pearson presciently observed that Canada's involvement in Indochina might "turn out to be as onerous as it certainly was unsought."[23] Pearson and Lett would have been even more worried had they known that shortly after the Geneva Conference ended, Secretary of State Dulles and President

Eisenhower had agreed that if things did not go as they wanted in Indochina, then they would use Canada to "block things."[24]

Pearson sent a nine-page letter of instruction to Lett describing the difficulties he was about to encounter. The letter added Canadian domestic and Cold War goals to Lett's ICC mission. He was directed to implement the Geneva agreements but also to encourage the development of a Southeast Asia Defence Organization to stand against Chinese aggression in the region; provide help in the region's economic development, preferably according to a capitalist model; and strengthen non-communist governments.[25] Lett was warned: "The task you will be undertaking on behalf of Canada in participating in the supervision of the cease fire in Vietnam, will be an extremely important and difficult one, and one for which there are no precedents in Canadian experience to guide you."[26] Pearson's letter promised the full cooperation and assistance of the external affairs department, with the caveat that Lett would have to rely on his own judgement regarding disputes within or brought to the ICC.[27]

Lett understood the breadth, complexity, and contradictions of his mission. He tried to tamp down unrealistic expectations. In a September 27 radio interview, he warned: "I should like to make it clear that the functions of the Commission are supervisory, judicial, and mediatory. It can make recommendations but cannot of itself enforce recommendations it may make."[28] And with that, Lett set out to risk his reputation, livelihood, and—given the volatility of the region—quite possibly his life.

LETT IN VIETNAM

On October 12, 1954, Lett kissed Evelyn and their daughters goodbye and headed to Ottawa. For three days he was briefed by external affairs officials and Chairman of the Chiefs of Staff General Charles Foulkes.

Lett enjoyed dinner with the prime minister, who asked him to thank Evelyn for allowing his mission to take place.[29] Arriving in London, Lett met with Canadian High Commissioner Norman Robertson. The experienced and highly respected Robertson expressed doubt that Lett's mission could succeed. He sat with members of the British Foreign Office, who similarly warned that there was no hope of stopping the communists from taking Vietnam.[30] It was then on to New Delhi for talks with Indian officials, who were only a trifle more optimistic, and then, finally, to Saigon.

With the three-hundred-day clock already ticking, Lett had little time to settle in. Less than twenty-four hours after assuming his post in Hanoi, he was told that the movement of civilians, soldiers, and materiel had begun well but problems were arising. An immediate crisis involved trouble with the relocation of Catholic refugees from the North. Catholics were a religious minority in a predominantly Buddhist society. They had been persecuted by Vietminh nationalist rebels and were cold to the North's anti-religious communist ideology, and so there was a natural desire among many Catholics to seize the opportunity to move south.[31]

Lett estimated that, if there were no restrictions on the movement of people from the North to the South, between one and two million might make the trek.[32] Ho Chi Minh's government could not allow such a significant drop in its population, the propaganda gift it would hand South Vietnamese prime minister Diem and the Americans, or the economic and military boost it would afford South Vietnam. Therefore, it did all it could to stop the migration. Its tactics included propaganda, violence, and ruthless intimidation. Catholics specifically were targeted in the widespread practice of forcibly separating families and then telling parents they could have their children back if they pledged to remain in place. The worst violations of human rights were in the Catholic dioceses of Phat Diem and Bui Chu, where, since mid-May, many Catholics had been harassed, shot, and their houses burned.

Meanwhile, Diem was doing all he could to encourage a Catholic migration. Diem was a devout Catholic. His religion was a significant part of the reason that Secretary of State Dulles supported Diem. Dulles and other American leaders believed that Buddhists were passive and weak and would never stand up to the communists.[33] Plus, while the Americans conceded Diem's faults, he was a clever politician and a sincere nationalist whose dream of someday ruling a reunited Vietnam meshed with American goals. Diem saw waves of immigrating Catholics as an important weapon in fortifying himself and his government by providing a power base independent of the Buddhist majority. He needed to build that base because, at that point, his authority extended no further than he could see from his palace window.

Organized crime syndicates had worked closely with the French and still controlled Saigon. The syndicates and rival religious sects ruled much of the land beyond. The empty shell that passed for the Army of the Republic of Vietnam (ARVN) was undertrained and often unpaid, and its men felt little loyalty to Diem or Emperor Bao Dai. It didn't help that all knew the reluctant and largely ignored emperor preferred the food, opium, and prostitutes of Paris to Vietnamese affairs of state.[34] Having already fought off three coup attempts, Diem filled most important posts with family members he believed he could trust, such as his brother, Ngo Dinh Nhu, who became South Vietnam's internal security chief.

Lett learned that America's Central Intelligence Agency (CIA) was acting to discredit Ho while encouraging Catholics and others to move south in what the Americans called the Passage to Freedom. American air force colonel Edward Lansdale had successfully directed covert CIA support for the Philippine government and, in June 1954, he was dispatched to Vietnam to provide similar help to Diem. Under Lansdale's direction, the Saigon Military Mission saw CIA agents undertake a number of dirty tricks, such as contaminating an oil refinery that supplied Hanoi's public transit system, thereby damaging bus engines.[35] In a direct appeal to Catholics, Lansdale contrived impending Christian pogroms and popularized the slogan "God Has Moved South." He paid priests to leave and take their parishes with them.[36] Historian Seth Jacobs has concluded that the CIA's activities in bolstering the Catholic migration south "ranked with the most audacious enterprises in the history of covert action."[37]

It was amid this jumble of political agendas and a looming humanitarian crisis that Sherwood Lett met with Canadian officials and then his Polish and Indian counterparts at the ICC's Hanoi headquarters. Since August, American and French ships and planes had been moving mostly Catholic refugees south, but 200,000 remained stuck in makeshift camps around Hanoi and the port city of Haiphong, while those in Northern Catholic areas continued to be harassed and prevented from moving.

The Polish ICC delegates adamantly supported Northern efforts to stop the Catholic migration. They claimed that few really wanted to leave and insisted that no ICC action was necessary. The increasingly frustrated Canadians worked to forge a compromise that would allow ICC mobile teams to be dispatched to investigate the camps, the movement of refugees, and conditions on the ground in Phat Diem and Bui Chu. With so much conflicting information, Lett asserted, the ICC needed to do its job.[38]

The Canadians, Indians, and Poles worked through the night. Different groups grappled with aspects of overlapping problems and where or whether to send mobile units. Lett walked from meeting to meeting to keep everyone talking by reminding them of their mandate to help people cross the 17th parallel and of the necessity to save lives. He was engaged in a number of private conversations, including phone calls to French, American, and Northern and Southern officials. Unanimity was finally won. Messages were relayed, orders issued, and mobile teams dispatched. Their presence eased tensions and mitigated the crises in Catholic regions and in the camps, while allowing the movement of more people.

The quick and decisive manner in which Lett had handled himself was commended by his staff and others. His cool under pressure was to be repeatedly tested. Every day brought new and disturbing messages from jungle hamlets and cities where even those doing their best to disentangle themselves from one another were meeting insurmountable challenges. ICC personnel oversaw Northern villages emptying and city apartment buildings being abandoned as families made their way to Haiphong and other port cities, where $93 million in American aid and ships from the U.S. Seventh Fleet helped them move south. At one point the French Air Force was transporting 3,400 refugees a day.[39]

The port city of Haiphong, east of Hanoi in North Vietnam, was of critical importance. It was a staging area for Northerners moving south while at the same time the city of over 100,000 people was being transferred from French to DRNV administrative control. Thousands of prisoners of war needed to be swapped, and at one point Vietminh prisoners threatened to riot when told they would be released but not allowed to migrate south. An ICC mobile team negotiated a settlement. When the city's administration and essential services nearly collapsed because enemies refused to cooperate in the transition of power, another ICC team intervened to smooth the transfer of files, equipment, and personnel. French and Vietminh forces argued about the ownership of military equipment, and an ICC mobile team intervened to settle the matter.

Lett was constantly involved in helping to negotiate troubles, find compromises, and keep the tensions in the city from escalating into violence that could have instigated another nationwide war. In the end, the transfer of Haiphong from one power to the other while the Americans simultaneously led the transfer of Northerners to the south through the city was among the ICC's most remarkable accomplishments.

By December 1954, there were 25 Canadian diplomats and 135 Canadian military personnel in Vietnam.[40] Lett came to rely upon the wisdom of his senior political advisor, Marcel Cadieux, who was replaced in February by the experienced and hard-working Saul Rae (whose son Bob would later be Ontario's premier). The Poles had about 160 people, and the Indians, because they constituted most of the administrative personnel, numbered over 1,000. In total, about 1,400 people were directing the delicate dance where at any moment a bad decision by a local political or military leader, an ICC diplomat or soldier, or some teenager with a homemade bomb or purloined rifle could ignite a new war. Miraculously, and despite spasms of violence, the hard and tenuous peace held.

Fixed six-person ICC teams, each containing Canadians, Indians, and Poles, operated in fourteen zones throughout the North and South. Fourteen border crossing points had been created. Every day Lett and the Polish and Indian commissioners directed mobile teams of three people each to hot spots and evaluated the reports of others. About 250,000 French, Vietminh, and ARVN soldiers and untold guerilla fighters, who had all been entwined throughout the country, were on the move. About 200,000 tons of difficult-to-haul military equipment was being transported.[41] While thousands of civilians were en route one way or another, no one knew how many more wished to go.

The ICC established a number of committees to administer their mandate, including Operations, Administration, and Legal. Its Freedom Committee invited anyone to petition for redress if their freedom to move, associate, or generally carry on with their lives, as promised by the Geneva Agreement's 14th clause, was denied. By December 10, 1954, the Freedom Committee had received 17,397 petitions.[42]

Lett reported to Ottawa that neither North nor South Vietnam appeared interested in cooperating with the ICC and that both were using it to score propaganda points. Ho's government actively restricted its people from submitting petitions to the ICC, Lett explained, while overwhelming the ICC with complaints about Diem's violations of the Geneva Agreement in an attempt to discredit what it considered his

illegitimate government. Meanwhile, Diem encouraged petitions from
his people, hoping to demonstrate that the Vietminh were still operating in the South and so the Geneva Agreement was crumbling and,
therefore, the Americans needed to intervene. Lett's reports indicated
that he saw through both Ho and Diem and knew about the ongoing
CIA operations that were complicating an already complex situation.
His reports also revealed a man growing increasingly frustrated in his
sincere efforts to do his job.[43]

It was impossible to thoroughly examine and respond to each case
brought to the ICC's attention but the commission averaged ten major
investigations a month. Nearly everyone led to strained debates among
the Canadians, Poles, and Indians. It was determined that the best way
to approach snags and scuffles was to seek solutions either without
laying blame or by assigning it equally to both sides.

Lett and his colleagues found it increasingly difficult to believe
anyone or anything. In a letter to Evelyn he suggested that she ignore
all press stories coming from Vietnam. He explained that he might be
dealing with reports of a series of murders in a village and then: "The
same day we might get an urgent complaint that 24 people have been
murdered in a certain place, 300 have been massacred by troops and a
half dozen buried alive as a torture against Communist agents. We then
[investigate and] find that 24 people were arrested in a riot in some village of whom possibly 20 had been released and four held in custody."[44]
Things were often not as bad as reported, he told her, but sometimes
they were worse.

In the fall of 1954 the CIA's Colonel Lansdale convinced Prime
Minister Diem of a plan to extend his government's rule beyond the
cities by rooting out opponents in rural areas. In December Diem
ordered the launching of a pacification campaign. Every hamlet, village, and town in South Vietnam was soon witnessing mass arrests,
savage beatings, torture, and the extrajudicial murder not just of suspected Vietminh sympathizers, agents, and spies but also of anyone

expressing anti-Diem views. Concentration camps were established but, in Orwellian doublespeak, they were called education centres.

Lett reported to Ottawa that sections of the South were experiencing a total collapse of law and order. North Vietnam's General Vo Nguyen Giap submitted a letter of complaint to the ICC, citing nine specific incidents in which the Geneva Agreement was being blatantly violated by Diem's terror campaign. He detailed incidents of intimidation and torture and the imprisonment of Vietminh soldiers arrested while dutifully marching north. Giap demanded redress.[45]

Lett and his Indian and Polish counterparts conferred. Poland demanded quick action but India demurred, advising a detailed investigation. Lett was in a difficult position. He was aware of the violence being perpetrated but also that his instructions were to support the South Vietnamese government, not institute actions against it. He had already reported to Ottawa that, while many Vietminh soldiers were moving north, many others were still in the South leading destabilization activities.[46] Lett saw Diem's pacification campaign as a misguided but necessary effort to rid the South of the Vietminh subversives who were endangering the implementation of the Geneva Agreement.

In what was far from the ICC's best moment, it was decided that Giap's letter should be dismissed because it quoted the wrong article of the Geneva Agreement. That letter, however, was but one of 1,328 complaints received by the ICC about Diem's pacification campaign. The ICC observed and reported but could do nothing to stop it, and the horror continued. (In 1959 Diem's government released a report confessing that the pacification campaign had imprisoned 180,843 people, but no mention was made of incidents of torture and murder.)[47]

In an action similar to the wanton brutality of Diem's campaign, Ho's government unleashed an ill-conceived and ruthless effort at land reform. Northern government officials indiscriminately tossed farmers off their land and punished those who resisted. People deemed insufficiently loyal were beaten and many were imprisoned. Appeals to the ICC were forbidden. By the end of December, even Ho had become repulsed. He stopped the worst atrocities and dodged personal responsibility by dismissing the senior officers in charge, who shouldered all the blame.[48]

Lett came to know all the major players. At a dinner party held in his honour by Ho Chi Minh, the Canadian found the communist leader "charming" and "quite a man." He was impressed with Ho's fluent English, Russian, Mandarin, French, and Vietnamese, and called him an extraordinary character with an extraordinary intellect.[49] But he was not fooled into thinking him a benign figure. In a report to Pearson, Lett described Ho as leading a "dictatorial, totalitarian, ruthlessly efficient regime."[50] He enjoyed a number of dinner and reception conversations with Giap during which the two generals shared battle experiences. As for South Vietnamese prime minister Diem, Lett found him inscrutable and untrustworthy.

As 1954 came to a close, Lett and the ICC could feel proud of having done some good, but their investigations and actions were being increasingly sabotaged or blocked by both the North and South. Travel permits and entry to particular areas, especially in the North, were being denied. Rules stated that only government vehicles could be used in certain areas but then, somehow, no vehicles could be found. The North insisted that its army had to provide guides for all ICC mobile teams, but then guides often failed to appear. Canadians reported that Vietminh soldiers regularly stopped ICC vehicles at checkpoints and removed refugees. At one refugee station, a Vietminh soldier appeared and simply confiscated all the paperwork from an Indian commissioner, ordered the station closed, and arranged for the fleeing people to be taken back north.[51] The ICC became increasingly impotent. Vietnam was teetering on the edge of chaos.

At Christmas, Lett attempted to raise the spirits of those under his command by adorning offices with tinsel made from cigarette package paper and other crazily contrived decorations. He arranged for turkeys and hams to be delivered to ICC personnel throughout Laos, Cambodia, and Vietnam. He increased the pay of the military staff who were primarily doing fieldwork so that it more closely matched that of the diplomatic staff. He improved mail service.

ICC members were hard-working and courageous and did their best to adjust to the heat, food, and water of questionable quality. Many suffered from intestinal diseases. They learned to boil drinking water, take anti-malarial drugs, and sleep beneath mosquito netting. The Canadians grew used to water buffalo steak but not Vietnamese or Indian music. They laughed as their Indian and Polish comrades gamely struggled to sing along with "Alouette."[52] Those dispatched on mobile teams had no time for such trivial matters as they made their way into remote villages, bounced over jungle roads, and worried that the next skinny teenager they encountered toting a Russian-made AK-47 could end their lives.

There was also no escaping the heartache of being away from loved ones and the knowledge that at any moment the place could spark into a war zone. Lett was reminded of this fact every morning as he walked five blocks to work past North Vietnamese armed guards at his hotel, more soldiers on street corners, and still more at the Burma Shell Building that served as the Canadian ICC headquarters and the Chamber of Commerce building where the commission met. If trouble erupted and the buildings were attacked, he knew there was no telling which way the guards would shoot.

The non-stop work and stress took a toll on Lett's health. In March 1955 he was tested and x-rayed by a French doctor, who suspected the occasional pain and constant discomfort he was feeling could be amoebic dysentery or even cancer. Fortunately, nothing was found. Pain medication was prescribed and Lett carried on.

Meanwhile, Diem began a new propaganda effort designed primarily to win greater support in the cities. His Denounce the Communists campaign linked communism to the widely reviled colonialism. Writers were hired to produce anti-communist articles, novels, plays, and songs. Police and political cadres imprisoned anyone who complained about the new campaign or Diem's government, along with those suspected of being communists or communist sympathizers.

Lett and the ICC addressed numerous complaints and dispatched mobile units to investigate the worst human rights abuses. Numbers were difficult to certify but it is estimated that from 1955 to 1960, Diem's pacification and Denounce the Communist campaigns saw from 25,000 to 184,000 arrested and 1,000 to 5,000 executed without trial.[53]

In April Lett travelled back to Ottawa to brief Pearson on ICC progress. He arrived just as the influential *Toronto Star* published a series of articles that characterized the mass migration as being sabotaged by the "reds" and criticized the ICC as ineffective and perhaps corrupt.[54] Lett told a reporter: "New countries are always touchy and our task is therefore much more delicate . . . but everything is going smoothly. . . . A reasonable degree of co-operation has been given by both sides—the French and the North Vietnamese."[55]

A number of newspapers joined the *Toronto Star* and Members of Parliament in criticizing Canada's role in Vietnam. It was suggested that the ICC was failing to stop or even properly acknowledge Northern actions that were impeding the movement of people who wished to travel south. Pearson said in the House that ICC actions could not stop all violations of the Geneva Agreement but that it was reducing the number of violations and for this reason its efforts should be applauded.[56]

Lett recorded a nine-minute radio broadcast outlining all that was going on in Vietnam, Laos, and Cambodia. He spoke of the mission's danger and the hardships being suffered by Canadians serving on the ICC's mobile teams but said all were in good health and spirits. He reminded Canadians of the immensity of the task and reiterated that the commission was permitted only to observe, inspect, and make recommendations. "The fact that hostilities have not been resumed in any one of the three countries, that decisions have been made by the Commissions and accepted by the parties," he concluded, "is perhaps an indication of some degree of success."[57]

Lett was being modest. He and ICC members deserved to take pride in the work they were doing. Despite the sporadic violence, it had to be conceded that the disentanglement of the combatants, mass migration of civilians, release of prisoners, and movement of military equipment were all going better than even the most optimistic had hoped. Cambodia and Laos, although still experiencing problems, were moving quickly toward self-rule. But storm clouds were gathering in Vietnam. There was an election to plan.

THE ELECTION

Geneva's Final Declaration had promised that the ICC would begin preparations a year in advance of the scheduled July 1956 Vietnamese election. In March 1955, Lett wrote a six-page memorandum to Pearson expressing grave concerns. He advised that, because everyone knew that Ho Chi Minh was poised to win the election, American secretary of state John Foster Dulles had been in conversation with Diem about stalling or cancelling it.[58]

Lett recommended that, regardless of who might win, Canada should do everything in its power to ensure that the election happened. For one thing, he argued, Ho Chi Minh would be correct in interpreting a cancelled election as a "double-cross."[59] Cancellation or even an effort to postpone it, he warned, might "carry with it the consequences of a renewal of hostilities."[60] Further, he wrote, the Geneva Agreement could be interpreted as stating that Canada's ICC duties would end with the election and Vietnam's subsequent reunification. If the election was not held, he warned, then Canada's commitment in Vietnam

could go on forever, surely something neither Pearson nor Prime
Minister St. Laurent wanted. He concluded, "For Canada, therefore,
the question of elections is not a theoretical but an intensely practical
one."[61] Lett suggested that, to avoid the crisis that would be caused by
the election's cancellation and ensure that Canada could leave Vietnam
on schedule, the Geneva Conference should be reconvened. It should
grant the ICC more money, people, and power to make the election
happen in as free and fair a manner as possible.[62]

Pearson conferred with St. Laurent and then with his French and
British counterparts. It was decided that bringing the conference
together again would threaten the fragile peace in the region and stir
greater animosity between China and the United States, who were, at
that moment, taking steps toward war over a disagreement regarding
Formosa (Taiwan). Lett was told to make do with what he had. Publicly,
Pearson said: "We are willing to continue our work on the commission
in Vietnam as long as there is any possibility of that work being useful
in the maintenance of peace there and the establishment of conditions
of stability."[63]

Lett had no choice but to accept his instructions. But he soon
reported to Pearson that three circumstances were moving Vietnam
toward catastrophe. First, Diem's government was becoming more
stable, because he had crushed his opposition and taken greater control of South Vietnam's financial institutions while appealing to
Vietnamese nationalism. Diem knew that an election would inevitably
end his government and all he had worked to accomplish. Therefore,
Diem would never allow the election to happen.

Second, ICC mobile teams had uncovered and confiscated arms
and ammunition depots created in the South by retreating Vietminh.[64]
Lett had also learned that while thousands of Vietminh were moving
northward, Ho had successfully arranged for thousands of other
Vietminh to blend in and remain in the South. It was later estimated
that there were six to ten thousand of these "stay behinds."[65] The

Vietminh fighters and all those guns were part of Ho's plan to take the South by force of arms if the election was cancelled.

Finally, Lett had been told that, despite the humanitarian outrages that were still occurring in the North, Ho remained massively popular. Ho's humility, simple dress, closeness to the people, and plain-spoken nationalism also resonated throughout the South. Lett was told that most Southern folks professed loyalty to Diem but slept with a picture of Ho under their pillows. If the election was cancelled, there would be outrage among the Vietnamese people who could legitimately contend that their wishes and right to self-determination had been denied. No one could predict how that anger would be expressed.

As if all that were not enough, Lett reported another growing concern: if the communists appeared to be winning the campaign, or if they won the election, there was no telling what the Americans would do. Odds were good, he wrote, that they would more actively intervene and thereby end Vietnam's moment of peace. Lett knew that the United States was already pressuring members of the recently created Southeast Asia Treaty Organization (SEATO) to publicly state their support for Diem and oppose a Vietnamese election.[66]

Lett's concerns led Pearson to dispatch External Affairs Deputy Minister John Holmes to Vietnam. Holmes's painful puns betrayed his frustration—while amusing staff—when he said things like "Stop Hanoi-ing me!" and "Let Saigons be Saigons."[67] He met with Diem in June 1955 and spoke with Lett and the Canadian ICC staff. All agreed that Diem's government, while corrupt and pitiless in dealing with both its citizens and enemies, was more stable than ever. Holmes learned that the Americans and Diem were exaggerating the number of infractions of the Geneva Agreement and that the ICC was doing the best it could to investigate and address those that it uncovered or were brought to its attention. Holmes became certain that, regardless of what the ICC did, an election could never meet Canadian free and fair standards.

In the end, despite ongoing problems and no matter how the election question was resolved, Holmes believed the ICC should remain in place and Canada should stay as part of it. To leave, he wrote, would tip the region into anarchy.[68] Plus, the Americans had clearly decided to disallow the elections and, according to the popular Washington aphorism, to "sink or swim with Ngo Dinh Diem." To stand publicly against Diem and demand that the elections take place would threaten Canadian-American relations.[69]

On June 13, 1955, Lett received new instructions from Ottawa. Nothing Canada or the ICC could do would change the minds of Diem or the Americans, and so the election would not happen. Lett was no longer to encourage ICC pre-election discussions.[70] He responded by repeating his prescient warning that if an election or some other means did not reunite Vietnam, the North would attack the South to bring about that end and, in all likelihood, win. Either way, the country would be united under a communist government, the only difference being that thousands of innocent people would die.[71]

Lett's warning would be his last, for, with his one-year term completed, he received word to return home. He was in Saigon concluding final meetings with his senior staff in their fourth-floor hotel suite when they were interrupted by a loud and boisterous parade passing on the street below. Red banners were flying, there were chants and songs, and a loudspeaker mounted atop a Jeep was blaring political slogans. Ominously, the parade stopped and turned toward the hotel. The crowd morphed into a mob, surged forward, and began hurling rocks. Police and military guards were mysteriously absent. Amid the cacophony of breaking glass, angry shouts, and a screeching speech blaring through the loudspeaker, the anxious Canadians hurriedly gathered up classified papers and blockaded their doors. Lett looked out between drawn curtains and saw the commission's white cars on fire. He heard furniture being smashed in the rooms above and below him.

As gunfire crackled on the street, Lett's door was smashed in and, armed with thick poles, an angry group of men burst in and demanded to know if he was hiding any Vietnamese people. Lett maintained his composure, said no, and watched as they searched and ransacked the suite. After several tense minutes, they stormed back into the hallway.[72] Only when the street mob began to disperse did the police arrive and fire a few shots into the air. Lett and the Canadians were escorted to safety in the opulent residence of the French commissioner-general.

It was July 20, 1955, and Diem had proclaimed the Geneva Agreement's first anniversary a "Day of Shame." All South Vietnamese public buildings and schools had lowered flags to half-staff. Schools were closed and workers were given the day off. Protesters had been transported by government vehicles to locations outside Saigon's Canadian, Indian, and Polish ICC offices. A subsequent ICC report asserted that Diem had personally either organized or sanctioned the violent protests.[73]

Two days later, after a heartfelt send-off from senior staff gathered at the airport, Lett's plane swept through the steaming heat and left Saigon. After stopovers in London and Ottawa, he was finally home with Evelyn. He promised to never leave again, assuring her, "It will take more than Mike Pearson and Louis St. Laurent to pry us apart for any more fancy jobs."[74]

Meanwhile, Diem delivered a long and terse speech in which he reminded all that, since the government of South Vietnam had not signed the Geneva Agreement, it was not bound by it. On October 26, he proclaimed the Republic of Vietnam. He manoeuvred Bao Dai's resignation and appointed himself president. Not a single communist or non-aligned country offered official recognition of the new country, but thirty-four Western countries did, including Canada.

The election didn't happen. The world watched communist powers insisting on a democratic election while the democratic West refused to allow it take place. With the scuttled elections preventing the peaceful reunification of Vietnam, Ho Chi Minh implemented his plans to reunify by force. All the Vietminh weapons in all the depots hidden throughout the South were retrieved, and all the "stay behinds" took them in hand. They were supported by all those in the South who wanted the latest imperial power gone and to have one country, with Ho Chi Minh as their leader. Lett took no satisfaction in having been proved right.

From the outset, St. Laurent and Pearson had known what they were up against. Their reasons for accepting the Geneva Conference's appointment that put Canada in Vietnam were principled and sound. Lett had a clear understanding of the challenges he faced in trying to carry out his tricky mandate. There was nothing naïve, sentimental, or surprising about the government's policies or Lett's mission.[75]

Lett returned to Canada physically and emotionally drained. Since accepting the assignment, he had lost twenty pounds. But he could take satisfaction in the fact that by the time he left, in the summer of 1955, his efforts and those of the ICC had assisted 900,000 Northerners to move south of the 17th parallel, about 85 percent of whom were Catholic. Prisoners had been exchanged, 30,000 French troops left for home, 90,000 Vietminh moved north, and 200,000 tons of military equipment had been shipped. One-third of Vietnam's territory had peacefully changed hands, including cities such as Haiphong.[76] There had been violence, but the ceasefire had held. Even those efforts, however, could not help the estimated 500,000 to 1 million who had wanted to relocate but had been prevented from doing so.[77] Lett left for home having earned the respect of everyone with whom he had served.

Perhaps Lett said it best in a letter to his wife in which he observed: "I cannot prevent many things from occurring which have occurred, but I can have some influence in preventing them happening again. And what has occurred is only a drop in the bucket compared to what would have occurred had the Commission and its teams not been here and functioning."[78]

CHAPTER 2

BLAIR SEABORN AND
A CHANCE FOR PEACE

The weather in Hyannisport, Massachusetts, was awful. A biting wind blustered in from the choppy Atlantic, tousling President Kennedy's thick brown hair as he watched the helicopter alight gently on the expansive lawn of his family's six-acre compound. Ducking beneath the chopper blades, Canadian prime minister Lester Pearson emerged and smiled at his host.

It was May 11, 1963, and although Pearson had come to office just the month before, the two leaders had respected each other for some time. Pearson admired Kennedy's intelligence and intellectual curiosity. Kennedy appreciated the Canadian's storied diplomatic career, his insightful articles addressing international affairs, and his having won the 1957 Nobel Peace Prize for helping to coax superpowers back from the brink of war when they had faced off over Egypt's nationalization of the Suez Canal.[1] Kennedy and Pearson shook hands and, beneath furiously flapping American and Canadian flags, walked briskly to the sprawling main house.

In meetings that afternoon and early evening, Kennedy, Pearson, and their staffs resolved a number of irritants that had been souring Canadian-American relations. Later, with Kennedy settled into a rocking chair and Pearson on a couch, they sipped drinks before a fire. In the course of their wide-ranging conversation, Kennedy asked what he should do about Vietnam. Without hesitation, Pearson replied, "I'd get out." Kennedy smiled and said, "Any damn fool knows that. The question is how?"[2]

How indeed. The fragile peace was holding; thousands of people had moved to their chosen side of the 17th parallel, soldiers had retreated, and a great deal of military hardware had been shipped away. Still, Vietnam was in many ways a bigger mess than when Sherwood Lett had arrived nine years earlier. By April 1956 French troops and nearly all French officials had left Vietnam. While this was a positive step for the country, their departure meant the collapse of the Joint Commission that had been chaired by France and the Vietminh. The International Control Commission remained in place but it was suddenly an orphan with no one to whom it could report and no one to enforce its recommendations.

After the promised July election was scuttled, the ICC's mandate blurred and its ability to influence events dwindled. The governments and armies of North and South Vietnam withdrew their liaison officers and, where they had barely tolerated ICC personnel before, now they often ignored them outright. Ever-tightening bureaucratic entanglements curtailed mobile unit travel, and then access to military bases was denied. In April 1957, South Vietnam's Diem government announced that it would no longer allow the ICC to investigate complaints forwarded by the North. As the North terrorized the disobedient and the

South killed the disloyal, the ICC could do nothing.[3] According to a Vietnamese joke, Indian officials passed their days gazing at the moon and yearning for home while the Poles read long, sad Russian poems and the Canadians drank.[4]

With the silent passing of the election deadline, Canada could have declared success and departed. After all, Cambodia and Laos were relatively stable and the ICC's primary goals in Vietnam had been met. Prime Minister St. Laurent's cabinet discussed announcing mission accomplished and bringing the Canadians home, but Pearson made the point that their departure would likely end the ICC and shatter the peace. He believed that working with India on the ICC was important in advancing Canadian-Indian relations. Plus, he said, ICC participation would continue to afford Canada a role in international discussions regarding Vietnam and the region. ICC partners Poland and India, as well as the Soviet Union, Britain, and the United States, urged Canada to stay. So, despite misgivings, Canada remained in Vietnam.[5] In 1957 Canada allocated $4 million to the mission and posted 137 diplomats and soldiers.[6] It remained a dangerous posting. On April 12, ICC diplomat Albert Edward Lucien Cannon was followed home and stabbed to death in his Saigon apartment. His murder was never solved.

In April 1958 the ICC headquarters were moved from their cramped and inadequate offices in Hanoi to a somewhat more adequate space in Saigon. The ICC did less and its partners bickered more. In its first year, the ICC addressed ten major cases a month and 81 percent of its decisions were settled unanimously. In all of 1960, the ICC addressed only eighteen cases and a mere three were unanimously settled.[7] While the communist Poles had begun as somewhat fair arbiters, by 1960 they were as blatantly and consistently voting to support the North as Canada's votes were backing the South.

As for the Americans, they continued to rely on Canada's tacit support for their still largely secret counterinsurgency endeavours. State Department briefing papers written to prepare President Kennedy for his May 1961 trip to Ottawa stated: "The Canadian government shares our view that the situation in Viet-nam is serious and we can count on their continued efforts to serve Free World interests in the ICC."[8] A month later Kennedy went through the motion of asking for ICC permission to deploy 1,500 more American advisors, along with more planes, helicopters, trucks, and assorted weapons and equipment. Over Poland's objection, the ICC approved the request; but Ottawa got word to the White House that the American troops should stagger their arrival rather than showing up in a conspicuously large group.[9]

Hugh Campbell, who served as a Canadian ICC commissioner in Vietnam from 1961 to 1963, later confessed: "I was bloody ashamed of the things I was required to do. . . . I don't recall any occasion when I saw anything in print that we should cover for the Americans, but at the same time, if you did not, you would be in a very difficult position."[10]

Meanwhile, Ho Chi Minh's goal of creating a unified, sovereign Vietnam remained the same as it had been since he penned his 1919 letter to President Wilson at Versailles. With Chinese backing, he built up his military and used a series of roads and trails through Laos to funnel money, personnel and weapons into the South to bolster the growing popularity of the National Liberation Front. The NLF was a political organization formed in 1960 to overthrow the South Vietnamese government and bring about the unification of Vietnam. The NLF's military arm, the Viet Cong, pursued those goals by supporting the North Vietnamese regular army though guerilla warfare. South Vietnam president Ngo Dinh Diem, of course, still dreamed of someday ruling all of Vietnam. But the increasing effectiveness of the Viet Cong led him to become more reliant on American help.

When Kennedy took office in January 1961, there were about nine hundred American military advisors in Vietnam. At the time of his death nearly three years later, there were over sixteen thousand.[11] He had steadily increased financial and logistical support for Diem's government in the hope that it would eventually stand on its own. He spoke publicly about doing everything necessary to stop a communist victory, but also said that the South Vietnamese people had to win the war themselves. Despite repeated urgings from advisors and generals, Kennedy had steadfastly refused to order the bombing of North Vietnamese targets or the deployment of American troops.[12] He had hoped that secret counterinsurgency methods would discourage the North and strengthen the South but came to doubt they would ever be enough, so he was planning a phased withdrawal of Americans from Vietnam to begin in late 1963.[13]

But then Kennedy made a tragic error. In August 1963 his advisors debated whether Diem should be overthrown due to obvious corruption and a brutal crackdown on Buddhists, followed by a dismissive reaction to monks who protested by publicly setting themselves on fire. In the end, Kennedy approved a coup that would be supported by Americans but led by South Vietnamese generals. On November 2, in an act Kennedy had not sanctioned, Diem and his brother, security chief and principal advisor Ngo Dinh Nhu, were assassinated. Just weeks later, Kennedy was struck down in Dallas.

Vice-President Lyndon Johnson was sworn in as the new president and he kept Kennedy's cabinet and principal advisors. They saw problems in South Vietnam intensify when Diem's assassination caused a power vacuum that led generals to fight each other more than the Viet Cong. Following another coup in January 1964, General Nguyen Khanh formed a government. Johnson was stuck fighting an intractable enemy, in support of an untenable government, to save people who had largely joined the other side.

The increasingly powerful general secretary of the Indochinese Communist Party, Le Duan, convinced Ho Chi Minh to take advantage of the uncertainty that followed the assassinations. Le Duan led efforts to ensure that North Vietnam's regular army (NVA) and Viet Cong insurgents operating in the South were afforded more political and material support. In January 1964 the National Liberation Front convened its second Congress and announced that it would reach out to South Vietnamese leaders in an attempt to resolve matters of contention. Ho announced that he hoped the Americans and South Vietnamese would agree to the political solution put forward by French president Charles de Gaulle. De Gaulle had proposed the idea of neutralization, whereby the Americans would withdraw from Vietnam, allowing the North and South to negotiate a settlement that would remove the country from foreign interference and Cold War machinations.[14] Much of the international community, including United Nations Secretary-General U Thant, agreed with de Gaulle.

Also in support of a negotiated settlement were formidable American opinion shapers such as the *New York Times*, the *Washington Post*, and *Newsweek*, along with influential syndicated columnists Walter Lippmann, David Halberstam, and James Reston. Reston had published an article in November 1963 asking, "Why a Truce in Korea and Not in Vietnam?"[15] While many congressmen privately spoke of their opposition to military escalation in Vietnam and the need for a diplomatic solution, powerful voices such as Senate Majority Leader Mike Mansfield and Senate Foreign Relations Committee Chairman William Fulbright went public. Mansfield, for instance, urged the South Vietnamese government to sit down with the NLF. "Perhaps among themselves they can come up with a solution," he said.[16]

A clearly frustrated Johnson complained to National Security Advisor McGeorge Bundy of the tightening Gordian knot: "Vietnam just worries the hell out of me. I don't see what we can ever hope to get out of there with once we're committed. . . . What the hell is Vietnam worth to me? What is Laos worth to me? What is it worth to this country? [But] if you start running from the Communists, they may just chase you right into your own kitchen."[17]

Johnson's falling back on domino theory fears is fascinating because in May 1964 he had asked CIA analysts to assess what would happen to the rest of Southeast Asia if Laos and Vietnam came under North

Vietnamese control. On June 9 the CIA reported to the president: "With the possible exception of Cambodia, it is unlikely that any nation in the area would quickly succumb to Communism as the result of the fall of Laos and South Vietnam. Furthermore, a continuation of Communism in the area would not be inexorable and any spread which did occur would take time—time in which the total situation may change in any number of ways unfavorable to the Communist cause."[18] Therefore, before he committed American troops to Vietnam, Johnson knew the domino theory that had motivated Eisenhower and Kennedy was suspect and that staying in Vietnam to stop the spread of communism was unnecessary. Johnson could leave but, just as Kennedy had said to Pearson, the problem was finding an honourable way out. Intensifying his exasperation was Johnson's desire to focus on other matters, primarily his ambitious domestic agenda and winning the November 1964 presidential election.

A consummate deal maker, Johnson thought a way to silence critics demanding negotiations and perhaps to get out of the Vietnam trap altogether could be to appear to be standing firm against the communists while secretly reaching out to Ho Chi Minh. The trouble with that option was that the two had no way of speaking with each other. There was no American ambassador in Hanoi, and no personal or back-channel communication between the two governments had been established.

Secretary of State Dean Rusk was tasked with finding an emissary. He considered asking Britain, Yugoslavia, Japan, or even the United Arab Republic but, after consultations with the hard-nosed American ambassador to South Vietnam, Henry Cabot Lodge, Rusk recommended asking Canada. The Canadians were considered ideal for several reasons: they had experience as peacekeepers and a well-earned reputation as successful diplomats; they knew Vietnam through eight years with the ICC and could move stealthily through the country; they and the North Vietnamese both spoke French; and they were reliable American allies.[19]

On April 29, 1964, Prime Minister Pearson and Secretary of State for External Affairs Paul Martin (father of future prime minister Paul Martin, Jr.) welcomed Secretary Rusk to Ottawa. The intelligent and politically ambitious Martin had visited Vietnam in 1956, met with Diem, and closely followed developments in the region. Rusk briefly outlined his take on the current situation, portraying South Vietnam in somewhat glowing terms, indicating that Prime Minister Khanh was a stable leader who was bringing order to his country and effectively stopping Viet Cong incursions. Rusk said that President Johnson wanted peace in Vietnam. Given nearly a decade of America's blatant disregard for the Geneva Agreement and those charged with overseeing its implementation, he somewhat disingenuously asserted that Johnson also wanted all the region's players to adhere to the agreement's terms. It was in pursuit of these goals, Rusk explained, that the president wanted Canada to take a message to Ho Chi Minh. Because the top-secret operation was meant to return with a deal, it was codenamed BACON, as in "bringing home the bacon."[20]

Pearson and Martin were skeptical about whether the mission would work and whether Canada should be involved. Pearson told Rusk that current Canadian ICC commissioner Gordon Cox did not share Rusk's confidence in Khanh because his government's survival was entirely dependent on American support. Nor was Pearson convinced that the Viet Cong's strength was waning. Rusk insisted on the accuracy of his intelligence.

It was 1954 all over again. Canada was being asked to ignore misgivings about a dangerous mission with more certain risks than potential rewards. Also, as in 1954, an essential ally was asking for help, the Cold War goal of protecting a democratic state from a communist incursion could be pursued, and if the mission was successful, a war could be averted. Plus, a successful mission meant the Canadians in Vietnam could finally come home. These considerations led Pearson and Martin to agree to participate.[21]

Rusk reported that Ambassador Lodge believed that Canada's Geoffrey Murray, whom he had known at the United Nations, could be trusted to lead the mission. But Pearson and Martin told Rusk that the man soon to become Canada's new ICC commissioner would be even better.

Born to a large, upper-middle-class Toronto family, J. Blair Seaborn was a soft-spoken, well-respected, red-haired, forty-year-old diplomat enjoying his seventeenth year with external affairs. After graduating from the University of Toronto and serving three years in the army, he had considered becoming an economist but opted instead to join the enthusiastic team who were making it such an exciting time to be part of Canada's diplomatic corps.[22] He had worked at the United Nations, The Hague, in Paris, and, for three years, as a counsellor in Canada's embassy in Moscow. In the spring of 1964, he was head of Ottawa's East European desk. Seaborn was known for his intelligence, quiet professionalism, dedication to duty, gentle sense of humour, and stoicism—all qualities that made him a good man in a crisis.[23]

Rusk agreed on Seaborn and the deal was struck. Rusk, Lodge, and their staffs then set to work developing talking points for Seaborn to take to Hanoi. Intense arguments arose over what Seaborn should say. Secretary of State Rusk wished to emphasize the carrot—the advantages to be gained by the North through peaceful negotiations. Ambassador Lodge wanted Seaborn to wave the stick—the all-out war that would befall Ho Chi Minh if he did not surrender to American demands.[24] The two camps finally agreed, and a Pearson-Johnson meeting was arranged.

On May 28 the media was told that the two leaders were just coincidentally in New York City at the same time and so would meet "casually" at the Hilton New Yorker Hotel. Behind closed doors and with McGeorge Bundy at his side, Johnson reiterated Rusk's message: all he wanted was peace. He outlined the agreed-upon talking points. Most important was that Ho must stand down and Khanh be allowed to remain standing. Seaborn's mission, the president said, was a last chance to avoid a war that he did not want.[25]

As he had in Ottawa, Pearson challenged American assumptions and assertions. He told Johnson that he, along with most Canadians and other Western allies, would oppose an escalation of the war. Pearson said that wars are easy to start but hard to stop and expressed his long-held fear that greater military action in Vietnam could lead to the use of nuclear weapons. Johnson repeated that he wanted only peace and that if military action was needed, then it would be limited.[26] After the thirty-minute meeting, Johnson said nothing to the media and Pearson told reporters the two had discussed issues regarding the Great Lakes.

While the prime minister was speaking with the president and then misleading the press, Blair Seaborn, Paul Martin, and three other senior Canadian officials were ensconced in Martin's office with the CIA's Chester Cooper and Rusk's special assistant and head of the interagency Vietnam Coordinating Committee, William H. Sullivan. Sullivan began on the wrong foot by saying that Rusk would communicate directly with Seaborn. Martin said no; Seaborn was a Canadian acting under the direction of the Canadian government and would not be an American agent. Martin insisted that Seaborn would report only to him and that all American communications would go through him. Sullivan backed down.[27]

Sullivan then reiterated the peace-or-peril message that Seaborn would offer and briefed him on the information he should seek. Martin was even more direct than Pearson in his insistence that Canada would never support the war's escalation, stating that Canada's primary reason for accepting the dangerous mission was to help the two sides step away from war. Sullivan said strategic and limited bombing might someday be necessary but that the president did not envision the introduction of American ground troops. Martin went on to say that he and his government did not agree with the details or scope of the message

Seaborn was being asked to deliver because it seemed more like an ultimatum than an invitation to negotiate. It would be better for all, he argued, if the Americans convened a new Geneva conference to seek a political end to a political problem.

Seaborn then spoke up, stating that if the carrot and stick messages were to be effective, then both needed to be more specific. Sullivan repeated that what Seaborn was to present had been carefully vetted and approved by the president and so it could not now be changed.[28]

The Canadians were clearly dissatisfied with the content of the message but ultimately agreed that it was worth delivering. They insisted, and the Americans finally agreed, that the Canadians would at least have final approval of the message's text.[29] With that concession, the Canadians agreed to deliver it faithfully. Martin allowed that even though the mission was not as he, Pearson, or Seaborn wished, he hoped that it would allow Canada to play a role in avoiding a new and wider Vietnam war.[30]

Seaborn later said: "All of us had doubts right along the line that a large increase of American force could produce an eventual settlement between North and South. At the same time, all of us were so concerned and preoccupied with the possibilities of a great escalation of the military situation in that area and what it might lead to."[31] Despite clearly expressed misgivings, Seaborn acknowledged that, with this much at stake and stopping a war at least a possibility, his assignment was one that neither he nor the Canadian government could refuse.

Seaborn had initially not been enthused about his assignment to lead the ICC, but the secret mission intrigued him.[32] He prepared carefully by reading all he could and consulting with everyone available to help him gain a greater understanding of North and South Vietnam, their people, and their leaders.

Seaborn's wife, Carol, like the spouses of all diplomats, understood the sacrifices families make when assignments change, and was aware that this posting was a potentially dangerous one. Carol nonetheless agreed that he should take it and that she and their two school-age children should move with him for the year in Vietnam. The clandestine peace mission meant that his departure date was expedited, and so Carol was left behind to rent their Ottawa home, sell their car, store furniture, and pack essentials. Throughout his preparations to lead the ICC, Seaborn whispered not a word of his secret mission—not even to Carol. Already worried, she had no idea of the real risks ahead.

SEEKING PEACE

A few weeks later, in June 1964, Seaborn settled himself into his quarters in Saigon and met his staff. On June 18, he was on a plane to Hanoi and then sitting, uncomfortably hot, in the back of a hulking black Russian-made car. He gazed out at the city's wide boulevards lined with old French mansions and ornate multi-storey buildings whose rounded edges and curves offered an air of grandeur. It was a city of bicycles that shared busy streets with cars, diesel-belching buses, pedestrians, and all manner of street vendors.

The car cruised to a halt in front of the former French governor's palace. Seaborn was shown to a huge ballroom, rich with Vietnamese art and antique furnishings. Within minutes he was shaking hands with Pham Van Dong. Silver-haired and handsome, the fifty-eight-year-old North Vietnamese prime minister had worked with Ho Chi Minh's Vietnamese Revolutionary Youth Association since the 1920s. He had been arrested by the French and suffered seven years of hard labour in Hoa Lo Prison; Americans later dubbed it the "Hanoi Hilton." His health had been destroyed in prison, where he acquired malaria and tuberculosis. Pham was Ho's most trusted colleague and advisor and had been the primary spokesperson for the Vietminh in Geneva. During his term with the ICC in Vietnam, Sherwood Lett had come to know Pham and to respect his intelligence, integrity, and openness.[33]

Seaborn and Pham wore conservative blue business suits. They sat facing each other on twin embroidered couches and exchanged pleasantries in French. The two men were friendly, calm, and confident. A North Vietnamese Army liaison officer silently scribbled notes. One would never guess that the fates of millions of lives, many yet unborn, were at stake.

Seaborn presented a letter of authority from Pearson, which Pham carefully read twice. Pham said that he sincerely appreciated the role Canada was playing in Vietnam and that he believed this mission to be of great importance.[34]

Seaborn assured Pham that the message he was about to convey came directly from the American president. To ensure that it was accurately relayed, he read from a prepared text. He said that President Johnson wanted peace in Vietnam, no permanent American bases, and the return home of all America's advisors. However, Johnson saw the current conflict as part of a global struggle between communism and liberal democracy and so it was of the utmost importance. Johnson was determined, Seaborn continued, that the Geneva Agreement's 17th parallel border be made permanent, with the governments of North and South Vietnam remaining in place. While the United States had no desire to attack North Vietnam or overthrow its government, it would not allow the Viet Cong–led insurgency to continue or permit the fall of South Vietnam's government. The solution proposed would be like Korea, with a communist North and a non-communist South.

Seaborn went on to reiterate what the ICC had declared in a 1962 report: the North Vietnamese government was solely responsible for the Viet Cong's violent activity in South Vietnam. If Ho ended his support for the Viet Cong and pledged to do nothing more to destabilize the South Vietnamese government, then the United States would be willing to leave and to provide economic aid for North Vietnam. Seaborn added that Canada would augment American economic assistance with additional financial aid. But, he warned, Ho must understand that American patience was limited. Johnson would do all that was necessary to defend his ally, and this could include a full-scale war that would be visited upon North Vietnamese cities. If such an escalation should occur, he said, there would be tremendous devastation and colossal loss of life.[35] Seaborn set aside the text and they sat in silence for a moment with their eyes locked. The carrot and stick had been delivered.

Prime Minister Pham had listened intently to everything Seaborn said, offering affirming sounds but no interruption. With a soft but firm tone, he then replied that his government had prepared for this meeting as the Americans and Canadians had, and so he was able to be clear. Ho Chi Minh, he explained, believed that a just solution involved four points: an immediate cessation of hostilities; a withdrawal of American personnel and military equipment; an agreement that the people of the South be allowed to determine their own future with the Liberation Front a part of the negotiations; and Vietnam's reunification.

Seaborn nodded, understanding from his study of Vietnam's history that the offer was essentially what Ho Chi Minh had proposed in 1919, and in 1946, and again in 1954. But there was more. Offering a way for the United States to save face and claim peace with honour, Pham said that reunification need not happen immediately upon American withdrawal. Further, the new Vietnam would stay out of the Cold War by becoming like India and, as de Gaulle had suggested, non-aligned and neutral.[36] Pham conceded that none of this would be easy for the United States to accept but that his government would be patient. He advocated an all-party "round-table" negotiation to settle matters in a peaceful fashion.

But then Pham met Seaborn's thinly veiled threat with one of his own: "The U.S. can go on increasing aid to South Vietnam. It can increase its own army personnel. I suffer to see the war go on, develop, intensify. Yet our people are determined to struggle." Leaning forward for emphasis, Pham said: "It's impossible, quite impossible—excuse me for saying this—for you Westerners to understand the force of the people's will to resist, and to continue. The struggle of our people exceeds the imagination. It has astonished us too."[37] In other words, if Johnson wanted war, bring it on.

Seaborn interrupted to repeat that the United States did not want war and would not escalate toward one without provocation but, again, American patience was not limitless. Pham merely nodded.

The conversation concluded with courteous bows and handshakes. The prime minister said he would respect the secrecy of the Canadian mission and offer no formal public statement. He also promised that while President Johnson considered all that he and Seaborn had discussed, his government would do nothing to provoke an American response. But, he pleaded, the Americans must be made to understand that they could never win a war in Vietnam, no matter how many soldiers they sent, how many bombs they dropped, or how many years they fought. Demonstrating that he kept abreast of American public sentiment, he referred to one of the country's most influential journalists and said, "Let me quote to you America's Walter Lippmann: 'There's no light at the end of the tunnel.'"[38] With these words of iron, Pham smiled and said that he looked forward to future talks and hoped that next time Seaborn could meet with Ho Chi Minh.

Seaborn was encouraged. He had found Pham Van Dong to be poised, intelligent, and "an impressive leader by any standard."[39] As he knew at the outset, the two sides had very different goals, the most glaring of which was whether there would be one or two Vietnams. However, if both sides really wanted peace, the conversation offered a road map to that end. If nothing else, neither side could later claim to have misunderstood the other's objectives or the price they were willing to pay to pursue them.

Besides delivering the message and assessing Pham's response, Seaborn had been instructed to determine whether Ho's government was being directed by China. His conversation with Pham and ICC personnel led him to conclude that the North Vietnamese government was in full control of their decisions and were not the Chinese puppets too often portrayed by so many in the American and Canadian media. This conclusion was supported by research he had done before coming to Vietnam regarding the historic distrust of China that lay in the hearts of the Vietnamese people. They wished to forge their own future, free of any foreign influence, including that of the Chinese.[40]

Seaborn had also been tasked with determining whether the North Vietnamese people were loyal to Ho and weary of war. To make his assessment, Seaborn enjoyed a few days travelling in and around Hanoi. He saw the good and not so good parts of the city, visited tourist sites, and was driven through the surrounding countryside, where he marvelled at the spectacular natural beauty. His fluent French allowed him to speak with people about their government and hopes regarding their country's future.

He also worked in Hanoi's rather run-down, roach-infested ICC offices, where the Canadians were laughingly protected by a single bored North Vietnamese soldier who lounged across the street, only occasionally glancing over at his charges. Seaborn met with the under-worked and frequently exasperated Canadian political officer, the sergeant, and the corporal who comprised the entire staff. Like those from Hanoi's many embassies, they often escaped the oven-like conditions of their offices to pass steamy afternoons in nearby air-conditioned bars, where they traded gossip with other Westerners and sipped cold drinks with locals among the ever-present prostitutes.[41]

Seaborn observed food on Hanoi's store shelves, goods in the shops; the children were in school and their parents at their jobs. It was a city that was working. There was deep and broad support for Ho Chi Minh and no evidence of divisions within his government or factions among the people. He saw nothing betraying a fear of the United States or anything that could be described as war weariness. Most government officials and citizens seemed convinced, he observed, that the United States would never bring the war to the North due to its fear of provoking the Chinese and possibly starting a third world war.[42]

Shortly after Seaborn's return to Saigon, the nature of his secret mission was troublingly called into question. He learned that on the day before his meeting with Pham Van Dong, General William Westmoreland, recently placed in command of American forces in Vietnam, had conducted a press conference during which he stated that he could not rule out attacks aimed directly at Northern cities. Hours later, the State Department had released previously classified testimony in which Assistant Secretary of State William Bundy had told a senate committee that the United States would do all that was necessary to end the insurgency in South Vietnam, which could include American-led attacks on the North.

The news release and press conference had obviously been timed to emphasize the big-stick portion of the message that Seaborn carried to Hanoi. They also made clear that the Americans were preparing for war while Seaborn was offering peace, and that Johnson saw Seaborn's mission not as genuine but as coercive diplomacy. It appeared that Seaborn had been dispatched to ask Pham not to negotiate but to capitulate.

Seaborn composed three long and detailed cables to Martin that were forwarded to the State Department. They faithfully reported all that he and Pham had discussed, all he had seen, and his conclusions. North Vietnamese (DRVN) leaders, he wrote somewhat ominously, "are completely convinced that military action at any level is not, repeat not, going to bring success for the U.S. and government forces in South Vietnam." Supporting what Johnson was hearing from his embassy in Saigon, Seaborn further reported on the North Vietnamese conviction that "the Khanh government is losing ground on the local political front and . . . that in the fullness of time success is assured for the Liberation Front supported by the DRVN."[43] Seaborn could not have been clearer—the Americans were losing now and, if they pressed matters, they would lose in the long run. As Sherwood Lett had done before him, Seaborn was providing a clear view of a certain future, but this time, directly to American decision makers.

Seaborn's reports were carefully analyzed in Washington, but were not well received. Like most other Americans who weighed in, Secretary of State Rusk's special assistant William Sullivan dismissed the road to peace that Pham offered and Seaborn supported. He called Seaborn's report sobering but said it simply mirrored the least optimistic of the options being offered to the president.[44] The state department's P.H. Kreisberg summarized the content of the cables and agreed with Sullivan. He nonetheless added that the tone and content of the Seaborn-Pham discussions suggested that further talks would be beneficial. Kreisburg suggested that Seaborn would be needed again because there appeared to be no appetite for direct contact between the North Vietnamese and American governments.[45]

After considering Seaborn's report, Rusk let Paul Martin know that there would be no official American response to North Vietnam. Seaborn was asked to delay his planned second visit to Hanoi so the United States could demonstrate its 'steadfastness.'"[46] There was trepidation in Ottawa about what that might mean.

With his reports submitted, Seaborn turned to the task of leading Canada's ICC delegation. Like every predecessor since Lett's departure, he found the experience vexing. After running into Polish intransigence and the bureaucratic rats' nests contrived by both the North and South Vietnamese, he pondered whether Canada and the ICC were doing any good at all.[47] Historian Robert Bothwell later quipped, "The Canadians pressed, the Poles obstructed, and the Indians dithered."[48]

Seaborn's frustration was somewhat alleviated in late July with the arrival in Saigon of Carol and the children. The family settled quickly into their new life and temporary home—a large, yellow stucco house within an old French villa. They enrolled their son, Geoffrey, in a French school. Their daughter, Virginia, attended an international school run by Belgian nuns who inexplicably frightened the children into obedience by relating stories of Viet Cong atrocities. The family enjoyed tennis and swimming. It was as if there was not a war brewing, except for a couple of bracing incidents: the occasion when the plane they were flying in was shot at and forced down; and the time when a bomb exploded at the American military headquarters next to Virginia's school.

SECOND TRY

Canadians and Americans tuning in to enjoy the antics of the crew of *McHale's Navy* or the contrived competition on *Hollywood Talent Scouts* were disappointed on Tuesday, August 4, 1964 when their television programs were interrupted by a speech from the White House. Frowning sternly through his dark-rimmed glasses, President Johnson spoke unnaturally slowly as he announced that on August 2, and again earlier that day, two U.S. Navy destroyers, USS *Maddox* and USS *Turner Joy*, had been victims of unprovoked attacks in the Gulf of Tonkin, ten miles off the coast of North Vietnam. Two of the attacking ships had been sunk. There were no American casualties. He said that, in a "limited and fitting response," American air attacks were at that moment being launched on North Vietnamese ships and land targets. Johnson said he did not want a wider war but would continue to defend American ships and personnel while protecting the people of South Vietnam from the terrorist violence being perpetrated upon them by the communists. He also noted that he had spoken with congressional leaders of both parties and that they promised quick passage of a resolution authorizing him to do whatever he deemed necessary to protect American interests in the region.[49] On August 7, after little debate, in an 88 to 2 vote, the Senate passed what became known as the Gulf of Tonkin Resolution. The House of Representatives passed it unanimously.

Just three days later, on August 10, Seaborn was on his way back to Hanoi aboard an old Boeing Stratoliner. It was one of three pre–Second World War planes owned and operated by the French company Aigle Azur that, although seemingly barely able to remain aloft, were used by the ICC for travel. Seaborn had grown used to the rumbling, bouncy journeys and non-attentive French crews but was nonetheless rattled during one flight when a couple of stewardesses who were drinking in the rear of the plane were joined by the captain. As the captain wove his way back toward the cockpit with a full glass in hand, Seaborn asked him if drinking champagne was a good idea. The captain shrugged and offered only that, if it disagreed with him, then perhaps Seaborn should not drink champagne.

Due to the Gulf of Tonkin tensions and the rather slapdash manner in which the Americans had prepared his talking points, Seaborn was even less optimistic about his second Hanoi mission. His job was to douse the sparks of war, but his message was neither new nor conciliatory. He was to insist that the response to the unprovoked attacks on the *Maddox* and *Turner Joy* had been "limited and appropriate" but that future actions would not be if the United States was again tested. Seaborn was to repeat that if Hanoi did not withdraw from the South and end the insurgency, then the United States would initiate air and naval action that would wreak havoc on North Vietnamese cities.[50] America, Seaborn was to advise Prime Minister Pham, was not a paper tiger.

Pham and Seaborn met in the same grand room as before, but this time there was no polite small talk. The prime minister was angry. Without allowing Seaborn to speak, he shouted that the first attack on the *Maddox* was in response to illegal American actions in the Gulf of Tonkin involving American and South Vietnamese incursions on North Vietnamese islands. Further, he claimed that the United States had invented the second attack; the American goal must have been to employ the ruse to bring the war to the North in order to find a way out of the political impasse in the South. Barely containing his rage, Pham seethed, "Up to now we have tried to avoid serious trouble; but it becomes more difficult now because the war has been carried to our territory." To emphasize the dangerous steps the Americans were taking, he warned, "If war comes to North Vietnam it will come to all of South East Asia."[51]

Seaborn ignored the threat and delivered his own. He also repeated the offer of economic aid if Pham's government would pledge to end hostilities directed at the government and people of South Vietnam and give up on dreams of reunification. Pham waved Seaborn off and declared that after absorbing enormous costs, North Vietnam would eventually prevail in a war with the United States. Economic aid was unnecessary; compromise was unnecessary; his government understood the peril of the moment and were not hiding it from the people. "The people will have to make many sacrifices," he said, "but we are in a state of legitimate defense because the war is imposed upon us."[52] The only way to avoid war was for the Americans to leave and allow the Vietnamese people to plan their own future. As he had in June, Pham cited French president Charles de Gaulle, who for two years had been publicly calling for that solution.[53]

With harsh messages heard and delivered, the tone of the conversation calmed as the two agreed that they must continue to talk in order to avoid a war that would be devastating for so many innocents. As they were leaving, Pham gently laid an arm over Seaborn's shoulder and said: "My son, you have your experiences with the Americans and we have ours. They are not the same."[54] They shook hands and Pham expressed hope that the Canadian channel of communication would remain open.

As on his earlier visit, Seaborn spent a few days in and around Hanoi. He was shocked at how the city had changed in just two months. Buildings were being reinforced, protective walls and bomb shelters constructed, and defensive slit trenches dug. There were daily air raid drills. Preparations were being made to evacuate mothers and children.

Reporters had been told in June that the Seaborn-Pham meeting was merely a routine courtesy call by yet another Canadian ICC commissioner, and so it had been ignored. No one in Ottawa or Washington had leaked Seaborn's cables. The August meeting had also been secret and again there were no media reports of its having occurred.

Back in Saigon, Seaborn composed a detailed report. It expressed many of the same points he had made before but emphasized that the American attacks and threats had not shaken but steeled North Vietnamese resolve. Bombing to win concessions had not worked; he expressed doubt that further bombing would bring a different result. He also noted Hanoi's increased war-readiness, again emphasizing that the North Vietnamese were willing to accept the losses that an American war would inflict, secure in the confidence that they would eventually win. For this reason, as Pham had said in June, the North Vietnamese wished to negotiate a settlement to reunite their country now, rather than after a destructive and bloody war.

Seaborn's August report proved problematic because it contradicted the narrative then being spun by Secretary of Defense Robert McNamara and others of influence in Washington. It offered nothing to support the consensus within the American administration as to how all would unfold. The report was read and dismissed.

Nonetheless, American leaders understood the value of Seaborn's experience in Hanoi and so regularly asked for briefings. General Maxwell Taylor, former chair of the Joint Chiefs of Staff had succeeded Lodge as American ambassador in July 1964 and often asked to speak with Seaborn. Seaborn also briefed General William Westmoreland and important American visitors such as McNamara and, although he did not yet hold an official government position, Henry Kissinger.

The deteriorating situation in Vietnam was reflected by the increasing frequency of gunfire in Saigon and echoes of mortar and rocket fire in distant hills. Seaborn and his wife discussed whether she and the children should return home but decided they would stay, for the time being.

In September, Seaborn flew to Tokyo to meet with Secretary of State for External Affairs, Paul Martin, who was there on a trade mission. After a long day of exhausting trade meetings, Martin repaired to his hotel pool. Seaborn borrowed a pair of pink shorts from the Canadian ambassador that were far too large for his slight frame, and the two discussed Vietnam while paddling in the warm water. Seaborn was blunt in his assessment and followed it up with a more detailed written report to Martin in which he concluded: "We are deluding ourselves if we think that by our participation in the ICC we are making any contribution . . . to peace and stability in this part of Southeast Asia, to a truer knowledge of what is happening, or restraint upon the parties. If we are not doing anything really useful, why do we not pull out, if need be, unilaterally?"[55]

Withdrawal from Vietnam was again seriously debated in Ottawa, but the already expressed arguments carried the day. Martin contended, and Pearson agreed, that Canada's voice may have little volume in Vietnam or Washington at the moment, but if the Canadians pulled out it would fall silent. Seaborn was told to be prepared for another secret mission to Hanoi and meanwhile to continue to make the ICC work as well as possible, even if that meant isolating Canada still more from its Polish and Indian partners.[56]

In November 1964 Lyndon Johnson won the presidency in a landslide, taking 61 percent of the popular vote. Martin asked Rusk if, with the election settled, the president would like to launch a new Seaborn mission with a more substantive message that might this time spark a negotiated peace.[57] American officials had not been considering using Seaborn again but agreed the idea had merit. Martin and Seaborn were soon in the old position of asking for something more substantive and specific to take to Ho. But Johnson offered nothing new.

Seaborn arrived in Hanoi on December 10. An indication of the shrinking value of the Canadian contact was made clear when Pham, once he had welcomed Seaborn, left the room to the Canadian and North Vietnam's ICC liaison, Colonel Ha Van Lau. Seaborn delivered the stale carrot of unspecified economic assistance and the vague stick of retaliations for continued Viet Cong aggression. The colonel listened without comment. He then repeated Ho Chi Minh's four-point plan for peace.[58]

Seaborn wrote another report that was dutifully sent through Ottawa to Washington, stating once again that the North Vietnamese people and government were ready for war, ready for its bloody costs, and assured of their eventual victory. He repeated that escalation in terms of ground troops and bombing would change nothing. He emphasized his belief that negotiations were the only way out of certain catastrophe.[59] As with Seaborn's August report, there was no response from the Americans.

LIES WITHIN SECRETS

Throughout their sincere if perhaps overly idealistic attempts to play a diplomatic role in stopping the march to war, Pearson, Martin, and Seaborn guessed, but had not known for sure, the degree to which the Americans had for some time been opposing genuine diplomacy. Back in the spring and summer of 1963, President Diem's brother, the mercurial and powerful Ngo Dinh Nhu, had publicly stated that the Americans should leave Vietnam. Seaborn and the Canadians had no way of knowing that it was that threat, along with CIA reports that Diem and his brother were opening negotiations with Ho Chi Minh to create a coalition government, that had frustrated President Kennedy.[60] A negotiated settlement of that nature would have contradicted American goals in Vietnam and so could not be allowed to happen. Diem was soon dead.

Pearson, Martin, and Seaborn also did not know that Johnson was as spooked as Kennedy by the prospect of South Vietnam negotiating a separate peace with Ho Chi Minh. The president's fears were rendered more intense when, in December 1963, Secretary of Defense McNamara told him there was growing support in South Vietnam for de Gaulle's idea of creating neutralist regimes in Southeast Asia, including in Vietnam. At Johnson's behest, McNamara led the charge to kill the idea. The effort included, in part, expanding the war to strengthen America's bargaining position before any sort of peace negotiations could gain traction.[61]

While planning Seaborn's first mission, the Canadians had not been told that Secretary of State Rusk had prepared—but not shared—a document entitled "Further Outline for Mr. Seaborn." It provided much greater detail about the carrot and stick to be offered than the talking points Seaborn eventually received. The economic aid that would be offered to North Vietnam would include grants of food, guaranteed trade, and help to support and stabilize its currency. The United States would recognize the government of North Vietnam and encourage its allies to do the same. The Americans would offer full amnesty to Viet Cong fighters and North Vietnamese soldiers. All prisoners would be unconditionally released. Further, within a year, the 23,000 American advisors in South Vietnam would be reduced to 350—the same number that had been present at the signing of the Geneva Agreement. Martin and Seaborn had asked for this level of specificity, but the Americans had refused. Ambassador Lodge's hard line had won the argument over Rusk's attempt to provide more detail in America's offer, and so the document had been filed. Seaborn's mission had thereby been sabotaged before he boarded the plane for Hanoi when all the specific advantages the North would win by ending their aggression had been removed, leaving only ambiguous promises and nebulous threats.[62]

The Canadians were also unaware that in January 1964, five months before Seaborn's first mission, Johnson had approved Operation Plan

(OPLAN) 34A.[63] It called for covert attacks on North Vietnam to demonstrate the risks inherent in continuing to support the Viet Cong insurgency in the South while buying time for the stabilization and strengthening of the South Vietnamese government. North Vietnamese bombing targets were chosen and logistical plans made to hit them. It was OPLAN 34A being put into action with attacks on North Vietnamese islands that had instigated the Gulf of Tonkin incident.

Few knew that in early May, a month before Seaborn arrived for his first meeting in Hanoi and three months before the Gulf of Tonkin confrontations, Assistant Secretary of State William Bundy had written a draft Congressional Resolution affording the president the legal authority to wage war without a formal declaration.[64] It was Bundy's pre-written draft that was pulled from a drawer when the second Gulf of Tonkin attack provided the excuse for its employment. Bundy's memo became the Gulf of Tonkin Resolution and the basis for all that followed.

Finally, the Canadians did not know, because no one outside of a select few in Washington knew, that North Vietnam's prime minister was right when he told Seaborn that there had been no second Gulf of Tonkin attack. Johnson had lied to Congress and to the American people. The president also did not reveal that the military was able to retaliate and hit five North Vietnamese naval bases and an oil depot that day because the targets had been set months earlier.

United Nations Secretary-General U Thant was also unaware of the secrets and lies when, in 1964, he tried to initiate a peace mission similar to Seaborn's. After failing to gain adequate American support for his efforts, U Thant conducted a news conference in February 1965 in which he said that the United States was withholding the truth from the American people about the possibility of ending the war by refusing to participate in genuine diplomacy.[65]

If Seaborn, Pearson, and Martin had been aware of the truth behind the American lies, their participation in the North Vietnamese negotiations could be dismissed as a cynical sham. However, because so much was kept from them and so many convincing lies were told, their efforts to stop the Vietnam War can be accepted as sincere. The Canadians were hopeful but not naïve. They were idealistic, perhaps, but never delusional about their power in Hanoi, Saigon, or Washington.[66] Pearson also knew that among his first priorities was to maintain good relations with the United States, and agreeing to send Seaborn addressed that priority.[67] Of course, the Canadian people had been left completely in the dark regarding the missions and machinations.

THE END OF THE BEGINNING

On February 12, 1965, the North Vietnamese government ordered Seaborn and the Polish and Indian commissioners to have the five fixed ICC teams located in the North withdrawn to Hanoi. The move created even more limits on the ICC's shrinking range of operations and its overall effectiveness. The ICC became a ghost that could appear occasionally, remind those with real power of past promises, but do little.[68] Meanwhile, Canadian ICC officials continued to provide valuable intelligence for the Americans. In May 1965, for instance, Canadian ICC commissioner David Jackson reported to the American embassy from his station in Hanoi: "Trench and shelter construction and military drilling persist on extensive scale. . . . MIG aircraft are to be seen almost daily over city."[69]

On March 2, a hundred American bombers crossed the 17th parallel into Northern territory. Shortly afterward, bridges, roads, factories, ports, oil depots, and rail lines were destroyed. The ongoing bombardment was code-named Rolling Thunder. With death and destruction raining down, aimed at infrastructure but also killing people, the Americans reached out to Seaborn again. Johnson would order a temporary halt to the bombing and then Seaborn would meet with Prime Minister Pham to determine whether Rolling Thunder had shaken Ho's resolve. Seaborn would again test the degree to which China was exerting leverage on the North Vietnamese as a way to sap American strength.[70] Seaborn left the ICC's Saigon headquarters and flew to Hanoi but again was only able to meet with ICC liaison Colonel Ha Van Lau. The conversation was short and bereft of diplomatic niceties. Seaborn reported to Ottawa and Washington that the bombing was not weakening but strengthening the North's determination to fight. Further, as he had written before, Ho's government had China's support but was acting alone.[71] Johnson had been told by his advisors that North Vietnam would be begging for peace within two weeks of Rolling Thunder's attacks.[72] Seaborn declared those advisors dead wrong. He was ignored.

On March 8, 3,500 Marines landed at the South Vietnamese port city of Da Nang. Their mission was to protect the American air base. To do so, the troops expanded their perimeter and moved farther into the jungle and through hamlets. With each excursion they encountered more Viet Cong resistance and gained a clearer realization that the locals could not be relied upon for support. In a tactic that came to typify the war's banal violence, villages began to be destroyed in order to save them from the Viet Cong. The war that all said they did not want had leapt from the shadows and was covert no more.

Seaborn watched as Saigon descended further into madness, with crime and corruption more rampant and indiscriminate violence more common. Carol and the children returned home to Ottawa. Seaborn became increasingly frustrated with the ICC's incessant infighting and withering impotence. A fitting metaphor for the worsening conditions appeared one evening when the Australian ambassador, a dinner guest at Seaborn's home, found a water rat swimming in the toilet.

At a June 17, 1965, press conference, President Johnson let slip that there were people, not linked to his government, who were negotiating with the North Vietnamese on his behalf. Seaborn was listening on the radio and intuited immediately that his cover had been blown.[73] Days later, Terence Robertson, a reporter from *Maclean's*, Canada's national news magazine, asked to meet with Seaborn.

The November 15, 1965, *Maclean's* cover showed a frowning Seaborn beside a carved dragon with an amusingly similar scowl, and the title "Vietnam Trouble Shooter." The article began, "While two giants, the United States and China, wrestle—if unofficially across the killing grounds of Vietnam—a 41-year-old Canadian, James Blair Seaborn, moves quietly behind both fronts in a frustrating, vital search for a formula for peace."[74] The article portrayed Seaborn as hard-working and modest. Seaborn is quoted explaining that the ICC's terms were established when Vietnam was ending a civil war but that changes in big power concerns had eroded the commission's ability to operate. He stated in the bluntest terms possible: "So now we have a situation in which those same powers all but ignore we exist. The Soviet Union and China send missiles and arms into North Vietnam, and the U.S. sends an entire war machine into South Vietnam."[75]

To his relief, Seaborn learned that he had apparently not been outed after all and that the timing of the interview was just a coincidence. It became clear that the reporter was unaware of the secret missions and so asked no questions about them; Seaborn, of course, offered nothing. But Robertson did ask about Seaborn's having met with North Vietnamese foreign minister Nguyen Duy Trinh on May 31.

The two had spoken for an hour in Hanoi. Trinh had said only that, with the war escalated, the only way to begin negotiations would be for the Americans to immediately and unilaterally leave. The Rolling Thunder bombardment served to fulfill Seaborn's prediction, rendering the conditions under which the North would initiate negotiations tougher and the likelihood of an escalated war greater. *Maclean's* readers remained unaware that, seventeen months before, Seaborn had offered a way to avoid the war.

More American troops were shipped to Vietnam. More North Vietnamese regular divisions joined the fight. More Viet Cong moved south and more in the South became Viet Cong. And more innocent people died. In October one of the three rickety French Stratoliner planes plunged into the jungle. It had been carrying nine ICC officials, including Canada's permanent representative in Hanoi J. Douglas Turner, the army's Sergeant J.S. Byrne, and Corporal V.J. Perkins. The plane was never found and the reason for the crash remains a mystery.

Seaborn's Vietnam assignment ended in November 1965. He enjoyed a reunion with his family and a brief break but was soon back to work. There were long debriefing sessions with Paul Martin and external affairs officials. He was invited to dinner with Prime Minister Pearson and McGeorge Bundy, where he learned that President Johnson was going to again try to use another bombing pause, this time over Christmas, to urge the North Vietnamese to the bargaining table. Seaborn told Bundy that it wouldn't work. It didn't.

In 1966 Martin pushed the Americans to back another Canadian-led peace initiative to Hanoi. It would be led by respected retired Canadian diplomat Chester Ronning. The White House didn't really want it but reluctantly agreed. Ronning met twice with Prime Minister Pham. They echoed many of the same points raised at the Seaborn meetings. Ronning's reports were presented to President Johnson but dismissed without comment.[76] Dean Rusk had come to view Paul Martin as little more than a nuisance and the Ronning mission as a waste of time.[77]

Seaborn had left Vietnam but the country's problems followed him home. The secrets and lies were leaking, and the Canadian people were learning that the war that seemed so distant was not really so far away at all. It was affecting their jobs, their communities, and their families. The Vietnam War that Seaborn had tried to stop was already Canada's war.

CHAPTER 3

CLAIRE CULHANE:
PERSISTENT RESISTANCE

n the 1960s *Weekend Magazine* was a popular supplement that was inserted into the fat Saturday editions of forty-one newspapers across Canada. Its May 27, 1967, cover showed a young woman in a knit cardigan holding a baby and the text "Louise Piché and the Orphans of Vietnam. A nurse from Quebec, she is part of a Canadian medical team helping the sick and wounded in this troubled country."[1]

The article lauded Canadian nurses and doctors who, since 1964, had been working with an American-sponsored program to treat sick and injured civilians and the wounded of both armies. It also told the story of a thirty-five-year-old Canadian doctor named Alje Vennema. As director of Canadian medical assistance to South Vietnam, Vennema was overseeing the building of a new Canadian hospital near the South

Vietnamese coastal city of Quang Ngai, midway between Saigon and Hanoi. The facility was to help the region's one-in-seven people suffering from tuberculosis. The $250,000 Canadian government seed funding was being funnelled through the Colombo Plan, an organization created in 1950 by Commonwealth countries seeking to staunch the spread of communism by building economic and social capacity in southeast Asia.

Among those who read the article was Claire Culhane, a forty-eight-year-old hospital administrator living in Montreal. Culhane was so struck by it that she immediately wrote to the external affairs department and offered to work at the Quang Ngai hospital. Within two weeks she was in Ottawa being interviewed by external affairs personnel director Jean Arsenault. While Culhane was back home completing a mountain of forms, the RCMP checked her background—perhaps a little too quickly.

Born Claire Eglin in 1918, she had grown up in a poor Jewish family that had fled the anti-Semitism and poverty of eastern Russia for Montreal. She moved to Ottawa as a teenager for training as a nurse but was expelled after several incidents of insubordination, mostly for minor infractions such as arriving at the hospital on a hot afternoon without the required girdle and slip beneath her starched white uniform. Back in Montreal, with a job as a stenographer, she was caught up in the fervour of the Spanish Civil War and at one point looked into going to Spain to fight the fascists. Her sympathy for striking garment workers led to her working with the Office Workers Union and the Retail Clerks Union. The politically engaged eighteen-year-old was appalled by the corruption rampant in the Quebec and Montreal governments. Identifying with working people fighting injustice, she joined the Communist Party of Canada. Its popularity was growing at the time, having elected a Member of Parliament and become a force in the labour movement—but when its leadership refused to support Canadian Second World War aims, the federal government had the party banned. Shortly afterward, Claire Eglin's home was raided and the RCMP opened what would become a thick file.

She fell in love with a handsome fellow communist, Garry Culhane, who was in a loveless marriage from which strict Quebec divorce laws allowed no escape. Because both were also under RCMP surveillance, they went underground and fled to British Columbia. Adopting Garry's surname and using a nickname, Claire Eglin became Kayla Culhane. She delivered speeches and wrote articles as the educational director for the Communist Party, which had rebranded itself the Labour-Progressive Party. In 1948 Culhane became disillusioned with more talk than action and left the party—but she remained on the RCMP's radar as an active member of the Ban the Bomb Movement. In June 1953 she led protests at Vancouver's American consulate, trying to stop the death sentences meted out to convicted American spies Julius and Ethel Rosenberg. Her prominence was such that Rosenbergs' attorney interviewed Culhane about possibly adopting the condemned couple's children.

Culhane had given birth to two daughters, Roisin in 1945 and Dara five years later. Garry had become a prominent labour leader but turned resentful when his influence waned. His bitterness affected their relationship. In 1958 they attempted to rekindle their love by starting a new life in Garry's native Ireland, but after a year it had become clear that the relationship was truly over. Culhane left Garry and teenaged Roisin, who chose to stay with her father, and returned to Montreal with Dara.

She found work as a medical typist, first at the Montreal Neurological Institute and then at the Grace Dart Tuberculosis Hospital. It was there that she learned medical record keeping and completed a two-year course to become a registered medical librarian. For the next decade, Culhane was a working single mom who gave up her political activism and went back to using her real first name. By the time she decided to go to Vietnam, the RCMP had either lost track of her or lost interest, and so all the political activities that had been of such interest to the police for so long were missed or ignored, and her overseas employment was approved.

Culhane left her job, got her shots, and packed her bags. Roisin had returned to Canada in 1963 and was now happily married and living in Vancouver with a two-year-old daughter. Culhane arranged for the seventeen-year-old Dara to stay with a friend. She would be gone for a year, living and working in the most dangerous place in the world.

IN COUNTRY

In August 1967, just two and a half months after being inspired by the *Weekend Magazine* article, Culhane found herself hungry, hot, and tired at Saigon's Tan Son Nhat Airport. After four hours of waiting alone and without local currency for food or drink, she gave up on the Canadian consulate that was supposed to have sent someone to meet her and found British Embassy officials at the airport who helped her to contact the Canadian ICC office. ICC legal advisor Gordon Longmuir rushed to her aid and set her up at the ritzy Continental Palace hotel.

After a shower and a meal, she wandered the neighbourhood and was shocked by the smell, heat, noise, and crowds. She was repulsed by the sight of children begging American soldiers and Westerners for gifts, picking their pockets, and offering them trinkets, or themselves.

The presence of people like Culhane in Vietnam stemmed in part from the Many Flags program initiated by President Lyndon Johnson in April 1964. The United States did not really need any help from its allies but wanted to convince international and domestic critics that its efforts in Vietnam enjoyed broad support. The thought was not new. President Kennedy had worked unsuccessfully to the same end. In his Ottawa meeting with Canadian prime minister John Diefenbaker in May 1961, for example, Kennedy had asked that Canada boost its foreign aid to South Vietnam. Diefenbaker refused and Kennedy dropped the matter.[2]

Three years later, however, it was a different war and Johnson was in even greater need of political cover. American officials urged, cajoled, and bribed countries to send troops or other aid.[3] By the end of 1964, only fifteen countries had offered direct but tepid military support. Thailand, South Korea, and the Philippines received American economic assistance in return for sending small contingents of soldiers. For their part, expressing a desire to stop the spread of communism in the region, New Zealand and Australia sent troops in 1962 without being bribed to do so. By the war's end, over three thousand New Zealanders and sixty thousand Australians, many of them conscripts, had seen action in Vietnam.[4]

In September 1965 Johnson wrote a personal letter to Prime Minister Pearson requesting Canada's help in Vietnam. The president argued: "Our people are growing restive over the fact that we are carrying virtually all the burden of a conflict in whose outcome—as we see it—all our friends have just as great an ultimate stake as we. . . . Such a contribution would have a value to our friendship and our common purpose far beyond its immediate cost."[5]

Pearson well understood the implicit threat and announced that Canada would maintain its ICC commitment but would not send Canadian troops to Vietnam. However, between 1964 and 1967, Canada's foreign assistance budget increased by a whopping 280 percent. The majority of the funds were dispensed in Southeast Asia through the Colombo Plan.[6] In 1965–66 Canada sent $1.2 million in direct financial aid to the government of South Vietnam, and the following year the amount increased to $2.6 million.[7]

That combination of American pressure and Canadian attempts to appease an ally contributed to Culhane's being in Vietnam and, on a hot August afternoon, in a small car sitting beside a Belgian doctor. They wove their way along bicycle-clogged avenues on a tour of local medical facilities. The doctor told her that shortly after construction began on the Quang Ngai tuberculosis (TB) hospital, Canada had agreed to also fund the construction of a Rehabilitation Centre in the coastal city of Quy Nhon, 109 miles south of Quang Ngai.[8]

The next day, Culhane was on her way to Quang Ngai. She gripped her knees and held her breath as the unmarked CIA plane rocketed straight toward the ground to avoid being hit by anti-aircraft fire and then suddenly jerked up, just in time to land. She then bounced along five miles of rough road in an American Jeep, arriving dusty and rattled at the two-storey white stucco building called Canada House, which for a year would be home. Her room was tiny, stuffy, and un-air-conditioned, with a cracked cement floor.[9]

The hospital's director, Dr. Vennema, was away in Saigon for meetings, but Culhane met the six-member team she would be working with: two Vietnamese assistants, a Canadian radiologist, and two French Canadian nurses, one of whom was Louise Piché, whose *Weekend Magazine* cover photo had spurred her to action. Culhane asked about the lack of security and was assured that the absence of fortifications or even a fence around their quarters signalled to the Viet Cong that they were neither a military base nor a threat. Her colleagues taught her to memorize a Vietnamese phrase that they said would help keep her alive: "I am Canadian. I am not American." She struggled to sleep that night amid the cacophony of mortars, rockets, and distant gunfire, accompanied by dogs and roosters voicing their lost ability to distinguish day from night.

Culhane was appalled by the conditions at the hospital. X-ray machines and other specialized medical equipment needed for tackling TB cases were on back order, along with other essential equipment such as a generator. The twenty-three-bed hospital was nonetheless treating sixty patients, about 80 percent of whom had been wounded by American artillery, the others by napalm and poison gas. A separate children's ward was addressing battle wounds and what in Canada would have been preventable illnesses. About twenty to thirty people a day arrived at the hospital, on foot or by scooter, and sometimes on American helicopters. The staff did what they could, but had to contend with sporadic electricity, no hot water, and a shortage of medical supplies, including bandages and morphine.[10]

The region was suffering its second year of vicious fighting. The Viet Cong controlled the rural areas around Quang Ngai. American attempts to win back territory had resulted in the destruction of 70 percent of the province's villages and the creation of 138,000 refugees—one of every five people.[11] Dr. Vennema estimated that about 80 percent of his patients were Viet Cong, but it was hard to attach political labels to suffering children.[12]

Between shifts in the hospital, Culhane and the nurses walked half an hour up the road to volunteer at the Quan Provincial Hospital. The 400-bed facility was overrun with 700 patients. Eighty percent were women and children suffering from malnutrition and ghastly war wounds. Culhane was sickened by what she saw—wide-eyed children writhing in the tortuous agony of napalm-seared flesh; a dead mother with a baby still suckling her breast; a teenage girl with her breasts sliced off and a bottle shoved into her vagina.[13]

By December the necessary equipment had arrived and so the Canadian hospital was treating TB cases among its 100 to 150 patients a day. Culhane worked as an advisor and administrative assistant to the director, often toiling until two in the morning on office work as well as helping with patients.[14] She created a meticulous record-keeping system noting personal details and the medical history of each patient. Culhane also oversaw the hospital's monthly $30,000 budget, which was hand-delivered by a Canadian embassy official, in cash, in a big steel box.

After being frustrated in her attempts to obtain equipment and supplies through official channels, Culhane began a direct correspondence with Canada's external affairs minister Paul Martin, demanding that bureaucratic red tape be cut and the hospital's budget increased. She wrote, for instance, that while a much-needed $2,000 generator had finally arrived, it had cost another $2,300 in bribes to have it success-fully dodge the thieves and black marketeers on the way from Da Nang.[15] Her letters seemed to help, for equipment and supplies began to arrive more regularly.

Culhane and the Canadians often toiled through sixteen-hour days and still couldn't keep up. They treated TB patients while continuing to accept scores of others too sick or injured to make it to the provincial hospital. Nevertheless, when Canada's current ICC commissioner, Ormond Dier, paid a visit, he expressed his surprise that the staff were working so hard. The hospital was simply a symbol of good intentions, he explained, so it didn't matter if a single patient was seen.[16] Dier's remarks led Culhane to seek a deeper understanding of what was really happening around her.

After leading Canadian medical efforts for six years and being invested into South Vietnam's Order of Merit and the Order of Canada, Dr. Vennema left in January 1968 to pursue advanced medical studies in London. He was replaced by a twenty-eight-year-old Montreal doctor named Michel Jutras. Dr. Jutras followed rules and procedures to the letter. He instituted strict office hours and shocked the staff by declar-ing that the Quang Ngai hospital was for TB patients only; all others were to be immediately transferred to the provincial hospital. The twin policies meant turning out and turning away wounded, sick, and dying people. Many were forced to walk or drag themselves to the provincial hospital or back to their homes, many of which had been burned or reduced to shell craters. Culhane could not stay silent. She told Dr. Jutras that the Geneva Conventions declared that those taking no part in hostilities had to be treated humanely and that shipping them out to lie untreated in the provincial hospital's dirty hallways or to die at home was clearly inhumane. She lost the argument.

Shortly thereafter, Culhane's close scrutiny of her patient files led her to discover that Jutras was sharing them with local CIA agents, who were using them to identify Viet Cong and Viet Cong sympathizers. She later found out that the files were being used to help the joint CIA–South Vietnamese counterinsurgency program code-named Phoenix. Beginning in December 1967, the secret program saw counterterrorism teams descend on villages to interrogate male adults and kidnap, torture, or kill those suspected of hiding information or being Viet Cong. In many cases, entire villages were burned. After the war, critics did not mince words, calling Phoenix a killing machine. Highly decorated Navy SEAL Joel Hutchins admitted that tragic excesses occurred, "with officials using the cover of the operation to eradicate present or future political or personal foes."[17] Phoenix made an already bad refugee problem worse and led to the creation of teeming camps where disease, including TB, became even more rampant. Culhane confronted Jutras, passionately arguing that helping the CIA meant that the Canadian hospital was nothing more than an American instrument of war, creating more victims than it could ever help.[18] Again, she was ignored.

On Culhane's final round of hospital wards on the evening of January 30, 1968, a Vietnamese patient whispered to her in French, "The VC come tonight."[19] One minute after four in the morning, a powerful explosion flung Culhane from her bed. She scrambled to the window and saw the sky alive with bursts of metal, noise, and light. It was the Tet Offensive. Vietnam's lunar new year, or Tet holiday, always saw thousands of people travel to be with friends and family. North Vietnamese forces had used the holiday to infiltrate every major South Vietnamese city with fighters and weapons and, at the appointed hour, attacked them all.

Culhane's first thoughts were for the patients. Out of habit and a faint hope that it would protect her from attack, she donned her white uniform. Resisting the urge to run, she ignored the booming sounds of battle and walked boldly down the middle of the deserted road to the hospital. Casualties were soon crowding in. The Vietnamese hospital staff were not allowed past roadblocks, leaving Culhane and the

Canadians to work tirelessly on their own to treat the wounded while still tending to those suffering the indignity and pain of tuberculosis.

Six days after the initial attack, a South Vietnamese platoon occupied the hospital's second floor. Artillery pieces were secured on the roof. Dozens of patients were transferred to the pandemonium of the provincial hospital and many others were given a ten-day supply of antibiotics, wished good luck, and told to walk home.

The Canadians did what they could for the dire TB cases that remained. One afternoon they stood at a window and gazed in slack-jawed horror in the direction of the makeshift Viet Cong prison compound a few miles away. American planes rocketed past at treetop level, dropping bomb after bomb until the camp and its occupants were pounded to dust.[20]

On February 6, with the last patients transferred or released, the Canadians were evacuated ninety miles north to heavily defended Da Nang. Culhane and the others volunteered for a few days at a local hospital and a refugee camp until they were transported south to Saigon. The Americans had retaken most of the city's neighbourhoods, but others were still being destroyed in house-to-house fighting.

Culhane and the others were eventually returned to Quang Ngai, but by then the hospital had become a military base. Much of the delicate medical equipment had been damaged or destroyed. Dr. Jutras told them that the hospital might soon reopen, but Culhane was done. She had known she was in trouble weeks before when, after months of hearing American GIs brag about things like throwing prisoners from helicopters or firing their weapons on fleeing farmers, she realized that she no longer found the stories horrifying. She had become numb, and that scared her.

Culhane also knew she could no longer work with Dr. Jutras. She had sent numerous letters to Paul Martin, reporting that Jutras kept hours that suited himself and not his patients; was prescribing drugs in a harmful, wasteful fashion; was arming the hospital in violation of the Geneva Conventions; and was shady with his expense account. Even worse, in Culhane's eyes, was that the medical records she oversaw were still being shared with the CIA, whose operatives became even more ruthless after Tet.

In a letter to Dr. Vennema she explained, "It's no longer possible to rationalize my way out, of not really being part of the Amer. War machine so long as we had to have anything to do with them."[21] To Paul Martin she wrote, "In my capacity of Administrative Assistant I found that I was no longer able to discharge my duties in a reasonable, responsible, honest and moral context, due mainly to the corruption and dishonour of the forces with which I was obliged to work."[22]

She whispered a tearful goodbye to a group of Vietnamese people whom she had befriended, saying, "I cannot work with the Americans who are destroying your people and your country. I cannot work with Dr. Jutras, who works with the Americans. I think the best way I can help you is to go back home and try to stop the war."[23] She wrote a final letter to Martin to say that she was forfeiting half a year's pay and a possible foreign service career and coming home.

Culhane had been training a local girl named Nga to assist her as a hospital secretary. Nga accompanied Culhane to the airport and cried as they hugged and waved goodbye. Before resuming her duties, Nga returned to visit her home village, six miles north of the Canadian hospital. Days later, she was dead, murdered along with her family and five hundred others by American soldiers at My Lai.

THE UNDERSTANDING

Upon her return to Canada in April 1968, Culhane reported to the Canadian International Development Agency. She met with its president, Maurice Strong, and human resources director, Jean Arsenault, the man who had approved her appointment. Culhane carefully explained the problems with the hospital and all it represented and said that, as a result, she could no longer in good conscience serve in Vietnam. Strong reproached her, saying that the hospital and her work were worth the money and effort if even a few people were helped.[24] Culhane asked whether helping twenty innocent civilians while being complicit in the death of thousands was a good bargain. Beyond assisting the CIA, she asked, how can it be right that one department of the Canadian government builds hospitals while another sanctions the manufacture and sale of military hardware that helps fill them with patients? How can the government say Canada is neutral while helping only South Vietnam?[25] If decision makers fully understood the nature of Canada's involvement in the war, she insisted, things would change.

Culhane was mistaken. The fact, of course, was that the decision makers to whom she vaguely referred understood all too well. That understanding had led three prime ministers to publicly support the war while swallowing their qualms—and a fourth would soon join their ranks. Until the war was almost over, there were only two notable exceptions to the self-imposed reticence. The first came from Lester Pearson, expressed in an April 1965 speech at Philadelphia's Temple University. Pearson offered support for America's war aims and congratulated the United States for its restraint and global leadership, but he went on to question the tactical value of American bombing. It should be paused to allow Hanoi an opportunity to seek a negotiated end to the war, he said.[26]

Shortly after leaving the dais, Pearson was invited to join President Johnson at Camp David the next day. The president walked Pearson to a terrace and harangued him, at one point grabbing him by the lapels, lifting him, and screaming, "You don't come here and piss on my rug."[27] The next day, Pearson composed a long letter to Johnson explaining the point of the Temple speech and reaffirming Canada's support for him and America's leadership.

Soon afterward, Pearson's finance minister, Walter Gordon, went further in a speech in which he argued that the United States had become involved in a civil war "which cannot be justified on either moral or strategic grounds." Gordon said Johnson should immediately stop the bombing and withdraw American forces.[28]

A Canadian political storm ensued, leading Pearson to issue a statement: "We hope the U.S.A., as the strongest of the warring parties, will take the initiative by bringing the bombing to an end and demand that talks begin at once for an armistice and a settlement."[29] Pearson took back control of Canadian-American relations from his troublesome minister and ensured, much to the consternation of the growing number of anti-war Canadians, that his government's mouth was henceforth clamped shut.[30]

A few months earlier, in January 1965, Pearson had been at Johnson's Texas ranch to discuss a number of issues, including the Auto Pact (Canada–United States Automotive Products Agreement), which would integrate the Canadian and American auto sectors. The meeting started badly when, standing before reporters, the president had welcomed "Prime Minister Wilson." When later told what he had done, Johnson called to apologize and Pearson replied, "Don't worry about it, Senator Goldwater."[31]

In the private meeting in Texas, Johnson had again asked Pearson to consider sending Canadian soldiers to Vietnam and again Pearson had said no. Auto Pact negotiations nonetheless continued unabated. Months later, after the Temple University and Gordon speeches added insult to Canada's refusal to provide more help in Vietnam, Johnson could have punished Canada in a number of ways, including ending the Auto Pact or stalling its passage. He did not. Nor did he publicly admonish Pearson. He ignored Gordon and from that point forward he all but ignored Canada.

Johnson's absence of a public reaction or retaliation revealed that Canadian-American relations were manifest in an ever-shifting

network of social, political, economic, and diplomatic interactions
that went beyond the circumstance of how two leaders got along.
They survived disagreement even on something as important as war.
Washington's official silence following the speeches and another
refusal to send troops also suggested that the Canadian government's
fear of standing up to the Americans on Vietnam had been ill-founded.
The sun rose the next day. And the myriad ways in which Canadians
and Americans interacted continued with nary a hiccup, whether
vacationing in each other's countries, doing business, or in the many
interactions between lower-level government officials who conducted
their affairs away from the disruptive interference of politicians.

For decades, Canadian leaders had understood the overlapping and
sometimes contradictory variables to be considered in stick-handling
Canada's relationship with the United States. They all knew and
accepted the game's high stakes. The Vietnam War only made the
stakes higher and the game more intense.

The economic-defence web that rendered Culhane's questions
about Canada's involvement in Vietnam so tricky began to be woven
in 1914, when Britain declared war on Germany and Canada automatically followed. Canada nearly bankrupted itself borrowing British
money to support its own war effort while helping to supply food to
British tables and supplies to British soldiers. By 1917 Britain was
nearly broke.[32] Canadian prime minister Robert Borden turned to the
American government, which backed loans and agreed to purchase
Canadian military products. In terms of military procurement, the
border was blurred.[33] Ensuing military cooperation paved the way to a
greater integration of the postwar Canadian and American economies,
with many American branch plants finding homes, workers, and markets north of the border.

The Second World War continued Canada's move from the British to
American orbit. In August 1940, President Franklin Roosevelt and Prime
Minister William Lyon Mackenzie King sat in a railcar in Ogdensburg,

New York, where they approved the creation of the Permanent Joint
Board on Defence, which would coordinate North America's sea, land,
and air defence. To assist a nearly bankrupt Britain, FDR created the
lend-lease arrangement, whereby Britain would pay later for the gift
of old American ships and other support. In April 1941, Mackenzie King
and FDR met again, this time at Roosevelt's Hyde Park estate. They
agreed that American goods purchased by Canada and then transferred to Britain would be counted as part of the land-lease effort. The
deal stabilized Canada's teetering dollar and bolstered its economy.
They also agreed that Canada and the United States should provide
each other with the war materials they were best able to produce, and
that military procurement should be coordinated to meet joint military and economic needs. The twin agreements survived the war and
guaranteed a further integration of American and Canadian economies and defence strategies.

On October 1, 1956, with Cold War tensions rising, Canada and the
United States signed the Defence Production Sharing Agreement. It
went even further than the Ogdensburg and Hyde Park agreements in
stating that Canadian companies would receive the same consideration on all American defence contracts as American companies. Raw
materials needed for production could come from both countries. It
guaranteed the standardization of military equipment and spare parts.
It cemented a Canadian exemption from the Buy America Act's 6 to 12
percent tariff on foreign companies vying for military contracts. It
eliminated the 12 to 17 percent custom duties on defence products that
were subcontracted from the United States. Four years later, it was
agreed that Canadian companies could also do research and development work for the Pentagon.

The fully integrated continental defence, production, and procurement arrangements were further solidified in 1957 with the creation of
the North American Air Defense Command (NORAD). Like the relative
sizes of the American and Canadian economies and defence budgets,

NORAD and the Defence Production Sharing Agreement were unbalanced and asymmetrical but mutually beneficial.

Canadian defence contractors knew that Canada's annual defence budgets had been on a downward trajectory since the end of the Korean War in 1953, a trend that continued throughout the 1960s.[34] With the Canadian domestic arms market unable to purchase sufficient goods for industry to maintain profits and employment levels, defence contracts needed to be found elsewhere, and there was nowhere better than America's permanent war economy.

Successive Canadian governments enacted programs to bolster the over-production of war material. In 1959 Diefenbaker approved $17.2 million in grants and loan guarantees to defence industries. In 1966 Pearson approved $10.6 million in grants to help Canadian defence contractors modernize their plants. Pearson also boosted the budget and personnel of the Canadian Commercial Corporation (CCC), the Crown corporation created in 1946 to help Canadian firms secure Pentagon contracts. The U.S. defense department worked with the CCC and, through it, with Canadian and Canadian-based American branch plants to ensure that Canadian laws and regulations did not hamper sales.[35]

By the time the Vietnam War had begun in earnest in 1965, Canadian companies and American branch plants were producing and selling to the United States a wide range of goods that included ammunition, air craft engines, grenades, gun sights, TNT, generators, military vehicles, spare parts, napalm, and more. Canadian defence production minister Charles "Bud" Drury estimated that in 1966 American defence contracts were responsible for 13,000 to 15,000 Canadian jobs, with spin-off jobs probably totalling 110,000.[36] In that year, the new auto pact and the ramping up of war-related production helped Canada turn a trade deficit with the United States into a trade surplus of $481.1 million.

MONEY OR MORALITY

It was all of this history, all these security arrangements, and all of that money that Culhane was challenging as she sat berating Maurice Strong in April 1968. She was not naïve, but she was determined. She was not suggesting, as Marxist analysts later would, that Canada had involved itself in Vietnam simply to turn a profit. Rather, she was arguing that Vietnam was not just another war offering simply another chapter in the story of interdependence that had begun with the First World War. She was insisting that the story needed to be changed or ended altogether, because it was immoral to be making money from an immoral war.

Culhane was unaware that for two years Cabinet had been struggling with that difficult idea. On February 9, 1965, perhaps with Blair Seaborn's reports in mind, Secretary of State for External Affairs Paul Martin had advised the Cabinet: "The United States was now embarked on a hopeless course since the [South] Vietnamese people had no will to fight and there were no prospects for strong civilian leadership."[37] And yet, on September 8, Martin tabled a report for Cabinet that said: "The United States Department of Defense had increased its procurement recently in Canada of a number of items destined for use in Viet Nam. These included Caribou and Buffalo aircraft, and a tracked vehicle which was being tested in Viet Nam at present. Some technicians from Canadian companies had also been sent to Viet Nam in connection with the provision of this equipment."[38]

All cabinet members knew that for decades Canada had been swapping sovereignty for security and principle for jobs, but the Faustian bargain was acceptable when the threats and wars were believed to be just. Martin's two reports were presenting Culhane's point, for what were cabinet members to do with the bargain when a war was known to be unwinnable, increasingly unpopular, and, to some, immoral? The problem had led Pearson to try to avoid publicly discussing Canadian involvement in the war and, when pushed, to insist that Canada was neutral. It had led Martin to say that, because of its ICC commitment, Canada was rendering no military assistance to South Vietnam.[39]

Cabinet decided to change not the situation, but how it was spoken of. Since so much Canadian-made war material was being shipped to the United States, it would be argued that the government had no way of tracking whether Canadian-made goods were ending up in Vietnam.[40] That talking point, however, would not withstand scrutiny for long.

In January 1966, the *Globe and Mail* reported that the sale of parts and ammunition from de Havilland were about to be shipped directly from Vancouver to Vietnam. In his only intervention in arms sales to the United States, Pearson had the sale stopped. "The shipment of Canadian military supplies to Vietnam would be incompatible with our role in the International Control Commission," he explained.[41] Other arms sales, however, continued.

A year later, in March 1967, a *Toronto Star* headline read: "Vietnam War Boosts Canadian Sales to U.S."[42] The story detailed how the war was expanding Canadian exports of oil, aluminum, ores, pulp, paper, and timber. U.S. war manufacturing lifted Canadian steel and iron exports by 54 percent. The majority of the nickel used by American plants for building war planes, missiles, and armoured vehicles came from Canada.[43] Between 1965 and the end of the war, American defence contractors purchased $2.34 billion worth of Canadian nickel.[44]

The *Star* and *Globe and Mail* articles, and others that followed, didn't account for indirect Canadian arms sales. By 1967 over three hundred Japanese companies were selling war material to the United States for use in Vietnam. They were also repairing damaged American military ships, aircraft, and tanks. Nearly all these activities involved Canadian mineral products.[45] Forty percent of Japan's copper and 50 percent of its aluminum, for example, both essential to its war production and repair industries, came from Canada.[46]

For most Canadians, Canada's claim to neutrality in a war while economically benefitting from it was lost in the happy celebrations marking the country's centenary. Sales of Canada's new and distinctive flag boomed. Expo '67 was a national birthday party to which the world was invited. Centennial projects saw communities build fountains, parks, and other expressions of national pride. For many Canadians, the heightened patriotism came with a helping of anti-Americanism and a desire that Canada should be more independent of the United States. A part of that growing shadow on the positive patriotism that tainted the happy festivities were questions about Vietnam.

In a November 1967 episode of the popular CBC television program *The Way It Is*, economist Gideon Rosenbluth spoke of Canada's involvement in the global arms trade and cited specifics regarding sales to the United States in support of the Vietnam War.[47] Panelist Robert Reguly of the *Toronto Star* called Canada's arms sales to Americans blatantly hypocritical. In the weeks following the program's airing, a number of articles in newspapers and popular magazines such as *Maclean's*, *Saturday Night*, *Canadian Forum*, and the *United Church Observer* criticized Canada's support for the war through arms sales.

Pearson did not publicly react to the program or the subsequent articles but, in a letter to University of Toronto professor Peter Hughes, he argued for a broader perspective. He wrote that a withdrawal from the Defence Production Sharing Agreement "would be interpreted as a notice of withdrawal on our part from continental defence and even from the collective defence arrangements of the Atlantic alliance."[48]

Beyond that argument, the economic benefits of feeding the war's insatiable appetite could not be denied. Jobs directly related to defence production were spread across the country with 21,700 in Toronto, 20,000 in Halifax, 7,000 in Winnipeg, 5,700 in Vancouver, 5,200 in Edmonton, 39,500 in Montreal, and more elsewhere.[49] As the war escalated, the number of jobs increased. In March 1968, Treasury Board President Edgar Benson stated, "Unemployment would rise if arms shipments to the U.S. were stopped. It is to our benefit to continue the program."[50]

Not all politicians were onside. New Democratic Party leader Tommy Douglas rose in the House of Commons to add his voice to the growing chorus of Canadians opposed to the war and Canada's role in it. He said, "Canada will not come before the bar of historic judgement with clean hands, because there is blood on them—blood money to the tune of more than $300 million a year."[51]

THE GADFLY

The turning point came in 1968. In January, the Tet Offensive made clear to all but the willfully blind that the Johnson administration had been lying about winning in Vietnam. Then, over the course of six months, student protests rocked Paris; Soviet tanks rolled into Prague; police clubbed protesters at the Democratic Party's National Convention in Chicago; and at Montreal's Saint-Jean-Baptiste Day parade, Front de libération du Quebec (FLQ) domestic terrorists threw rocks at Prime Minister Pierre Trudeau. In Ireland, the Troubles began. In the United States, Martin Luther King and Robert Kennedy were assassinated. The happy songs and determined optimism of Canada's centennial year and the Summer of Love seemed a lifetime ago.

It was into this tumultuous moment of anger, angst, and growing anti-war activism that Claire Culhane took her private protests public. In April, she delivered her sixteen-page report to Maurice Strong, Jean Arsenault, and External Aid Director Earl Drake. It outlined her experiences in Vietnam and made recommendations regarding Canadian war policies. It concluded that Canada should end its no-longer-veiled complicity in the war by stopping arms sales, withdrawing all personnel, and ending all financial support for the South Vietnamese government. "Very simply," she wrote, "let us stop making money out of this war."[52]

Strong, Arsenault, and Drake each sent a perfunctory thank you letter but said there was really nothing they could do.[53] Strong ended his letter on a patronizing note: "Please accept my sincere thanks for your interest in our medical aid program in Vietnam."[54] Culhane's report was shown to no one.

Shortly after learning the fate of her report, Culhane met with her old mentor Thérèse Casgrain. The seventy-two-year-old firebrand had founded Quebec's suffrage movement in 1921. She hosted a political radio program, led the Quebec wing of the Cooperative Common-wealth Federation, and in 1961 was a founding member of the Quebec branch of the Voice of Women for Peace (VOW).

Founded in 1960 by women concerned about nuclear disarmament, the Canadian VOW earned national attention in 1962 with a protest that involved the collection of baby teeth to prove they contained dangerously high levels of strontium-90—evidence of nuclear testing fallout. VOW had evolved into a national organization dedicated to a number of issues, including fighting for an end to the Vietnam War. In fact, with ties across the country and in the United States and Europe, VOW became Canada's only national and international organization with an anti-war stance. VOW and Canada's growing anti-war movement brought together students, workers, feminists, and academics, along with Quebec nationalists who sympathized with Vietnam's anti-colonialism.

Casgrain's continuing work with VOW and the Fédération des femmes du Québec, which she had formed in 1966, helped introduce Culhane to influential women across the country. On May 22, Culhane addressed a VOW-sponsored meeting at Montreal's Sir George Williams University. The audience was shocked by her stories describing what she had witnessed and experienced in Vietnam, and by her report's conclusions and demands. The speech led to a meeting with Notre-Dame-de-Grâce MP Warren Allmand and, through him, with other MPs and external affairs officials. Shortly afterward she was elected to

VOW's National Council and would later become president of its Quebec chapter.

Culhane's activism contributed to strengthening a link between the anti-war protests and feminism's Second Wave. The Second Wave had begun with the 1963 publication of Betty Friedan's *The Feminine Mystique*, which argued against the Freudian idea that one's biological sex dictates one's role in society. The movement questioned assumptions underlying male-dominated power structures in government, business, religion, media, and popular culture. It also questioned commonly held expectations regarding family, marriage, and work. In seeking a more just society for all, women involved themselves in the Civil Rights movement and the struggle for gay rights, and in opposition to nuclear weapons, militarism, and the war. In both Canada and the United States, feminists already risked ridicule as "bra burners" and "man haters." Their anti-war stance led to accusations of being communists, unpatriotic, ungrateful, and, what some clinging to old ways considered the worst insult of all, "un-lady like."[55]

Culhane was in the middle of it all. She became a relentless correspondent, writing to newspaper editors, politicians, and various religious and political action groups. She began receiving both letters of support and vicious hate mail. Typical of the latter was an unsigned letter of June 28, 1968, asking if she was a real Canadian and telling her to move to Russia.[56] Several letters to the editors of various newspapers slammed her actions and advocacy as "un-Canadian" and "pro-communist." Some questioned whether she had served in Vietnam at all. She responded with letters to newspapers that had published the most heinous attacks and at one point threatened to sue a *Montreal Gazette* writer for defamation of character.[57]

Lester Pearson had retired in April 1968 and his justice minister, the charismatic Pierre Elliott Trudeau, had become the Liberal leader and prime minister. Two months later, in a flamboyant campaign in which the media coined the phrase "Trudeaumania," he led the party to a majority victory.

Culhane began directing her numerous letters to Trudeau, his new cabinet, and agency leaders. Trudeau's secretary of state for external affairs Mitchell Sharp wrote to Culhane thanking her for her suggestions but saying that the hospital in Quang Ngai would be staying open and Canada would continue to help in South Vietnam with similar ventures.[58] In 1968 the Canadian International Development Agency (CIDA) had replaced the External Aid Office, with Maurice Strong remaining its president. He replied that her opinions had already been considered and respected but, while there was acknowledgement of the difficulties, risks, and problems involved in Canada's helping South Vietnam, "our assistance should continue as long as it can contribute effectively to the relief of some of the suffering which the people of Vietnam are experiencing."[59]

Culhane's activities, connections, and correspondence led Strong to warn the ICC in Saigon that she was asking troublesome questions and so preparations should be made to defend Canada's presence in Vietnam.[60] Not coincidentally, Culhane's long-dormant RCMP file was reactivated. In June, ignoring the proper order of horses and locked barn doors, the RCMP sent a letter to Jean Arsenault saying that, after further investigation, it was advised that Culhane not be hired to work for external affairs.[61] Culhane was again deemed dangerous.

She did not rest. Culhane added a strong voice to the country's growing generational divide by taking her anti-war message to Canadian universities. While a number of concerns preoccupied students—including Civil Rights, feminism, and Quebec's Quiet Revolution—the anti-war movement was the central cause that unified and galvanized them across the country.[62] Students organized protests and wrote articles and letters to editors addressing numerous matters relating to the war, but they were most passionately vexed by Canada's involvement, especially its arms sales to the United States.[63]

Draining her savings and reluctantly accepting financial help from friends and supporters, Culhane travelled the country speaking and being interviewed by student leaders and by national, regional, and local media. With each interview and university speech, she advocated shifting the anti-war movement from demanding that America end the war to insisting that Canada end its involvement in it. Her editorials and columns continued to inflame. In a *Canadian Dimension* article, for example, Culhane wrote: "I wonder if anyone thought to send medical groups to Auschwitz to help care for those victims not yet consumed by the ovens?"[64]

On September 30, 1968, Culhane arrived on Parliament Hill ready to carry out a bold plan to take her activism to a new level. Having assured her worried daughters that she would be okay and secured a leave of absence from her job at Montreal's Neurological Institute, on that Monday morning, Culhane announced a hunger strike. A Voice of Women press release stated: "Mrs. Culhane hopes this Fast will point up the hypocrisy of profiteering from the sale of war materials while pretending to send aid to the Vietnamese people."[65] Culhane told reporters that she was particularly irritated that in a recent United Nations speech Canada's external affairs minister, Mitchell Sharp, had not acknowledged Canada's role in the war and had said that American bombing should end only after North Vietnam withdrew from the South. This waffling, she said, must end. Canada's support for the war must end.

Passing tourists mostly just stared or smiled at the grey-haired woman sitting quietly by the eternal flame, but several shared kind words of encouragement. Warren Allmand dropped by and offered the use of his office washroom and phones. A number of MPs and cabinet ministers came to chat. She received messages of support from across Canada and around the world, including the Stockholm Conference on Vietnam, which said her action should spur similar demonstrations in other countries.[66] Her protest was widely covered, and while many newspapers accurately reported her views, others, reflecting the ageism and misogyny prevalent at the time, dismissed her as emotional and shrill. Headlines included "Fasting Grandmother Camps at MPs' Doors" and "Granny Fasts on the Hill: She's Hungry but Not Alone."[67]

Culhane's hunger strike forced many parliamentarians to respond to questions they had been avoiding. Most hedged. Trudeau's powerful minister of citizenship and immigration, Jean Marchand, dropped by for a visit, which quickly turned into a heated debate. Culhane insisted that Marchand should support ending the Defence Production Sharing Agreement. He snapped: "Do you want to be the one to tell 150,000 workers that they're out of work if we discontinue producing war material for the U.S.A. under the defence contracts we hold with them?"[68] In just a few words, Marchand had expressed Cabinet's quandary and the essence of the national conversation.

Thérèse Casgrain was with Culhane on October 9, the day planned for the ten-day fast's end, when a message came from the prime minister. Trudeau wanted to talk. Culhane broke her fast with some fruit and juice. Casgrain and a weak but determined Culhane then slowly entered the prime minister's spacious office.

Trudeau rose, shook their hands, and offered that it took a great deal of courage to do what Culhane was doing. Unintimidated by the office or the man, Culhane replied, "It doesn't take much courage. You should be congratulating the thousands of Canadians who feel the same way I do but aren't here."[69] Trudeau said that perhaps Culhane was misinterpreting what Sharp had said at the United Nations, but she quickly produced a copy of the speech and offered to read the offending portion.

At that point, an aide entered the room and announced that the prime minister was needed at another meeting. All three laughed at what was so obviously a pre-planned interruption. Trudeau said gracious goodbyes but then paused at the door. He said softly, "You have no idea the pressure I am under." Culhane replied that she understood perfectly: "Why do you think I spent ten days out there, if not trying to bring on another set of pressures?"[70]

Culhane's fast may have raised awareness of the issues at hand but it did not end Canada's involvement in the war. The argument Marchand had articulated was too strong. Plus, Trudeau agreed with Pearson that there was no point in Canada's trying to hasten the war's end. He later wrote: "Barbaric, devastating, poisonous of human and international relations as were so many aspects of this conflict, there was no possibility of any third-party influence. The Nixon administration would brook no interference, countenance no criticism, and entertain no suggestions. . . . If effectiveness was to be a measure of Canadian foreign policy, Vietnam, sadly, offered no opportunity for influence."[71] With respect to Vietnam, quiet diplomacy would continue to be expressed as silent diplomacy within the complex web of Canadian-American relations. And the arms sales would carry on.

The ICC's new Canadian commissioner, Gordon Longmuir, the man who had belatedly welcomed Culhane when she arrived in Saigon, wrote to Ottawa that her hunger strike had been reported in Northern and Southern newspapers. The Hanoi press, he said, were using it as a propaganda victory. He wrote that the hunger strike would likely result in "a renewed onslaught on the subject of arms sales to the United States." He pledged to do as his predecessors had done and ignore questions and accusations.[72]

Two months later, VOW helped sponsor Culhane to be among two hundred international delegates attending the three-day Stockholm Conference on Vietnam. She enthusiastically supported the resolution stating that Canada and all other countries with medical teams and personnel in South Vietnam should withdraw their money and people. Countries should become truly neutral, the conference concluded, by offering help only through the International Red Cross, which supplied assistance to both sides.

From Stockholm, Culhane visited France, where she met two North Vietnamese delegates to the Paris Peace Talks, and then Britain, where she was feted by the London press. Back home in Canada, she undertook a nationwide speaking tour in January 1969. Travelling lightly and lodging with friends and supporters, she conducted numerous newspaper and radio interviews, and addressed large and small audiences in university lecture halls and church basements. She continued to write letters to the prime minister, cabinet ministers, MPs, and others. She was indefatigable.

On December 19, 1969, Culhane was back in Paris, where she made an impassioned presentation to the International Conference on War Crimes, which was co-chaired by influential philosopher Jean-Paul Sartre. To a hushed audience she repeated many of the stories of her time in Vietnam and her conclusion that Canada and all allied countries must immediately end their multi-faceted support for the war.[73]

The growing antipathy toward the war was seen back in Canada that month when, at the conclusion of their week-long conference in Montreal, the Canadian Council of Churches stated that Canada should end its involvement in the Vietnam War. It said, "We regret the continuing export to the United States of Canadian-manufactured products which become part of the American war machine. . . . This action by Canada indicates this nation's co-operation in U.S. military policies and gives tacit moral support to them."[74]

Still, the government remained unmoved. In fact, CIDA spearheaded even more projects in South Vietnam. While supplying weapons that helped create refugees, Canada was building a $535,000 refugee centre on the outskirts of Saigon.

Culhane decided that another high-profile protest was needed. On Christmas Eve, she and activist filmmaker Michael Rubbo led a candlelight vigil on Parliament Hill. To bring even more attention to the cause, they and a few supporters established a camp, but when the RCMP escorted them from the property, they moved to a nearby vacant lot beside a church. Culhane was determined to maintain the protest until January 12, when Parliament would resume sitting.

On the first night the temperature plummeted. Then it snowed. Supporters donated food, clothing, and blankets. Her flimsy shelter was soon surrounded by a small tent village. Culhane and others spoke with reporters, who showed up every day with clipboards, cameras, and coffee. The protest was debated on radio call-in shows and television news programs. Culhane asked Canadians to send letters and telegrams to their MPs and the prime minister containing only one word: *Enough.* They should demand that Canada call for an end to the war, withdraw all support, and stop all arms sales to the United States.[75] The makeshift camp became known as Enough Village. Culhane and her supporters criticized the prime minister for having recently taken the time to speak with John Lennon and Yoko Ono about peace, and making peace a prominent part of his Christmas message to Canadians, while doing nothing to end or even acknowledge Canada's role in the war. Dr. Vennema visited to offer encouragement. On New Year's Day, two opposition MPs, Progressive Conservative David MacDonald and the New Democratic Party's Ed Broadbent, dropped by with a warm lunch.

On the protest's last day, the prime minister's limousine stopped by the camp and Trudeau lowered his window. He said he admired Culhane's convictions. She said she was outraged that Canada was so intricately involved in the war and Trudeau responded, "I'm not sure that we are."[76] Culhane explained that Canada shared $4 billion in trade with the United States, including military sales. The prime minister countered: "[We're] friendly with the United States but we are not involved in the war." Culhane would not let him off the hook. Did he not feel guilty that Canada had sold $370 million worth of military equipment for use in Vietnam? How much, she asked, had companies that were profiting from arms sales donated to the Liberal Party? Trudeau dodged the question: "You don't seem to have a solution for ending the war tomorrow, beyond appealing to the United States to be more reasonable. I think President Nixon is very aware of the need to come to a responsible solution to this war."[77] They talked past each other for a few moments longer until Trudeau tired of the verbal ping-pong and left.

When the protest ended, she wrote to Trudeau, thanking him for the brief conversation but asking how much of the 21 percent increase in Canadians' cost of living was a result of American inflation caused by the war. She noted that he had said in an Edmonton speech that the overwhelming threat to Canada would come from the two-thirds of the world's people who were falling further behind in their standard of living—yet Canadian companies had earned $360 million in arms sales while his government had allocated only $260 million to development assistance. She asked again how much the Liberal Party was receiving from defence industry companies.[78] The only response came from one of Trudeau's secretaries, who acknowledged receipt of her letter.[79]

CHEMICAL DIVIDES

In 1970 Culhane moved to British Columbia to enjoy more time with her children and grandchildren. She continued to research, write, and speak out. In May she participated in a protest at the Defence Research Establishment in Suffield, Alberta. Nine hundred people camped out and chanted for three days outside the plant gates, drawing attention to Canada's continuing involvement in the research, development, and sales of chemical weapons used in Vietnam.

Among the companies implicated was Dow Chemical, founded by Herbert Dow, who was born in Belleville, Ontario. The Michigan-based enterprise had opened a plant in Sarnia, Ontario, during the Second World War. In the 1960s it manufactured napalm, a blend of gasoline, benzene, and polystyrene, which, when dropped from helicopter gunships or fixed-wing aircraft, burned the flesh of those it touched, destroyed fat tissues, and left victims writhing in insufferable agony. The fortunate died.

A growing awareness of the ghastly effects of dangerous chemical-based products led to protests against the companies producing them. Among those companies was Dow, which nevertheless increased production, including at its Sarnia plant. Dow became the focus of a number of protests, articles, and letters to editors across Canada. A short film entitled *Methods* showed the devastating effects of the use of chemicals in the war. Culhane showed the film at a number of her speeches, where she spoke of helping to treat napalm victims at the Quang Ngai hospital who were wrapped so tightly in Vaseline and gauze that she could not tell if they were men or women, alive or dead. She spoke of napalm-doused children dying slow and agonizing deaths. As the lights dimmed to view the film, she whispered, "We are party to everything you are about to see."[80]

Events at the University of Toronto were a microcosm of debates raging across Canada. In November 1967, faculty members and students staged a sit-in to protest Dow's plan to conduct job interviews on campus. Mathematics professor Chandler Davis wrote in *The Varsity*, the widely read campus paper, "As we would not invade Vietnam, we should not be a cog in a machine which is invading Vietnam."[81] Dow cancelled its visit. That decision led U of T engineering students to rise up against the anti-war protesters, arguing that they had a right to decide for themselves whom they worked for, regardless of a company's product or customers. The Engineering Society demanded that Dow recruiters be re-invited to the university. Its action inspired other students and student groups to protest the protesters.

After the Student Advisory Council (SAC) passed a motion condemning all Canadian companies that provided products for use in Vietnam, a 1,600-signature petition led to the resignation of SAC president Tom Faulkner.[82] Faulkner then ran for re-election and won by over eight hundred votes.[83] Dow's recruiters did not return to the university, but its Sarnia plant continued to make napalm and sell it to the Pentagon.

In 1972 people around the world came to know the effects of napalm on civilians through nine-year-old Kim Phuc, who, in perhaps the most famous photograph of the war, was seen naked, running, and screaming with other children after a napalm attack on their village. Kim Phuc suffered third-degree burns to much of her body and endured seventeen operations. After the war, she and her husband fled to Canada and found a home near Toronto.

Napalm was not the only controversial chemical agent used in the war. From June 14 to 16, 1966, American Army helicopters roared just over the treetops at Canadian Forces Base Gagetown, in southwest New Brunswick, dropping a fine chemical spray.[84] A year later, from June 21 to 24, they did it again. The Americans were testing a herbicide defoliant that burned the leaves from trees and shrubs. Variants of the chemical had been used in Vietnam since 1961 to rob the Viet Cong of jungle cover. In the program code-named Operation Ranch Hand, American GIs riffed on Smokey the Bear's slogan and joked, "Only you can prevent forests." The military nicknamed the chemicals after the colours of the bands that encircled their metal containers, calling them Agent Purple, Agent White, and, the most widely used, Agent Orange.

From 1962 to 1971, approximately 19 million gallons of the stuff was spread over 10 to 20 percent of Vietnam and parts of Laos, destroying 12,000 square miles of jungle and forest, and poisoning crops and water supplies. Later, scientists determined that the chemicals were carcinogenic and that those who ate contaminated food, drank contaminated water, or were exposed to the spray suffered dramatically increased incidences of cancer. Exposure also caused genetic damage resulting in the birth of terribly ill or disfigured children.[85] It was these chemicals that the Americans were testing at the base near Oromocto, New Brunswick. Because they were not registered for use in Canada, the tests were illegal. But there they were—twice.

Monsanto, Dow Chemicals, and five other American companies had contracted to manufacture Agent Orange but could not meet the

Pentagon's enormous demand. In 1956 the Uniroyal Chemical Company had begun producing Agent Orange at its plant in Elmira, Ontario, about eighty miles northwest of Toronto. It was used by Ontario's hydro corporation to clear forest for its lines and by its Department of Highways to clear brush from roadsides. Beginning in 1962, barrels of Agent Orange were regularly loaded onto trains at the Elmira station and shipped to Montreal for transport to Vietnam.[86]

Elmira's seven thousand citizens benefitted from the American defence contract as plant and spin-off jobs boosted prosperity. They accepted the sickly-sweet smell that wafted over their homes as just part of life in the small town. They accepted without complaint that plant waste was dumped into barrels and buried nearby. What they did not know, however, was that while the herbicide they were making was killing people in Vietnam, it was also slowly killing them. Due to long-standing manufacturing and disposal practices, Agent Orange and residue from other chemicals produced in the plant slowly seeped into the local aquifer, contaminating the water supply.[87] It would affect them long after the war ended.

SHE PERSISTS

On January 21, 1971, Claire Culhane appeared on the popular CBC television program *Viewpoint*. She expressed support for Prime Minister Trudeau's argument that Britain should end arms sales to South Africa because they rendered the British people complicit in apartheid. But if that logic was sound, she said, then Trudeau was making Canada complicit in the Vietnam War by continuing to sanction Canadian arms sales to the United States.[88]

Six weeks later, on March 4, Culhane arrived unannounced at Parliament Hill. She and Marie Taylor, an old friend and curator of drawings at the National Gallery, made their way to the House of Commons

visitors' gallery and took seats overlooking the external affairs minister. As Question Period began, Culhane slipped a lock and chain from
beneath her baggy clothing and secured her ankle to a chair leg. She
then shouted: "Why is Canada building hospitals in South Vietnam and
also supplying bombs in Vietnam? Why was there no investigation of
the Canadian member of the ICC who admitted he had given information to the CIA? Why is the government refusing to release reports
made by me and a former director of the Tuberculosis Hospital about
conditions there?"[89] NDP leader Tommy Douglas stopped his remarks
and, to laughter from his colleagues, quipped, "Mr. Speaker, I am used
to being interrupted. I have been married for a long time."[90] Culhane
threw handfuls of leaflets that fluttered down on government members. Four security guards quickly descended and, after fumbling with
the chain, led her away. The stunt made the front page of the *Globe
and Mail* and was widely reported across the country. Culhane was
charged with creating a disturbance and, on April 19, appeared in an
Ottawa court, but the case was dismissed because the Crown had not
adequately proved the charge.

Two weeks later Culhane was in Washington. She met with a number
of congressmen regarding Canada's involvement in the war. On June
14 New York Representative Bella Abzug read into the congressional
record a copy of the 1968 report that Culhane had prepared for Maurice
Strong. Abzug concluded: "The implication which one draws from her
disclosures is that not even a medical unit functions in Vietnam without having American political interest as their foremost consideration.
The report made by Mrs. Culhane demonstrates clearly how the most
humanitarian of programs can become distorted and diverted to war-
making purposes. I respect Mrs. Culhane for her undeterred efforts to
make these facts public."[91]

While many Canadian newspapers noted Abzug's remarks, the
headlines remained dominated by the previous day's publication in
the *New York Times* of what became known as the Pentagon Papers. The

revelations were stunning. A series of articles based on secret information relating to three American administrations' handling of the Vietnam War laid bare the many lies that had been told over the years. Among them was that Prime Minister Pham Van Dong was correct when he told Blair Seaborn that the second Gulf of Tonkin attack in August 1964, the attack that was the pretext for all that followed, had never happened.[92] The opposition Progressive Conservatives pounded the government on what the Pentagon Papers revealed about Canada's secret role in Vietnam. Mitchell Sharp rose in the House on June 17 and admitted that the Seaborn missions had indeed taken place and that the government had kept them from the Canadian people.[93]

In November 1972, Culhane released a book entitled *Why Is Canada in Vietnam? The Truth About Our Foreign Aid*. Her main point was summarized in the first chapter: "In every war, medical programmes have been used as a 'front' for intelligence activities, but we should have the right to decide whether our programme be permitted to continue, given its main purpose is to serve the military needs of the U.S. in Vietnam, and not the needs of the Vietnamese people."[94] She quoted the director of the US-AID program in Vietnam, who had been asked by a reporter about charges that aid in Vietnam was simply a cover for CIA operations. He replied, "Well, I just have to admit that that is true."[95] Culhane embarked on a cross-Canada book tour.

Culhane continued to win as many enemies as friends. Her book and tour helped to continue shape the national conversation about Vietnam. In this way, the war contributed to the evolution of a new consensus about who Canadians were and who they aspired to be.

CHAPTER 4

JOE ERICKSON AND THE NEW UNDERGROUND RAILROAD

On a cool September morning in 2012, Joe Erickson was in his Peterborough County barn with his horses. The fit, tanned sixty-eight-year-old with the trimmed white beard and old beekeeper's straw hat hummed to himself as he brushed the big Belgian. Erickson loved his horses. Stories handed down about his deceased grandfather and lessons he'd learned from his father could be summed up in the ancient agrarian proverb "There is something about the outside of a horse that is good for the inside of a man."

But on that morning, he was saying goodbye. He changed out of his barn clothes, enjoyed his last sip of tea, bid goodbye to his wife, Tina, and set out down the gravel road that began the long journey home to his native Minnesota. From his home near Keene, about midway between Ottawa and Toronto, he travelled north to loop over the top of Lake Superior and took in the rugged beauty of the Canadian Shield. He was headed for the fiftieth anniversary of his high school graduation and to see family and friends he had not visited in a long while.

Erickson pulled his dusty blue Hyundai to a stop at the Grand Portage–Pigeon River border crossing. He smiled and said a friendly hello to the American agent as he handed over his Canadian passport. The agent checked his computer screen, frowned, glanced at the passport again, stared at Erickson for a second and then gazed back at the screen. Holding on to the passport, and without explanation, he pointed to where he wanted Erickson to park and then remain in his car.

Two agents led Erickson into the stale, sterile building and to a cold, windowless room with a steel table and metal chairs. He was ordered to wait. The steel door locked behind him with an alarmingly loud clunk. After he had sat alone for several minutes, fighting apprehension and wondering what he could possibly have done wrong, the agents returned. As they grilled him, he was shocked at the details of his life contained in their file and by their deeply personal questions. They would not reveal how they knew so much or why he was being detained. Finally, after over an hour of stressful interrogation, with neither explanation nor apology, they gave him his passport and let him go.

Erickson was shaken. He had crossed into the United States many times without trouble and had expected none on that day. Just over the border, he checked into a small hotel. The next morning he stopped for breakfast in Grand Marais, where he met up with his nephew Peter, and neither could guess what the problem had been. Six hours later Erickson was at the home of his sister Beth Jansen and her husband, Keven, in Alexandria, Minnesota. Erickson told them of the border ordeal and was surprised when Beth waved it off, saying, "Oh, that's just the old FBI stuff." His sister was about to reveal a secret his family had kept for decades.

—

Pope County had been a terrific place to grow up. Situated on the gently rolling transition between the prairie and the northern woods and lakes, it boasted the rich, black corn-belt soil that generations ago had attracted Scandinavian homesteaders. Harold and Emmalyn Erickson's 220-acre farm offered Joe and his sisters, Verona, Beth, and Pam, spacious horizons to explore. There were forts and rafts to build, ponds to skate on, hay ropes to swing from, and horses and ponies to ride.

A popular young man, Erickson excelled at school, especially in student government, debate, theatre, and music. He was active in the 4-H club, where, at every meeting, he pledged his "head to clearer thinking, heart to greater loyalty, hand to larger service, and health to better living for home, club, community, and country." As the state's 4-H club vice-president, he attended the Farm Bureau National Convention in Chicago, where Minnesota senator, and later vice-president, Hubert Humphrey recognized him, thrust out his hand, and said, "Hi, Joe, how are things? Are your folks still on the family farm?" Later that day, Joe was thrilled to share the speaker's platform with Humphrey.

In 1962 Erickson enrolled at the University of Minnesota's College of Agriculture. That October, the Cuban Missile Crisis terrified the world with the possibility of nuclear annihilation. Erickson was unnerved by a demonstration at the university where male students chanted their ability to pass the military's health test and their eagerness to fight communists: "Hey! Hey! We're all 1-A." Their enthusiasm for war frustrated Erickson, for he knew that if they really wanted to fight they would have already enlisted. Besides, because they were in a post-secondary institution, they earned a deferment from the Selective Service System and so would not be drafted.

Erickson grew unhappy with his chosen program and, inspired by President Kennedy's call for service, joined the Peace Corps. In 1966, he served in Medellin, Colombia, as a community organizer. He lived simply, while encouraging and enabling local leaders to advocate more effectively for social and economic justice. He became dispirited with the local administration of the well-intentioned program and then heartbroken when Mary, the girlfriend he had left back home, stopped writing. After six months, he returned home.

Erickson re-entered the University of Minnesota and concentrated more on theatre and drama. He re-established his relationship with Mary, who was a talented actress and drama student. After only a year away from campus, he noticed a pronounced change in its atmosphere. As at nearly all other universities and colleges, groups of students were fighting for sexual freedom, racial and gender equality, and greater influence over their curriculum—and against the Vietnam War. The national media covered anti-war activities at elite universities, but sentiments were as passionate and actions as ambitious at state schools like his.[1] In fact, students at those places of learning had more reason to be upset, because many of their schools were funded by Pentagon research grants.

As in universities and colleges across Canada and the United States, only a minority of U. of M. students fought to end the war. They faced hostile opposition from administrators, faculty, and other students, but their determination and numbers grew. While Erickson opposed the war and engaged in debates, he questioned the effectiveness of mass demonstrations. He was also uncomfortable with the anti-war culture, especially the prevalence of drugs.

After completing university in 1967, Joe and Mary were wed. They worked in the local theatre and opera community. When he had turned eighteen, as required by law, he had registered with the United States Selective Service System and passed his mandatory physical examination. With the war escalating, more young men were leaving for Vietnam, and because Joe was no longer a university student, he and Mary knew his time would come. They had a decision to make. They agreed that he would not fight in a war they believed was morally wrong, and so there were three choices. He could portray himself as a conscientious objector, but that would be a lie. He could go to prison.

But there was a third option. After many long and difficult discussions, he and Mary decided they would escape to Canada.

FOLLOWING THE NORTHERN STAR

Americans had sought Canadian sanctuary even before there were Americans and Canadians. The American Revolution was a civil war in which only about a third of the British colonists actively supported the rebel cause. With Britain's defeat, about forty-six thousand of those who had remained loyal to the king fled the newly established United States to settle permanently and help shape what would become Canada. Of that number, about two thousand were Indigenous people who had fought with the British. Over three thousand were African Americans, some slaves, but most free.

The conflict over the monstrous shame of slavery led to the deaths of 750,000 Americans in the country's second civil war. For thirty years before Fort Sumter's cannons roared in 1861, thirty to forty thousand African-American slaves had demonstrated humanity's indomitable urge to be free by smashing their chains and fleeing to Canada. They found refuge in a land that, while not without the scourge of racism, had at least abolished slavery.

The Civil War's fratricidal butchery saw a desertion rate of 45 percent, and many fled to Canada.[2] Confederate soldiers having either deserted or escaped from prisoner-of-war camps found so many compatriots in Montreal that its swankiest hotel, the St. Lawrence Hall, proudly advertised the best mint juleps in town. So many of Maine's young men dodged the draft that a popular New Brunswick escape route was renamed (and is still called) Skedaddle Ridge.

A hundred years later a new war was turning Americans against each other. With the Vietnam draft, the government was again dictating that young men should cede their liberty to fight its war. Those who said no were rejecting the state's power to determine the trajectory of their lives. In moving to Canada, they became thieves: stealing government property by pilfering themselves away. In deciding to follow the northern star to freedom, Erickson and others like him were part of an American tradition as rich and long as settling political matters through military means.

Many of those leaving America in the 1960s believed it was really America that had left them. James Leslie, for instance, evaded the draft when, in December 1967, he drove his Volkswagen from San Francisco to Vancouver. He later explained, "There was an image of Canada as an alternate America. And I think a lot of people [thought]—I at certain times must have said it—that I'll go up there and I'll really be able to live the American dream, that that polity that was supposed to exist [in the United States] may in fact exist in Canada."[3] Like Leslie, the war resisters pledged allegiance to themselves rather than to their flag. They opted to identify more with their principles than their nationality.[4] In this way, perhaps those coming to Canada to live in a society that they believed more closely resembled Jeffersonian values were the most American Americans of all.

Joe and Mary told their friends of their plan and, to various degrees, were supported by all. Their parents were surprised but accepted the decision. In March 1968 they packed what little they had into their old Chevy—cursed with an aluminum block that never allowed it to start in cold weather—and an even older trailer.

They had done their homework and knew about the landed immigrant application forms that awaited them at the border. They wrote their carefully prepared answers and with great relief watched the Canadian border agent stamp their papers and wish them luck. Hours later, with the sun setting, they pulled into Winnipeg; a prairie city where neither knew a soul.

The couple were in their early twenties and, unlike many others fleeing at the time, they arrived with a little money. They also had some

drafting work from a family friend's business that they had arranged
to complete in Winnipeg and send back to Minnesota. They were therefore able to avoid living in a room or hostel and instead sought a house
to rent. In the working-class area of St. Vital, the landlord met them at
the door and asked where they were from. "You're from the States, eh?
What the hell is going on down there with this war?" They were immediately given a lease.

Mary quickly found work at the University of Manitoba and a neigh-
bour's asking Joe to help with an emergency cement pour led to a full-
time job. The neighbourhood introduced them to Winnipeg's vibrant
immigrant community, where stories of moving from war-torn Europe
and having to learn a new language and a startlingly new culture put
their own adjustment experience into perspective.

Erickson worked with people from around the world and, in deep
and intense conversations, he learned a great deal about war's human
costs. He picked up all he knew about carpentry from Guenther, of
German descent, who was tormented by how a proud people such as his
could have fallen into Nazism and been responsible for such horrors.
Erickson made a lifelong friend of Branko. In broken English, Branko
explained that for him it had come down to coming to Canada or facing
possible death due to the violence of the war between Serbia and his
native Croatia. Sigurd, a seventy-something Canadian veteran of the
First World War, explained how he and other privates had once opened
fire on an officer who had ordered them to undertake an obviously sui-
cidal charge. Maurice, the Saskatchewan Métis who hardly ever said a
word, added, "Yeah, we did the same in World War Two." Tony had left
Northern Ireland to escape the growing sectarian violence that became
the Troubles and once said, "For crying out loud, Joe, turn the radio
and television off the Friday before Remembrance Day, and don't turn
it on again until the Monday night after." Joe worked hard and picked
up important skills, one of which was learning to swear, convinced that
war in any form was so vulgar that only construction-site language was

appropriate when discussing it. His workmates and friends reaffirmed that he had made the right decision to avoid Vietnam—the concept of glory in war was only for recruiters and movies.

On a weekend when Mary was visiting family in Minnesota, Joe felt compelled to write a letter to his draft board back home in Pope County. He wanted to be honest and transparent by telling them when and why he had left and where he had gone. The letter also bluntly articulated his feelings about the immorality of the Vietnam War and his resolute intention to have no part in it. He urged members of the board to reflect on the role they were playing in supporting the war. He asked whether the Nuremberg trials had not shown that claiming to be only following orders absolves no one. Erickson felt a sense of relief when he dropped the envelope in the mailbox. He received no response and had no clue as to the chain of events he had just initiated.

He and Mary moved to a Victorian house on Osborne Street. After a year, however, there was growing stress in their relationship. Finally, they decided to split up, and so Mary packed their car and returned to Minnesota.

Now alone in the house, Erickson began hosting a weekly gathering of fellow war resisters. Young men and women would sit in a circle with a 24-case of beer in the middle. When the two-four was gone, the meeting was over. While war resisters were the main participants, actors, reporters, neighbours, and friends sometimes showed up to learn about the United States, the war, and the resisters' experiences. They shared information and ideas, vented about their troubles, and spoke of help they and others needed.

Resisters confessed to being worried about being forced back to the United States. One evening, members of the group spoke of the possibility of FBI infiltrators in their midst. Three newspaper reporters, who happened to be present that evening, said that they had, indeed, heard rumours that conversations that occurred in groups such as Erickson's were fed to the RCMP or the FBI. Erickson believed such fears were pointless distractions and said, "Listen—we're in Canada and we're safe here." He said he had been assured that fleeing Selective Service in the United States was not among the violations listed in Canada's U.S. extradition treaty and urged the group to avoid letting visions of FBI handcuffs haunt their dreams. However, Ryan, a resister and friend of Erickson's visiting from Saskatoon, had been cautioned at the University of Saskatchewan, where he was finishing his master's degree, to be careful what he said—the Mounties had ears everywhere.

As the saying goes, it's not paranoia when someone really is out to get you, and Erickson's group was justified in their concerns. The RCMP spied and reported on any groups or individuals who challenged the established political, economic, or cultural status quo— groups such as communists, union and university activists, Quebec nationalists, anti-war protesters, and war resisters.[5] Exiled Americans and the organizations that supported them were considered foreign radicals who needed to be watched because they were negatively influencing apparently naïve Canadian youth. The RCMP acknowledged in 1966 that, with respect to war resisters, it was working with the FBI and that its officers were always present when FBI agents conducted interrogations.[6]

Merritt Clifton, who founded a Montreal-based resister support group, said of the RCMP: "They were always polite and always in uniform, and they always gave us time so that anyone who was on the premises had time to hide or make a run for it. I don't think they really wanted to catch anyone, but they had to ask questions because they were supposed to be cooperating with the Americans."[7]

The fear of capture and return struck Erickson when, at four in the morning, he was jarred awake by his ringing phone. A stern voice identified the speaker as an RCMP constable. Erikson was ordered to report to the local detachment at five that morning. He arrived freshly showered and in his best clothes, and was told an FBI agent was in a room down the hall and wanted to see him. Erickson squared his jaw and said he was no longer in the United States and so insisted, incorrectly, that the FBI had no right to interview him. The RCMP officer smiled and said that he would begin with a few questions. The two had a rather pleasant thirty-minute chat in which Erickson spoke of where he was living, where he worked, and how he was finding life in Winnipeg. Satisfied, the officer left, presumably to confer with the FBI agent. He soon returned, shook Erickson's hand, smiled, and said he was free to go. "Really?" asked Erickson. "Young man," the officer said, "if I were you, I would have done exactly what you did."

While enjoying life in Winnipeg and his circle of friends, Erickson had been turning more of his attention to theatre. He learned of the thriving arts scene in Toronto and, in the summer of 1970, decided to begin again in Canada's largest and most culturally diverse city. He gathered a few essentials in a large backpack and stood with his thumb out on the Trans-Canada Highway. As fate would have it, a University of Toronto professor who had been in Winnipeg for a conference picked him up and they drove together all the way to Toronto.

WAR-RESISTER ORGANIZATIONS

By 1970 war resisters had been fleeing to Canada for five years. From the American west coast, they travelled to British Columbia and from New England they headed primarily to Moncton, Halifax, and Montreal. Many moved to rural and remote areas, living alone or in small groups of resister enclaves, while others formed communes, far removed from both the American and Canadian mainstreams. Like Erickson, though, most eventually ended up in or near Toronto. While the Canadian government knew how many Americans moved to Canada each year, neither it nor the American government kept track of how many were war resisters. University of Toronto sociology professor and author John Hagan, himself a resister, calculated that in 1965, 1,281 American war resisters came to Canada. The numbers rose each year: 2,543 in 1966, 3,549 in 1967, 5,173 in 1968, 6,284 in 1969, and in 1970, 7,991 war resisters settled in Canada.[8]

Of the 26,821 young people who between 1965 and 1970 left friends, families, and the hopes and homes they knew, nearly half were women.[9] Many of the women were like Mary, in that they travelled with a husband or partner who was avoiding the war. Also like Mary, nearly all played a major role in the decision to leave. Canadian border agents always seemed to ask the men numerous and detailed questions but, probably due to the predominant sexist belief at the time that women were merely doing as they were told, few women were asked anything.[10]

Among the many women who made the journey north and would contribute mightily to Canada's development was journalist, author, and activist Jane Jacobs. She moved from New York with her architect husband, Bob, in order to save their children from being drafted. Her revolutionary thoughts on city planning helped shape Toronto and other cities, including many in America. Another notable woman resister was influential journalist, author, teacher, and the first female editor of a national daily Canadian newspaper, Diane Francis. When her husband, Frank, received his draft notice in April 1966, they left New York for Toronto. They composed a letter to the Queen's draft board explaining that they had "pursued the American dream to Canada."[11] Renowned Canadian author Margaret Atwood returned to Toronto with her American first husband and war resister, Jim Polk. Atwood rose to the forefront of writers, actors, and publishers who joined university professors in supporting the transplanted Americans while shaping Canada's cultural community.

Many of the thousands of war resisters making their way to Canada were helped in their decision, journey, and settlement by resister organizations on both sides of the border. These organizations were needed in the United States because the government was certainly not about to help anyone evade military service, and in Canada because the government would not designate war resisters as refugees and so its support programs did not apply.

One of the most active of the seventy-five American resister organizations was Boston's New England Resistance (BNER). Like most others, BNER was staffed largely by volunteers and ran on a shoestring budget. It offered those considering the move to Canada advice regarding immigration law and provided helpful Canadian addresses and phone numbers. BNER volunteers also appeared at draft boards to discuss options with draftees and made impromptu and inflammatory speeches at military recruitment events. Their dedication to non-violence was often tested. In March 1966, for instance, BNER led a demonstration that saw resisters silently burn their draft notices before the South Boston District Courthouse. The police stood by as a mob of 250 fell on the young protesters and beat them senseless, sending many to the hospital.[12]

American resister organizations were in regular contact with their Canadian counterparts. Among the first and most significant was the Vancouver Committee to Aid American War Objectors. It was founded in 1966 by a lawyer and a group of University of British Columbia professors. Like many similar organizations, it was quickly overwhelmed by the numbers of those seeking help. Run by dedicated volunteers and a few paid staff, it rented office space in an old East Georgia Street warehouse. Other resister organizations, such as the Montreal Council to Aid War Resisters and Ottawa's Assistance with Immigration and the Draft, wrote or gathered and distributed newsletters containing useful information, including contacts for housing, schools, and employment.

Canada's most widely known and influential resister support group was in Toronto. The Student Union for Peace Action began in December 1964 at the University of Toronto and dedicated itself to fighting nuclear proliferation. Within a year, it had shifted its focus to helping war resisters. By 1966 the need to counsel the growing number of resisters saw it morph into the Toronto Anti-Draft Programme (TADP).

In 1967 a twenty-year-old Texas-born war resister named Mark Satin walked into the TADP's cramped and chaotic offices. Within months, his passion and unflagging energy led to his appointment as the director of its anti-draft program. Satin wrote and edited the *Manual for Draft-Age Immigrants to Canada*. Published in 1968 by Toronto's House of Anansi Press, the thin book went through six editions and sold over 65,000 copies. Sales were helped by articles written about it in the *New York Times, Life, Time, Reader's Digest,* and even the *Ladies' Home Journal.* It helped finance TADP operations and put House of Anansi on the road to becoming one of Canada's most successful independent publishers.

The *Manual* was available at or through every Canadian and American war resister organization and at American colleges and universities. A third of those who escaped to Canada after 1968 spoke of having been inspired and helped by the *Manual for Draft-Age Immigrants to Canada.*[13] John Hagan, who fled with his wife to Canada in August 1969 called the *Manual* "a manifesto for the mobilization of the resistance movement."[14]

The *Manual* was blunt in its stated purpose: "This is a handbook for draft resisters who have chosen to immigrate to Canada. Read it, cover to cover, and you will know how."[15] It explained Canadian immigration laws and suggested applying for landed immigrant status, which allowed a person to live, work, and attend school in Canada, and be able to apply for eventual Canadian citizenship. It offered hints on crossing the border, such as first getting a haircut and not arriving on a motorcycle. The *Manual* provided addresses of American and Canadian government agencies from which to obtain forms and information. It also listed the addresses and phone numbers of Canadian and American anti-draft organizations. Sections written by Canadian professors sketched the country's history, political institutions, culture, weather, and more. A section on housing sardonically began, "Most Canadians do not live in igloos."[16] Canada was painted as a more open, tolerant, and happy country than the United States, with a long history of welcoming immigrants in general and war resisters in particular. The

Manual also emphasized that war resisters might never be allowed to return home.

By 1968 the TAPD's Spadina Avenue offices, with their peeling paint and castaway furniture, were helping an average of seventeen new resisters a day. Many arrived with nothing but a knapsack. Those passing through the yellow door emblazoned with a white dove of peace found ringing phones, jumbles of conversations, and people rushing in and out. Mark Satin oversaw the barely controlled bedlam with an astounding memory for names and faces. When Satin was fired by the TAPD Board in May 1968 under a cloud of recrimination, Bernie Jaffe, assisted by Naomi Wall, took over. They were helped by staff members and dedicated young volunteers.

Most resister organizations earned revenue from the sale of literature, but all relied on direct and in-kind donations. Lawyers such as Toronto's Clayton Ruby, for example, did pro bono work. Essential to Canadian and American war resister organizations was the support provided by churches. In December 1969, American and Canadian clergy and representatives from the American National Council of Churches and the ecumenical body representing the world's widest range of denominations—the Canadian Council of Churches (CCC)— met in Windsor, Ontario. They agreed upon ways to improve and coordinate church efforts to support the resister movement. The Windsor Consultation led to a pledge of $100,000, which was funnelled through the CCC to Canada's war resister organizations. The CCC created the Ministry to Draft-Age Immigrants to oversee the ambitious initiative. Money moved through the CCC's new ministry from churches and church groups in the United States, Germany, Denmark, France, and the Netherlands.[17]

Individual Canadian Anglican, Presbyterian, Mennonite, Catholic, Lutheran, and United churches, Buddhist temples, and Jewish synagogues donated money to local resister organizations. They helped raise awareness and encouraged their congregations to offer money and direct assistance such as temporary housing. They either produced or helped distribute books, booklets, and pamphlets.

J. McRee Elrod was a Canadian Unitarian minister who led the creation of Immigration Aid to Refugees of Conscience. He took it upon himself to help those who came north, and encouraged others to follow them. He wrote numerous open letters to publications and groups in the United States that extolled Canada's virtues. Magazines as disparate as *Esquire*, the *New York Review of Books*, and even *Playboy* printed Elrod's letters. Typical was his January 1968 letter published in the *Christian Century*, in which he encouraged emigration to Canada, calling it "one of the few countries trying to create peace on earth."[18]

Churches and faith-based organizations cited overlapping motives for their war resister activities. First was the humanitarian urge to help those in need. In an August 1970 article in the *Christian Century*, a World Council of Churches spokesperson wrote, "These men are refugees and we do not make any judgement on the rightness or wrongness of their decision. We help them as human beings whom the churches in Canada are trying to assist."[19]

Second, the growing opposition to the war was often tinged with anti-Americanism. This motive was clearly seen in the National Council of Church's decision to appoint fervently anti-American Robert Gardner to lead its powerful Ministry to Draft-Age Immigrants. Gardner wrote: "The American dream has been punctured. The nation has lost its innocence. The greatest military power in history has been ground to a stalemate by revolutionary insurgents. . . . A generation of presidents and national leaders have been proven liars and inept fools. The economy doesn't work. The cities are unlivable. . . . The land of the free and the home of the brave has killed, crippled, jailed and exiled thousands of its young."[20]

Just as not all nineteenth-century fugitive slaves employed the help of the Underground Railroad or sought the assistance of support groups once they crossed the border, not all of those fleeing the Vietnam War turned to resister organizations for help. Joe Erickson was among those who didn't. He did not read Satin's *Manual for Draft-Age Immigrants to Canada*, nor did he and Mary visit or seek help from the Winnipeg Committee to Assist War Objectors. Similarly, upon arriving in Toronto, Erickson did not drop in at the Toronto Anti-Draft Programme's office. He was also not among those who participated in or helped organize anti-war protests. He had made the decision not to fight in the war or, beyond stealing himself, to fight against it. Instead, Erickson was among those who worked hard to quietly assimilate and gracefully become Canadian.

On his first full day in Toronto, Erickson met a fellow Minnesotan resister. On a drunken dare, he cold-called a number of *Globe and Mail* job ads, including one for a vocal music and art teacher at Don Mills Junior High School. At eleven the next day he was being interviewed. At noon he was a teacher.

While on the job and teaching himself how to teach, Erickson became involved with the University of Toronto's Drama Centre, where he acted and directed plays. Erickson was also soon teaching and acting at the Canadian Radio and Television Arts Centre. He became artistic director for Theatre in Camera at the Bathurst Street Theatre.

As Erickson was making his way, his Winnipeg friend Branko had moved to Toronto and started a contracting business. Although Erickson enjoyed the high school teaching experience, he left after a year to work with Branko. Together they formed a company that specialized in pre-Confederation rural historic buildings. Erickson became adept at restoring and reproducing timber frame and log buildings, exclusively hand-hewn, in private or museum settings. Despite these measures of success, adjustment continued to be difficult, away from family, old friends, and the touchstones of childhood.

Like Erickson, Jack Todd was a resister who experienced the pain of detachment from family and the familiar while building a new life in

Canada. In 1969 he settled in Vancouver, where he wrote first for the *Vancouver Sun* and then relocated and became a celebrated sports columnist with the *Montreal Gazette*. In a memoir, he later recalled the difficulties he and other resisters experienced in adjusting to Canada. Many of the problems were significant and led to heartaches, regret, and, for some, clinical depression. Some problems were trivial, akin to the discomforts felt by American tourists upon discovering that corner stores didn't sell Marlboro cigarettes or beer. Todd and his compatriots initially assumed that Vancouver's overall quiet, gentleness, and politeness were insincere, but they learned first to accept and then to enjoy it.[21] They adopted Canadian idiosyncrasies such as celebrating Thanksgiving in October and adding the letter *u* to words like *color* and *neighbor*. They were in agreement, though, that it would be time to leave if they ever fell into the Canadian habit of ending sentences with "eh?"

RESISTING THE RESISTERS

While many Canadians and Canadian groups welcomed the resisters and helped them adjust to their new lives, others hated the idea of so many Americans moving to Canada. A 1968 national poll indicated that 58 percent of Canadians believed the war resisters should not be allowed into Canada and only 28 percent supported their arrival.[22] The division over welcoming or rejecting resisters added to the rifts and reflections that were already forcing Canadians to seek answers to questions about core values that many would rather have left unasked.

Schisms in churches and faith-based groups mirrored the growing societal divisions. A 1968 poll conducted by the United Church found that 63 percent of its clergy but only 45 percent of its laity agreed with church support for resisters. The poll was repeated the next year and showed that 73 percent of clergy but still only 48 percent of the laity agreed with supporting the young Americans.[23]

A measure of the anti-resister sentiment was part of the 1960s generational and ideological chasms that had opened between those supporting traditional goals, attitudes, and values and those rejecting all three. In 1965 half of all Canadians were under the age of twenty-five.[24] Young people were filling universities, colleges, and urban neighbourhoods. Many became engaged in political causes while others were cultural refugees, interested more in lifestyle than politics. It was tough to distinguish the cultural and political rebels from each other and from the resisters, for all were around the same age and, by 1967, with their long hair and unconventional clothing, often looked much the same.

War resisters congregated in a number of Toronto's neighbourhoods, with the largest so-called resister ghetto on Baldwin Street. Those with entrepreneurial spirits transformed the neighbourhood with new businesses offering clothes, food, art, and a day care. Newspapers and magazines geared to resister needs and interests, such as *Harbinger* and *AMEX*, offered advice on settling in the city while also reflecting the counterculture's anti-establishment attitudes and political opinions. Not far from Baldwin Street was the Yorkville area, a magnet that drew the curious and disaffected to explore alternative lifestyles reflected in counterculture music, art, and fashion. Like Vancouver's Kitsilano district and similar neighbourhoods in many other Canadian cities, Yorkville became a crossroads for new ideas.

The haphazardly tumbling cultural and political agendas of American war resisters and Canadian youth merged into a heady social movement that challenged Old Canada. Old Canada rested on the British-oriented, white, patriarchal, political, and cultural norms that didn't need to be discussed, for most simply knew and accepted them as the way things were and should always be. It was the dominant attitude of the older generation steeped in the lessons of the Depression and Second World War. In the 1960s, this generation occupied positions of power. They wanted calm, not disruption; respect, not challenge. The Old Canada elite, comfortably ensconced in the private clubs and private schools of the Toronto–Ottawa–English Montreal axis of power, similarly expected and demanded a perpetuation of the status quo.[25] Anywhere outside was a region. Anyone questioning its hegemonic beliefs was an enemy.

In this context, the war resisters were even more dangerous than the young Canadians with whom they shared so much, because they were outsiders. As with many of the rebellious youth, the appearance, activities, and very presence of these hordes of young Americans seemed to be tearing down the old while offering nothing new.[26]

Many war resisters were indeed part of the counterculture movement, but there were divisions within both groups. Resisters like Erickson wanted no part of either. The American youth movement's radical left opposed resister flights to Canada. Students for a Democratic Society (SDS), for instance, was formed in 1959 and by 1965 had developed into a powerful and increasingly militant organization that lobbied decision makers and led demonstrations such as the occupation of government and university buildings and the enormously successful 1965 March on Washington. In 1967 the SDS passed a resolution opposing resisters' decisions to flee to Canada. The resolution claimed to understand the urge to run but asked those who had emigrated to come home and, if they would not, to at least help build international support for efforts to end the war.[27] In this way, war resisters were framed as traitors to both those supporting and those opposing the war.

Despite the divisions between and within the youth movement and the resisters, many Canadians linked them and hated them both. Many media reports did not help, as they conflated the groups when belittling or attacking rebellious young people. Disdain was clear in the utterances of many authority figures who despised expressions of youthful anti-authoritarianism. Toronto mayor William Dennison, for instance, said in 1968, "a few hippies and deserters are Toronto's only problem."[28] Vancouver mayor Tom Campbell was even more emphatic on CBC TV:

We've got a scum community, that have organized, have decided to
grow long hair, and decided to pretend to be hippies. They want to
take everything and give nothing. Half of them are American draft
dodgers who won't even fight for their own country, who are up here
for protection, if they were in their homeland, they could be in jail.
Now if we were in trouble, if they wouldn't fight for their mother
country, what do you think they would do for their adopted country?
Nothing. Which is exactly what they are doing now. Nothing.[29]

Campbell used old vagrancy laws to gather up those he deemed hippies and jail anyone suspicious or with no fixed address. War resisters
were caught up in the anti-hippie sweep and many found themselves
behind bars or with one-way bus tickets out of town. In 1969 the offices
of Vancouver's American Deserters Committee were raided by the
RCMP ten times.[30] Each raid came with a warrant approving a search
for drugs but ended with a ransacking of files in which the names and
addresses of draft resisters were recorded. After every office raid, hos-
tels and many of the homes of resisters were also raided and arrests
were made. Committee members assumed that the mayor knew about
the raids and that either they were held at the behest of the FBI or stolen
names were being forwarded to the FBI.[31]

When Simon Fraser University students demonstrated against the
war, Mayor Campbell reacted by seeing that police were issued longer
batons. He again took to the airwaves promising that he would rid the
city of hippies and resisters. Vancouver would not, he said, become a
"draft dodger, deserter, hippy haven."[32] Campbell also said, "I believe
the law should be used against any revolutionary whether he's a U.S.
draft dodger or a hippie. . . . I don't like draft dodgers and I'll do anything within the law that allows me to get rid of them."[33]

The resistance to resisters was also seen in Canadian universities.
With the explosion of new Canadian universities in the 1960s, and an

insufficient number of Canadians with PhDs, it had been necessary to hire American scholars, some of whom were resisters, to fill teaching and administrative roles. At the same time, many universities were offering very few Canadian-based courses. Canadian students were able to graduate without ever encountering a Canadian book. Universities, it was argued, were important among the places where community and beliefs were debated and developed, and so it was essential that Canadians and Canadian ideas be present in them. Respected Canadian author Robertson Davies wrote: "These professors see history, economics and literature as Americans see them and, with the effortless superiority of a greater people approaching the lesser, they assume that their view is the right one. In the course of a few university generations . . . it may be assumed that their attitudes will prevail in Canada."[34]

In November 1968, Carleton University English professors Robin Matthews and James Steele initiated the Canadianization movement. Its primary goals were to hire more Canadian university professors and administrators and have them offer more courses addressing Canada and Canadian ideas. They travelled the country, exploiting the Vietnam War's having heightened and for some validated anti-American sentiments. They argued that universities should not be the landing place for resister scholars and students and other Americans who were acting as imperialists, disparaging or squashing all that was uniquely Canadian.

The movement's leadership split over goals and tactics and it was attacked by a number of high-profile Canadian scholars. However, by the late 1970s, all universities were making efforts to hire Canadians and offer more Canadian courses. The federal government passed regulations requiring more Canadian professors. More Canadian stories would be taught to young people, who, it was hoped, would then seek and tell more and better Canadian stories.

DESERTERS

Many of the young men who trekked to Canada were like Erickson in that they left while at some stage of being drafted and were dubbed draft dodgers. Others were deserters. They had been drafted or enlisted, donned the uniform, and then during training or after returning home from a tour of duty, opted to leave. For the understandable reason that there was really nowhere to go, fewer than 1 percent deserted while in Vietnam.[35]

A great number of Canadians who accepted draft dodgers rejected deserters. Canadian resister organizations understood the prevalent attitude and so, afraid of jeopardizing their support and funding, most of them turned away deserters who appeared at their door. Federal law allowed draft dodgers into the country. After all, there was an obvious benefit to be gained from the best-educated group of immigrants to ever cross the border. However, the law allowed, and the government supported, discrimination against deserters.

The discrimination began in October 1966 when officials from the RCMP and the immigration department established a file on the growing number of American deserters. Three months later, newly appointed director of immigration J.C. Morrison wrote to all immigration border officers stating that their discretionary powers should be used to ensure that no deserters entered Canada. According to Morrison, deserters were unworthy of entering Canada because they had demonstrated an unwillingness to maintain "moral or contractual obligations."[36]

A year later, Canada's immigration laws and regulations were overhauled to end the racially discriminatory practices that had favoured European and American immigrants. The new system based entry to Canada on points allocated for attributes such as education, age, and language proficiency. Five of the nine categories related to job skills and employment prospects. Acceptance required earning at least fifty of a possible hundred points. Those with sufficient points could enter

Canada as visitors and then apply for landed immigrant status rather than having to apply from their home country or at the border.

The point system was a major step in Canadian immigration law, but an unforeseen consequence was that it ended up swapping biases from race to class.[37] This change affected war resisters because, as with Erickson, most draft dodgers had a post-secondary education and were easily able to earn more than fifty points. The American Selective Service System, whereby those in college or university were granted deferral from the draft, made poor and non-white Americans twice as likely to be conscripted and sent to Vietnam. Once there, they were twice as likely to be assigned to jungle and front-line positions rather than safer support roles and so, once home, more likely to suffer from post-traumatic stress caused by battle conditions. These factors meant that working-class and African-American soldiers were more likely to desert.[38] Canadian resister organizations learned this truth when they found that deserters at their offices were nearly all less educated, less employable, and less white than draft dodgers. In their efforts to adjust to life in Canada they suffered more housing and job discrimination.[39]

In the 1968 federal election campaign, Prime Minister Pierre Trudeau expressed a desire for what he called a Just Society. He also said that he had no wish to stop war resisters at the border. Nonetheless, resisters trying to cross into Canada discovered that, despite the new point system, Canadian gatekeepers were continuing to use their discretionary power to deny entry even to deserters who managed to earn the required number of points, in many cases because of their inability or unwillingness to prove their current military status.[40]

While some Canadians opposed deserters coming to Canada, others directed their anger at the regulations and practices that were keeping them out. The United Church and a number of newspapers accused the government of insensitivity and, perhaps worse, of pandering to the Pentagon and White House.[41] Opposition parties added to the growing discontent. NDP leader David Lewis risked losing the support of those who hated the idea of "coddling deserters" when he rose in the House and linked support for deserters to the expression of Canadian sovereignty: "I see no reason whatsoever, except a servile attitude on the part of Canada, for treating American young men who object to fighting an immoral war in Vietnam differently from the way we treated literally tens of thousands of immigrants all through the years who refused to accept military service in their countries for similar reasons."[42]

A number of resister organizations initiated a letter-writing campaign urging Minister of Manpower and Immigration Allan MacEachen to end the discriminatory practices. Representatives from the United Church confronted him at a speaking engagement and the Canadian Council of Churches appealed for changes. MacEachen publicly denied that border agents had been instructed to stop deserters. He then wrote a confidential memo to Cabinet arguing that it was a desire to please, or at least not to antagonize, the United States that was at the heart of the policy: "To grant asylum to deserters as refugees would constitute a blanket condemnation of the United States and its political and judicial system. . . . Many critics of the present policy are less interested in the welfare of the deserters than in using them as a focal point for a continuing campaign against the United States."[43]

In February 1969, five Canadian students from York University's Glendon College appeared at five different border crossings. They all carried phony papers identifying themselves as a real deserter named John Heintzelman. Each of the fake Heintzelmans earned more than the required fifty points but none was allowed entry. A *Montreal Star* story written by one of the students, Bob Waller, inspired a new tsunami of letters to MacEachen. Nearly all criticized him and the government for colluding with the Americans to stop deserters.[44]

The matter was discussed in Cabinet again but it was decided that nothing would be done pending a White House meeting the following month between Prime Minister Trudeau and newly elected president Richard Nixon. The president failed to raise the issue of war resisters at the meeting and so Trudeau remained silent. At a National Press Club appearance afterwards, however, Trudeau said something that would be quoted many times afterward:

> Americans should never underestimate the constant pressure on Canada which the mere presence of the United States has produced. We're a different people from you. We're a different people partly because of you. Living next to you is in some ways like sleeping with an elephant. No matter how friendly and even-tempered is the beast, if I can call it that, one is affected by every twitch and grunt. It should not therefore be expected that this kind of nation, this Canada, should project itself as a mirror image of the United States.[45]

In response to a reporter's question, Trudeau floated a trial balloon by saying that, while he personally believed those serving in the military had a legal obligation to complete their service, his government was reviewing the issue of allowing deserters to enter Canada. For now, though, "The status of being a draft-dodger doesn't enter at all into our immigration policy. You can have your draft card in your pocket; if you are dodging the draft, you're not even asked about it and you are admitted at the Canadian border. It is an irrelevant question from the point of view of our policy." The White House gave no response.

On May 22 MacEachen announced that he had reversed the regulation he had previously insisted did not exist. With that change, although deserters still needed to qualify through the point system, they could no longer be summarily turned back at the border at the discretion of individual officers. In the months that followed, resister organizations noticed a significant rise in the number of deserters—in many cities they began to outnumber draft dodgers.[46]

Their growing numbers added to the controversy over allowing deserters into Canada, which sparked more widespread resentment against all resisters. That bitterness grew when, in 1970, the Canadian economy began to tip toward recession. In July, a *Vancouver Sun* article blamed resisters, and deserters in particular, for adding to the British Columbia jobs crisis that saw 87,000 without work.[47] On January 25, 1971, a *Toronto Star* editorial attacked resisters for raising the city's crime rate. It also claimed that 200,000 American resisters were "stealing scarce jobs from Canadians."[48]

The growing unemployment rate was partly responsible for about a thousand fewer resisters crossing the border in 1971 than had done so the previous year. Another reason was 1970's October Crisis. Prime Minister Trudeau had used the War Measures Act to put soldiers and tanks on Quebec streets while suspending the civil rights of Canadians in response to the radical Quebec terrorist group, the FLQ, kidnapping a British trade commissioner and a Quebec cabinet minister. Many resisters had second thoughts about settling in a society that appeared just as authoritarian as the one they were considering leaving.[49] Despite these factors, 7,022 resisters arrived in Canada in 1971, and the next year saw another 7,290 cross the border.[50]

In November 1972, responding to the growing anti-resister sentiment and broader backlash against immigration, Trudeau announced a change to Section 34 of Canada's immigration regulations. People who entered the country as visitors could no longer apply for landed status from within Canada. Those suddenly stranded were told they had to leave the country and then apply to come back in. Some resisters were without sufficient funds to afford the necessary travel. All worried about being arrested when they stepped back on American soil. They could not go home and they could not become Canadian.

Church groups speaking on behalf of resisters and resister organizations joined the explosion of protests against the change, which they said violated Canadian values and the government's declared dedication to multiculturalism. In June 1973 the government bent to the pressure and Minister of Manpower and Immigration Robert Andras announced the Adjustment of Status Program. It was a "once and for all policy" whereby those who had lived in Canada since November 30, 1972, and suddenly become "illegals," had sixty days to apply for landed immigrant status, after which the window would shut.

Resister organizations snapped into action and did much of the government's work in undertaking a mass communication program. The Canadian Council of Churches allocated $110,000 to purchase advertisements in newspapers and magazines. Radio spots featured popular singer-songwriter Jesse Winchester, who, in 1967, had received his draft notice and left Memphis for Montreal. Posters were placed in resister communities in Vancouver, Winnipeg, Toronto, Montreal, and Halifax.

By the time the sixty-day window closed, 49,230 people had registered for landed status.[51] It is not known how many were resisters. It was assumed that thousands of people either ignored the "once and for all" opportunity or refused to participate because their distrust of government rendered them unwilling to expose themselves to authorities. Many resisters also missed the registration drive because they lived in remote communes or cabins where belonging to a particular country no longer seemed to matter.

The hectic sixty-day period and the debates that had led to it constituted another important moment in the long conversation among Canadians. Since neither the United States nor Canada kept track of the number of people who fled the draft or deserted, it is difficult to determine the exact number of resisters who by the war's end in January 1973 had made the journey north. Sociologists and historians have estimated the total at between 52,000 and 100,000.[52] While the number can be debated, what is indisputable is that, while adjusting and coping, fighting back or fitting in, war resisters altered both Canada and the United States by adding another element in the processes of national introspection and reinvention.

CARRYING ON

Joe Erickson answered a knock at his door one evening to find an old friend from Minnesota, Ron, on his doorstep. At university they had shared a love of classical music and Ron had been part of the group that sometimes heatedly debated whether to comply with draft notices. Ron had honoured his and spent two years in the army, stationed in Georgia. He had not been able to come to peace with that decision and after serving his time found it hard to transition back into civilian life. He lost jobs, friends, and pride, and eventually found his way to Toronto. Ron slept on Erickson's floor, drank heavily, wept inconsolably, and told wild stories of adventures that challenged credulity. He was broken.

Ron worked for a while with Erickson and Branko but, getting no better, returned home to live with his parents. A few weeks later, Erickson was staying at a cabin he was renovating north of Toronto when Branko showed up in the middle of the night. He passed on the terrible news that Ron had committed suicide.

Devastated, Erickson blamed himself for Ron's death. It led to an emotional crash. He never regretted leaving the United States but was torn by the belief that, because he did, some poor ghetto kid or hard-scrabble country boy had served in his place. Erickson's survivor guilt began a struggle with depression that therapists eased but could not truly end. In his darkest days, he was reminded of his mother saying that the Vietnam War was a worse calamity than the Second World War, to which she had lost a favourite brother, because there were no right choices. She said the war was ruining an entire generation of young men. Neither Ron nor Erickson saw action in Vietnam, but the war shattered them both. Somehow, with the mercy of time and hope of redemption, Erickson learned to carry on.

Erickson was among the vast majority of resisters who neither sought nor found the spotlight. Without fanfare he forged his new life, experiencing, as we all do, the good, the bad, and the sad. As his friend

Tony told him, "So, you get into trouble, then you get out of trouble. That's what makes life fun."

In the mid-1970s, Erickson was joined in Canada by Vicki, whom he had known from his younger days in Minnesota, and her two children, Shauny and Gregor. They welcomed a son, Karl, to their family in 1983. Erickson found no other role as rewarding or instructive as fatherhood. As time passed he experienced another divorce, new love, occasional illnesses, and all the other challenges and rewards of life.

Then, in 2012, when he was in his sixties, the sixties sought revenge. After his ordeal at the border, where he was detained and questioned, his sister Beth had slipped by making the offhand reference to the FBI. Once the high school reunion festivities were over, Erickson spoke with Beth, who was surprised he had not heard about all that had happened after he left for Canada, so many years before.

Beth said, "Look, I'm sick of this business, but as an older woman, I have earned the right now to some outrage and anger. I am totally fed up with what the FBI did to our family. Their tactics were over the top. They unnecessarily intimidated people they were dealing with." To a shocked Erickson, Beth told the story of how, after he left for Winnipeg, teams of FBI agents had repeatedly visited their parents at the farm. They always arrived during the evening milking. One agent would interrogate their mother in the house while the other questioned their father in the barn. The agents pretended to be seeking information about Erickson, but it was clear they knew more about him than the family did. The agents provided disturbingly detailed accounts of their son's life in Winnipeg and Toronto. They tried to massage feelings of resentment and abandonment in their father, saying it was the son's place to be there on the ancestral farm. They stoked their mother's fears, by portraying Erickson as a dangerous rebel the FBI and Canadian police were closely monitoring. They tried to manipulate both parents into revealing secrets about their son and to persuade him to return home. Their mother grew to genuinely fear that Erickson would be assassinated by the CIA or FBI. After a few FBI visits she no longer trusted her friends or her party-line telephone.

Beth enrolled at the University of Minnesota, Morris Campus, in 1968. In a speech class, she delivered an address entitled "American Values: Mom, Apple Pie, and the FBI." She explained what the FBI was doing to her family as a result of her brother having dodged the war. Days later, the FBI paid another visit to the farm. They threatened her mother, saying that Beth had not yet become radicalized but she should do everything possible to see that it didn't happen. The FBI were extremely effective at keeping the family frightened, isolated, and silent. Through it all, the family protected Joe by keeping it all to themselves.

Erickson came to understand that the FBI intimidation had profoundly altered the personalities and changed the lives of his parents and sisters, and he was shaken by the knowledge that it had all happened because of his decision to leave. He was in for another shock. After the high school reunion, he paid a nostalgic visit to the archives of the local historical society and found that he had been erased from the public record. He had apparently not attended the local school or won numerous debates and music competitions, not received a scholarship to attend university or the American Legion's "For God and Country" School Award, and not served at the state leadership level of the 4-H program. All records of his having been a part of the community were gone.[53]

It was time to go. Erickson's trip had taught him that despite the passage of over forty years, the Vietnam War was not yet through with him. The war's lessons were profound and its shadow dark and long. He pointed his blue Hyundai north and cranked Bach's B minor *Sanctus* to full volume. Erickson crossed the border at Sault St. Marie in the throes of a violent thunder and lightning storm. He smiled at the big Canadian flag flapping in the rain. He was home.

Doug Carey (right) in Hue

CHAPTER 5

DOUG CAREY: SOLDIERS
IN ANOTHER MAN'S WAR

The ship was massive, but mountainous waves off the coast of Taiwan made it bob and sway like a child's toy. Doug Carey was standing watch at the stern, white-knuckled, sopping wet, holding fast to the rail and convinced that the next wave could be the one that capsized them. Up the ship climbed, teetering for a second with the gigantic propellers thumping in mid-air, and then plunging down into salty brine, only to resurface to do it all again. Carey and the hundreds of other equally frightened, sick, and exhilarated young men were learning an important lesson. In this war, although people trying to kill you are the primary danger, another enemy is nature, in all its banal cruelty.

The circumstances that put nineteen-year-old Doug Carey on that ship and on his way to Vietnam could be traced back to his childhood.

He had grown up surrounded by veterans and police officers. His grandfather was the police chief in Cobourg, Ontario, and then justice of the peace. Many of his uncles, his father's friends, his teachers, and nearly every man in town had served in the Second World War or Korea. Doug grew up believing service was natural; it was expected. Carey's father was Canadian, his mother American, and they were living in Waterbury, Connecticut, when he was born. Three months later, his father accepted a position with his grandfather's furniture store and funeral home in Port Hope, Ontario. Carey's mother worked as an executive secretary. The eldest of three boys, Doug fell into frequent disagreements with his parents, which led to his being raised principally by his grandparents in Oakville, Port Hope, and Cobourg. He left high school before graduation in 1964 and enjoyed an adventurous summer hitchhiking with a friend to Vancouver and then to Halifax.

By the following summer he was working odd jobs and plotting his future when he saw two reports on the evening television news that altered the course of his life. He and his grandmother were moved by a particularly poignant item about American soldiers working to help civilians in a badly damaged Vietnamese village; a story then followed about draft dodgers coming to Canada. While he had been mulling the bold move for some time, he chose that moment to say that he had decided to do his bit and enlist with the United States Marine Corps. His strong and stoic grandmother, Kathryn La Fleur, was not surprised. She nodded and said, "Freedom is not free."

A couple of days later, on August 25, 1965, Carey was on a bus to Buffalo, New York. He walked into the massive downtown city post office building and into the recruitment centre. When he said he'd come from Canada, he was told that the process could take awhile. He completed paperwork and left. Before he could contemplate his next move, he heard the recruiting officer running to catch up with him on the sidewalk. Obviously having looked at Carey's forms, he asked if it was true that he had been born in Connecticut. When Carey nodded, the tall man in the crisp uniform replied, "Well, c'mon back in, son, and let's get this done."

Carey returned home to await a call for a physical and then hopped the bus back to Buffalo to easily pass it. He bided his time back home again until, a couple of weeks later, he received orders to report to boot camp at Parris Island, South Carolina.

Basic training had been reduced from twelve to eight weeks in order to help meet Vietnam's insatiable demand for new recruits. Carey endured the endless push-ups, running, sleep deprivation, yelling, and marching, but he enjoyed the weapons training. It was then on to North Carolina's Camp Lejeune for six weeks of advanced infantry training and yet more training at Camp Pendleton in California. He had grown tougher, fitter, and more disciplined than he had ever been. He was ready for war—at least, he thought he was.

WARRIORS AND BORDERS

Young people such as Carey who wished to take up arms and the governments that needed them to do so had never let a border get in their way. When, in 1861, Americans decided to butcher themselves in a civil war to determine if all men were truly created equal, the British colonies of Canada, New Brunswick, and Nova Scotia were officially neutral. Britain's 1818 Foreign Enlistment Act prohibited joining a foreign military, but approximately forty thousand British North Americans defied it to join the fight.[1] Canadian authorities ignored the young people heading south to enlist, just as American recruiters winked at age restrictions and citizenship. In fact, American recruiters were common sights in Canadian cities.

In 1914 Canada automatically followed Britain into the First World War, but the United States stayed out for the first three years of the four-year conflict. Even though the American Foreign Enlistment Act

precluded Americans from serving with a foreign military, so many of
them ventured north to enlist that five special battalions were created
for them. Collectively they were called the American Legion. Overseas, the American battalions were split up and their members joined
Canadian units, enduring the same gruesome trenches and falling
in no man's land next to Canadians boys wearing the same muddy
uniforms. By early 1917 Canadian volunteer rates were in decline, but
near some border towns, Americans made up 20 percent of new
recruits. By the war's end, over 35,000 Americans and Canadians who
had been living in the United States had enlisted in the Canadian
Expeditionary Force.[2]

Canada entered the century's second global war with Hitler's 1939
Polish invasion but, again, the United States remained out. But many of
the children of those who had moved to Canada to serve in the war that
was supposed to have ended all wars followed their fathers' paths northward. Even before Canada had entered the war, in March 1939, Canada's
renowned First World War fighter pilot Billy Bishop and American
First World War pilot Clayton Knight met with President Roosevelt. He
endorsed their idea to form the Clayton Knight Committee. It encouraged enthusiastic young Americans and experienced American pilots
to join the Royal Canadian Air Force. The United States Air Force made
up stories about why certain officers were being dismissed, knowing
full well where they were going.[3] Nearly 9,000 Americans took up the
Clayton Knight Committee's invitation to fly with the RCAF and 704
lost their lives. They were among the 29,000 Americans who served in
Canadian uniforms in the Second World War.[4]

When President Lyndon Johnson escalated the Americanization of
the Vietnam War in 1965, Canada's 1937 Foreign Enlistment Act was
still in effect. It had been enacted to stop passionate Canadians from
leaving to fight in the Spanish Civil War and stated: "Any person who,
being a Canadian national, whether within or without Canada, volun-
tarily accepts or agrees to accept any commission or engagement in the

armed forces of any foreign state at war with any friendly foreign state . . . is guilty of an offence under this Act."[5] In February 1966, an Opposition Member of Parliament raised the issue of Canadians violating the law by crossing the border to enlist in the American armed forces. Secretary of State for External Affairs Paul Martin laconically replied, "It's a free country." When asked by former prime minister John Diefenbaker if one could be prosecuted under the act, Martin replied with one word: "No."[6]

It is difficult to determine precisely how many Canadians joined the American forces to fight in Vietnam. Neither the American nor the Canadian government kept track of the numbers of Canadians serving. Many who enlisted and fought were born in Canada but had moved to the United States and, either as children or adults, had become American citizens and did not return to Canada after the war. Should they count as Canadians in Vietnam?

Many used enlistment to become American. Until 1986, there was no requirement that armed service members had to be American citizens. It usually took five years of residency to become a citizen, but in peacetime military service shrunk that period to three years and in wartime to only one. Common military practices made the process quite easy. Montreal's John Laurin, for instance, enlisted with the U.S. Army at Albany, New York, and in August 1968 was in Vietnam. Halfway through his tour he agreed to join a group of other "aliens" and was flown to Honolulu. About five hundred young people were asked rudimentary questions about American history, took the oath, and became citizens. They were then shipped back to finish their tours as Americans. Should Laurin count as a Canadian in Vietnam?

Doug Carey's mother was American and he was born in the United States, and so he was a dual citizen. However, he had lived in Canada from infancy and considered himself Canadian. He hoped to survive the war and return home to Canada. Should he be considered a Canadian in Vietnam?

The most popular recruiting stations used by Canadians were near the border at Buffalo and Plattsburgh, New York; Fargo, North Dakota; and Blaine, Washington. Along the Quebec border, recruiting stations displayed signs declaring "Bienvenue Canadiens."[7] Recruiters gave Canadians wishing to enlist a letter of acceptability that enabled them to qualify for a residency visa. They could then freely re-enter, live, work, and serve in the United States. Many recruiters sped the process along by using the old Civil War trick of listing the location of the recruiting station as a recruit's hometown, so that many young Quebecers, for example, were, on record, from Plattsburgh. Should they be counted as Canadians in Vietnam?

These factors have led to a range of guesses regarding how many Canadians served. Historian Fred Gaffen concluded that there were about twelve thousand.[8] A national organization of veterans called the Canadian Vietnam Veterans Coalition estimated that it was closer to forty thousand.[9] The struggle to determine a precise number is a reminder that issues related to the sanctity of the border and the definition of nationality are among the Vietnam War's important lessons.

Every Canadian recruit was in his late teens or early to mid-twenties. They watched and read the same news reports about the war, were immersed in the same Cold War consensus, and were exposed to the same anti-authoritarian siren songs and anti-American-tinged Canadian patriotism as those who ignored the war or, as it escalated, protested against it. Some of those protests were aimed directly at them.

On Sunday, April 25, 1971, for instance, when 200,000 anti-war protesters marched on Washington, there were similar marches in Nanaimo, Halifax, Winnipeg, Ottawa, and Montreal. About 1,500 people walked from Toronto's provincial legislature at Queen's Park to City Hall's Nathan Phillips Square, where they heard keynote speaker Claire Culhane chastise Canadians who were supporting the war by signing up to fight it. She cited the 1937 law prohibiting Canadians from joining foreign armies and said that the Trudeau government, "which insists so vehemently in the upholding of law, must state its intention to prosecute all Canadian citizens who are in the U.S. Army."[10] But no one was ever charged.

Edward Bowes was born and raised in Dorchester, New Brunswick. One sunny summer afternoon in 1968 he was in Ottawa and encountered a noisy anti-war demonstration outside the Parliament Buildings. Seeking to understand, he spoke with a number of the protesters who were about his age. His reaction was one of revulsion—he considered them hypocrites for demonstrating against a war they did not need to fight. He also thought their drug use was immoral. The incident inspired him to travel to Bangor, Maine, where he enlisted in the U.S. Army, after which he served a tour in Vietnam.[11]

Bowes reminds us that each young person who enlisted had his own reason for doing so. For many, like Carey, military service was simply a natural part of growing up. Others saw it as an exciting option. Winnipeg's Rob Purvis and three of his friends, Butch, Billy, and Larry, enlisted together in Fargo. Purvis later explained: "We were just young and very naïve kids when we signed up. We watched the war every night on the six o'clock news. We had just graduated from high school and we were looking around for something to do. There were no careers or jobs that were meaningful. We figured we would join the army."[12] They chose the American service because the Canadian military at the time was shrinking and morale was low due to a decision to unify its three branches into one. Plus, Canada was not at war. Purvis and the others wanted to go where the action was. Sadly, only three of the four high school buddies came home; Larry Collins didn't make it.

Many were motivated by a desire to fight communism—the monolithic bogeyman that, for a generation, the American and Canadian governments had taught citizens to fear and hate. Bob Beatty of Kingston, Nova Scotia, enlisted with the U.S. Marines. His reason? "The American government was telling us that the communists were trying to infiltrate into Southeast Asia. And the next step would be Australia and then from there they could come across and into Canada. I felt that if I'm going to fight communism I should fight it in a foreign country."[13]

Richard Dextraze left Montreal to join the Marines. He was killed when on patrol in April 1969. His father was General Jacques Dextraze who, from 1972 to 1977, served as Canada's Chief of the Defence Staff. The general echoed Beatty in observing: "People say they were cranks, that they were stupid to go over there because it wasn't our war. But this war was to fight a common enemy."[14]

A group of twenty-five members of the Mohawk Nation from Kahnawake, Quebec, enlisted in the Marines together and, in so doing, took General Dextraze's notion of a common Cold War enemy one step further. They believed in a concept that was unfathomable to Canadians heady with the fresh swell of patriotism, waving the new flag, and celebrating Centennial projects. Teddy Canadian was among the Mohawk group and explained it well: "There's never been any border for Mohawk people. To us, it's all one continent."[15]

IN COUNTRY

No matter how well trained or thoroughly indoctrinated, no one is ever fully prepared for war. War is always more physically demanding and emotionally wrenching than imagined or expected. Yet, Doug Carey observed, "The funny part about war is that when you are there you want to be home with your family but when you are home you want to be back with your fellow Marines in the heat of it all."

Carey and his comrades made it through the Pacific storm and in June 1966 landed at Da Nang, as shocked as anyone by the stench, heat, and soup-like humidity. Carey was a proud member of the 1st Battalion, 3rd Marines. They were charged with protecting the Da Nang base by conducting patrols in the surrounding hills, jungle, and villages. As such, they took on several roles. They were detectives who sought evidence of Viet Cong insurgents. They were cops enforcing ever-changing rules. They also served as bait—inviting action upon themselves so that air support could be called in to attack with death from the sky.

Carey learned that experienced Marines' greatest fear was not the Viet Cong, who set booby traps and sprang ambushes, but the jungle, and the FNGs—Fucking New Guys. Too many FNGs made too much noise and too many mistakes, thereby costing too many lives. The jungle offered ankle-breaking holes, foliage sharp as razor-wire, huge snakes, and ravenous clouds of mosquitoes carrying malaria and other diseases. One night a perimeter flare wire was tripped by a tiger and the camp lit up like noon, scaring both the tiger and the men. Another night, to protect himself from the rain, Carey fashioned his poncho into a tent. He awoke to find a dense and sticky web on and around him and, inches from his face, a poisonous spider the size of his fist.

Through it all, Carey kept his mouth shut. He questioned nothing and followed orders. Contrary to what he had been told in training, he learned that most men's core aim was not to win the war, and not really even to kill the enemy. The goal was to survive. While all other military branches served twelve-month tours, the Marines served thirteen, and everyone knew how many days they had left. Those with the biggest numbers were sent up front. Those with just a few days left were often sent to the rear. Carey learned quickly. He survived.

In October 1966, his unit was transferred to Khe Sanh. The Marines' combat engineers were building a large base and runway to stop Laotian border infiltration, while providing a home from which attacks could be launched. It was also to be a magnet, inviting the regular North Vietnamese Army (NVA) to launch a traditional assault. As they did at Da Nang, Carey and his compatriots fanned out into the jungle on missions that lasted hours and sometimes days. They were again the hunters and the hunted.

Carey was in and around Khe Sanh when the annual rains began. Every year the rain starts suddenly and falls with the power of a bathtub being emptied on your head over and over again, day after day, week after week. It was endless thunder on steel helmets. One man sought to escape the rain's relentless pounding by creeping under a tank to sleep. The mud grew softer in the night and the tank slowly sank, crushing him to death.

Everyone in Carey's unit knew he was from Canada. He was occasionally teased about it but no one really cared. He had met no Canadians during his training or tour but he knew others were there. One day a villager surprised him with the gift of a homemade knitted Canadian flag. He smiled, nodded, and a picture was taken.

At the completion of his tour, Carey was happy to be home in Oakville but found it disconcerting. Within forty-eight hours of being extricated from the jungle, he was watching TV from a comfortable couch and wondering if the thirteen months of hell and heartache had really happened. It felt like time travel, for he had lived a lifetime of experiences while things at home seemed not to have progressed a day. The Oakville paper celebrated his service, painting him a hero. Another local man was also singled out for praise: Captain Thomas Kenneth Crichton, who had been wounded in Vietnam but was expected to recover and return to combat.[16]

Carey's mind was still very much in Vietnam. He couldn't sleep. He was hypersensitive to the smallest sounds. He drank a little too often and a little too much with old friends. In October they attended Expo '67 in Montreal. He enjoyed touring the Canadian pavilion and others, but he was particularly impressed by the massive American steel dome, where the honour guards were Marines. When Carey showed his ID card, he was afforded a behind-the-scenes tour and then spent the night at their rooms quaffing beer and swapping stories.

Thirty days later, Carey reported to Camp Pendleton in California to start his second tour. After four weeks of training, he was transferred to Marine Corps Air Station Kaneohe Bay, Hawaii, where he was assigned to the 1st Battalion, 27th Marines. He was on a ship, approaching the Philippines, and taking part in a war game exercise when news broke about the January 1968 Tet Offensive. The ships headed for Vietnam.

From the deck of USS *Vancouver* in the Da Nang harbour, Carey watched firefights tearing up distant hills. He and the others gasped and cheered as AC-47 gunships strafed the ground with six thousand rounds a minute. With every fourth bullet a tracer, the giant planes appeared to be spewing red urine. The planes were nicknamed Spooky or Puff the Magic Dragon. It was during one of the strafing runs that Carey approached his sergeant to say how proud he was to be serving a second tour.

As part of the well-coordinated Tet Offensive, Vietnam's ancient imperial capital city of Hue had been overrun by ten thousand Viet Cong and NVA. The brutal and pitiless battle of Hue, in many ways the worst of the war, raged for twenty-four days. In March, Carey was among those dispatched to pursue the several thousand NVA soldiers who had been driven into the countryside east of Hue and were regrouping, possibly to counterattack.

The days were relatively peaceful, sometimes even boring, but darkness brought hell. Carey's platoon would establish a perimeter, protected by trip wires and Claymores, small mines set off by clapping together a two-pronged metal detonator. Everyone lived in fear and teetered on the edge of exhaustion. Rockets and mortars flew both ways overhead and tracers lit the sky. Firefights would erupt from nowhere, with the screams of wounded men barely audible over automatic weapon fire.

Even worse was listening-post duty. With two men per fighting hole, they would take turns remaining awake and staring into the darkness for any sign of enemy movement. On rainy or cloud-filled nights visibility was nearly zero. It was worse when the moon cast jungle shadows, leading tired and wired minds to conjure monsters. The man on duty clicked once on the radio every hour to indicate all was well. Repeated clicks meant something was wrong. One night at a listening post turned a young man old. Carey endured dozens.

On May 5, while on listening-post duty with Alpha Company, Carey spotted three NVA soldiers sneaking along the side of a small Buddhist temple and moving toward the fighting hole containing his closest friend, Ricky Lee Doye. In the ensuing firefight, Doye was hit. His body was recovered the next morning. He had crawled over twenty feet toward Carey, leaving a ghastly streak of blood, before finally succumbing to his wounds. Doye was nineteen.

Like all who served, Carey came to understand that the devil's wiliest trick in war is turning the extraordinary into routine. David Dear was another countryman who would come to understand the trick all too well. Dear was born in Parry Sound, Ontario, the son of a Canadian army captain. He joined the U.S. Army in January 1963 and trained to serve in the hospital corps. In October 1965, he was assigned to a Mobile Army Surgical Hospital (MASH) unit. The welcome periods when doctors, nurses, and staff had little to do were interrupted by incoming waves of broken, bloody, torn-up teenagers in soldiers' clothing. Dear was on duty one afternoon when the bloated body of an American sergeant was pulled from the Da Nang River and brought to his unit. The sergeant's hands were tied behind his back and there was a bullet hole in the back of his head. That his lungs were full of water meant he had been thrown in the river while still alive. The strings were cut that had roughly sewn his lips shut. Inside the tortured man's mouth were his testicles.[17]

Art Diablo was one of the twenty-five volunteers from Kahnawake who arrived in Vietnam in January 1968. The plane dispatching him at Da Nang landed and slowed but didn't fully stop, forcing Diablo and the others to jump from the back and then run for shelter. The heat and stench blinded his eyes and buckled his knees while officers yelled orders he couldn't hear. He was aghast at the men whose tours had ended and were silently assembling to leave, for they looked more like "jungle animals" than Marines.[18]

In May, while on a routine patrol, Diablo was hit by a rocket-propelled grenade. After two weeks in a Cam Ranh Bay hospital he was back in the jungle. During an ambush on his platoon, Diablo's left arm was hit. There were multiple compound fractures and the arm hung from his shoulder, held only by ripped and burned flesh. Diablo had been in Vietnam for only four months and was now heading home, physically broken and emotionally shattered.

In that same month, Carey's battalion was among those transferred south of Da Nang as part of Operation Allen Brook. The NVA had assembled a division and appeared to be preparing an attack. They had to be stopped. The fighting was fierce and losses were heavy.

Carey was in the thick of it when on July 19, 1968, he suddenly fell ill, suffering vomiting, fever, an intense headache, and confusion. The right side of his body was stiff and tingly. A helicopter lifted him to the hospital in Da Nang, where he was packed in ice to bring down his 107-degree temperature. A nurse and corpsman kept repeating that everything would be all right as Carey slipped in and out of consciousness. The doctors diagnosed him with Japanese encephalitis, a dangerous and sometimes fatal disease. After being shot at, shelled, and avoiding too many booby traps to mention, and after receiving thousands of insect bites during months in the jungle, a single infected mosquito had taken him down.

He was treated in Da Nang, then Japan, then at Naval Hospital Great Lakes in Chicago, and finally at the Bethesda Naval Hospital in Maryland. Electric stimulus rejuvenated atrophied muscles. He pushed himself through painful physiotherapy. By December Carey was down to 128 pounds and unable to walk but determined to get home for Christmas. On the short flight to Canada, responding to a question from a flight attendant, he said he was returning from Vietnam. The co-pilot was informed and he sat beside Carey for a while and spoke of how his brother was another Canadian who had served. On the tarmac in Toronto, the pilot asked all passengers to remain seated, and two RCMP officers boarded and helped Carey from the plane. One carried his bags while the other pushed his wheelchair through customs and to his smiling, crying parents waiting at the gate. Doug Carey was home.

THE END

In the spring of 1969, there were 550,000 American troops in Vietnam. As part of President Richard Nixon's Vietnamization strategy, whereby the South Vietnamese were expected to take a greater leadership role in fighting the war, American troops slowly began to be withdrawn. By the fall of 1972, the Navy and Air Force were carrying the brunt of the burden in supporting South Vietnam. The Paris peace talks were dragging on, as protests continued to bring people to the streets in cities around the world. To jar the North Vietnamese negotiators, on December 18 President Nixon ordered a massive, continuous bombing of Hanoi and important infrastructure. The punishment went on for twelve days and killed over 1,500 civilians. Fifteen American B-52 bombers and eleven other aircraft and their crews were shot down.

An enormous public outcry met the Christmas bombing. Pierre Trudeau's Liberals had been re-elected the previous October but with only two seats more than the Progressive Conservatives. Parliament resumed sitting on January 4 and many observers expected the government to fall on its first vote. But the sly prime minister knew how all New Democratic Party members and most Liberals felt about Vietnam and Nixon's latest operation, and so as his first act Trudeau brought forth a resolution that "deplored" the bombing. It passed overwhelmingly.

While the political manoeuvre saved and solidified Trudeau's government, there was collateral damage—it had incensed President

Nixon. He and Trudeau saw eye to eye on very little. Nixon considered Trudeau a leftist, pompous egghead and privately referred to him as a son of a bitch.[19] Trudeau respected Nixon as a politician but found him cold and uncomfortable in his own skin. He was concerned that the president so often deferred to national security advisor Henry Kissinger and others to explain the details of topics at hand.[20] The two had nonetheless always managed to remain professional in addressing even the stickiest of bilateral situations such as the so-called Nixon Shock of August 1971, when the United States suddenly placed restrictive tariffs on goods from a number of countries, including Canada. Nixon met Trudeau at the White House and, despite his personal feelings about the prime minister, had granted Canada an exemption.

Nixon reacted to the condemnation of his Christmas bombing by ordering that Canadian diplomats be shunned and invitations to meetings and receptions rescinded. Nixon even refused to send a letter of condolence when Trudeau's mother died, on January 16.[21] But that was all he did. Congress took no action. Trudeau's government had, at least for the moment, forgotten about quiet diplomacy and in so doing caught up with what had become the opinion of the majority of Canadians on the war. Trudeau's resolution proved again that, while it is nice when presidents and prime ministers get along, as Pearson and Kennedy had, it's not necessary. More important, it demonstrated, as Pearson had shown in his Temple University speech, that to stand publicly against the war and the American administration's policies in waging it was not as diplomatically unwise or economically perilous as so many had believed for so long.

Finally, the Paris negotiators reached an agreement. On January 23, 1973, Nixon appeared on television to announce the end of the war. The president explained that January 27 would mark the beginning of an internationally supervised ceasefire and a sixty-day period in which all remaining American troops would be withdrawn and prisoners of war released. Ho Chi Minh had died in September 1969 and so was unable to witness the retreat of yet another Western power from Vietnam.

Nixon had promised in his televised address that the United States would do everything the agreement required and that other interested nations would do all they could to ensure that it was carried out. Trudeau was happy that the war was over but understood Nixon's meaning: Canada could not yet come home. At a January 24 press conference, Henry Kissinger explained the Paris Agreement, including the creation of the International Commission of Control and Supervision (ICCS) to replace the moribund International Control Commission. It would comprise Hungary, Poland, Indonesia, and Canada.

In contrast to 1954, Canada had been consulted in advance of the announcement and had agreed to serve. Several times bitten by problems with the first multilateral commission, Canadian undersecretary of state for external affairs Ed Ritchie wrote a detailed report regarding how a new commission should effectively supervise the truce, and it was submitted to Washington. Kissinger either did not read or chose to ignore Ritchie's recommendations. His press conference made clear that the new commission's mandate and power would be as limited as the first.

Disappointed in having his department's report disregarded, but feeling less constrained by the dictates of quiet diplomacy than his predecessors, Trudeau's secretary of state for external affairs, Mitchell Sharp, publicly stated that Canada would participate but, no matter the situation at the time, would leave after sixty days. Further, Canada would not negotiate with the other members of the commission regarding what could or could not be investigated or reported. He promised that Canada would speak out on anything found to be in violation of the Paris Accords regardless of the perpetrator or the opinions of other commissioners. This became known as Canada's "open mouth" policy.[22]

Michel Gauvin was seconded from his duties as ambassador to Greece to act as Canada's ICCS chief. Gauvin had been a major with the

Canadian army, served in combat in the Second World War, and earned the Distinguished Service Cross. He was a clever and experienced diplomat who in 1955 had been in Vietnam with the ICC. He arrived in Saigon at three in the morning and demanded a meeting with his foreign counterparts at eight. When he observed the manoeuvring over who would chair their meetings, he took the gavel himself. He became the primary spokesperson for the ICCS and the Four-Party Joint Military Commission to which it reported. Gauvin set up his offices in Saigon's old ICC headquarters where Sherwood Lett and Blair Seaborn had served before him.

The 240 Canadian soldiers and 50 diplomats under Gauvin's direction were deployed with those from the other ICCS countries to 45 locations. It became immediately frustrating that only the Canadians and Indonesians had the authority to act on suspected violations without the delaying tactic of checking with home. The ICCS oversaw prisoner exchanges and observed Americans removing their people and equipment. But the Paris agreement had allowed North Vietnamese soldiers to remain in the South. Violent actions instigated by and directed at them made it clear that the civil war that had always coexisted with the American war was continuing. In many regions there was really no ceasefire to monitor.

The situation remained volatile and danger acute. ICCS members were frequently targeted. Gauvin successfully negotiated the freeing of Captains Ian Patten and Fletcher Thomson of the Royal Canadian Regiment, who had been captured by North Vietnamese forces and held for seventeen days. Canadian Army Captain Charles Laviolette was less fortunate. He had arrived in Vietnam in January 1973 but only two months later was killed when the clearly marked ICCS helicopter in which he was travelling wandered off course and was shot down by a North Vietnamese army unit.[23] Laviolette joined four other Canadian soldiers and diplomats who died while serving with the ICC and ICCS: Sergeant J.S. Byrne, Corporal Vernon J. Perkin, John Douglas Turner, and Phillip MacDonald. The forty-two-year-old Laviolette was the last Canadian to die in Vietnam.

The prisoner-of-war swap went well but was not completed by the sixty-day deadline and so Kissinger asked Mitchell Sharp to extend the mission. Before agreeing, Sharp led a fact-finding expedition to Vietnam. He heard what Pearson had been told nearly a decade before—even though the enterprise was a lesson in frustration; if Canada left, the commission would collapse and the fragile peace would tumble "like a house of cards."[24] Sharp's report led Cabinet to permit a 90- and then a 120-day extension. Trudeau announced that it would be the last extension and that no matter what the state of affairs after 120 days, Canada would leave Vietnam. When an aide told President Nixon of Canada's having put a firm deadline on its commitment, he swore and called Trudeau "an asshole."[25] When the White House tapes later revealed the insult, Trudeau shrugged and laconically commented, "I've been called worse things by better people."[26]

Gauvin extended his stay and continued to speak out, often to the consternation of the Polish and Hungarian ICCS members, who sought to hide and deny North Vietnamese breaches of the peace agreement. In the first six months there were 18,000 violations and 76,000 casualties.[27] However, nearly all the Americans had left and some 32,000 prisoners of war had been freed or exchanged. Finally, in July 1973, the Canadian deadline was reached, and the last Canadians left Saigon. Iran took Canada's place on the ICCS, and the commission limped on until 1975, when it was quietly disbanded.

Canada had been in Vietnam from 1954 to 1973—nineteen long years of hopeful, exasperating, and sometimes valiant service. One-third of external affairs diplomats had served in Vietnam. Trudeau observed, "This was the longest, and certainly the single most unhappy, offshore contribution ever made by Canada to the international community."[28] Unhappy, perhaps, but the soldiers and diplomats had done what they could. They served with dignity, honour, and diligence in a dangerous environment with both hands secured tightly behind their backs.

The war was over—but not really, as the people of Vietnam could certainly attest. It was certainly not over for those who had served, including the Canadians who had come home damaged, or for the families of those who had not come home at all.

THE WALL

The Wall—one needs say nothing more. In 1981, after a long struggle to determine the best way to commemorate those who served in Vietnam, the winner of a national design contest for a veterans memorial was announced: twenty-one-year-old Yale University architecture student Maya Lin's remarkable model was chosen over 1420 other designs.

Located beside Washington's revered Lincoln Memorial, the wall was dedicated in 1982. Many people initially hated it but then gradually learned to understand its power. Rather than stand before it, you enter it. You walk in, crouch a little, and read the first names engraved on the reflective black marble. As you descend and the wall grows taller, all fall silent. You feel it. It's sacred. You inevitably stop reading names as the wall grows taller and taller and the sheer number of names overwhelms. That's the point. The wall turns at 1968, Tet, and you slowly begin ascending, re-emerging from the darkness and into the light.

The 58,282 names on the wall honour those who died or are missing in action. Rob McSorley is among them. At seventeen he'd quit East Vancouver's Templeton Secondary School, craving the action and adventure of war. His distraught parents did all they could to dissuade him, but the young man was determined. He skipped across the border to Blaine, Washington, and enlisted.

After training, he was flown to Vietnam as a proud member of the U.S. Army Rangers 75th Infantry, L Company, 101st Airborne Division, nicknamed the Screaming Eagles. On April 8, 1970, McSorley's twelve-person unit was in the A Shau Valley at the Laos border. Mission Grasshopper involved infiltrating positions along the Ho Chi Minh Trail, reporting on Viet Cong or NVA movement, engaging if necessary, and calling for air support when needed. Most of the reconnaissance work was done through thick jungle that restricted visibility to barely a yard. The Rangers were battle-tested and combat-hardened. They relied on each other like the brothers they had become. At 1:30 in the afternoon, four helicopters dropped them at the designated landing zone just inside the Laotian border. Two of the helicopters were empty, to deceive anyone who might be watching about the group's size.

They immediately saw a number of NVA soldiers running down the hill, away from the landing zone. Others were spotted on a hill above their position. The Rangers quickly moved to set up a secure perimeter and waited for the inevitable attack, which for some reason never came. A single helicopter was called in to fake an extraction, hoping it would entice the NVA into the open.

The ploy worked. Bullets sprayed the helicopter, allowing the Rangers to spot enemy positions and return fire. The firefight quickly escalated, with the NVA attacking the Rangers' perimeter at McSorley's position. They put their M16s on rock 'n' roll—firing six automatic bursts—and McSorley killed two and wounded more. Amid the firing he yelled to Frank "Buff" Johnson: "Hey, Buff, I feel like John Wayne!"[29] They continued firing, with Johnson launching M79 grenades until, finally, the NVA withdrew. There was another quick exchange and another tense quiet.

With less than two hours of sunlight remaining, the Ranger group gathered their gear and prepared to return to the landing zone. McSorley's closest friend in the unit was another teenager, Bruce Bowland. Bowland was to walk point, leading the column through the jungle. McSorley smiled and said to his less experienced friend, "You forget who taught you to walk point?" Bowland nodded and McSorley took the perilous point position.

The men were slowly and quietly making their way with McSorley in the lead when AK-47 fire crashed in front of and around them. McSorley killed three NVA soldiers but then his weapon jammed. He took three shots in the chest and shoulder and lay wounded in open ground, more than thirty feet in front of the others.[30] Gary Sands crawled out and dragged McSorley back to safety. With McSorley moaning in agony, the firefight continued. Within fifteen minutes he was dead. It was just two weeks past his nineteenth birthday.

Days later, the doorbell rang at the McSorleys' Vancouver home. A hand-delivered telegram brought the news. Rob's parents were devastated. It was the wrong order. Children should not die before their parents. Time saw their grief and isolation grow, for no one they knew shared their experience of losing a child who was fighting in a foreign uniform in a foreign land in an unpopular war.

But a sliver of good came from the monumentally bad. Forty-five years later, Bruce Bowland observed: "Without Rob sacrificing his life for me, I would be gone, too. I wouldn't be here. I wouldn't have a son and two daughters. I wouldn't have a grandson."[31] Bowland's adult daughter said, "I feel that it is necessary to thank one very special person for my life. I don't even know him personally, but I do know that I would not be alive today if it had not have been for a man by the name of Rob G. McSorley."[32]

While McSorley's name is carved into the reflective black granite of Washington's Vietnam Veterans Memorial, the problem of defining exactly who is Canadian allows us only to estimate that between 79 and 160 other Canadians share that tribute.[33] Canadian visitors remember them by leaving small Canadian flags beneath each name. They were honoured in that fashion in September 1986, when a group of one hundred Canadian Vietnam War vets and two Silver Cross Mothers who had lost sons in Vietnam made a pilgrimage to the wall.

The visitors completed paper and charcoal rubbings, and left flags, red roses, and tears.

The group was organized by the Canadian Vietnam Veterans Association (CVVA). It grew from an informal meeting in the spring of 1986 in which Canadian Vietnam vet Rob Purvis chatted with three other vets in a Winnipeg coffee shop. They wrote letters to the editors of newspapers across the country, inviting other vets to contact them. They were stunned at the waves of mail that poured in. As in the United States, most Canadian vets had been largely silent about their service. They were nervous but pleased with the notion of a community of common experience. The CVVA inspired the formation of a number of local Canadian Vietnam vet groups.

Lee Hitchins called Purvis about forming an Ottawa group. Purvis sent him names of those in the area, and among them was Doug Carey, now living near Carleton Place, west of Ottawa. Carey and Hitchins met and then arranged a meeting of those who might be interested. They assumed that not many or perhaps no one would come. Instead, at a small deli called Little David's in the west Ottawa community of Bells Corners, twenty-five Canadian Vietnam vets showed up. Conversations began tentatively but Carey and the others were soon swapping stories, laughing, cursing, and wiping away tears. For nearly all of them, it was the first time they had been able to speak freely about their experiences —the first time they did not feel misunderstood, forgotten, and alone.

At the second meeting, they arranged to participate in the Washington pilgrimage. Carey was among those who took part. He was moved by the wall and stood with his hands on the names of some of those he had known, including Ricky Lee Doye. Carey was comforted by sharing the emotional experience with people who understood what he had gone through and the many painful ways in which he was still haunted by the war. The Ottawa group continued to provide a point of contact for veterans in the area. Like the other branches, it invited and allowed more vets to emerge from the shadows.

The Washington pilgrimage inspired a desire to find ways to formally honour Canadian Vietnam vets. Purvis began small by asking the Royal Canadian Legion to allow the laying of a wreath at Winnipeg's Remembrance Day service. The Legion said no. The decision was consistent with the fact that Vietnam vets could not be members of the Legion or participate in Legion services because Canada had not officially sent troops to the war.

The rejection began a long battle between the CVVA and the Legion. In June 1987, the CVVA made the case that Canadians killed in service during the Vietnam War should have their names inscribed on hometown war memorials. The Manitoba and Northwestern Ontario District of the Legion declined the request. A delegate explained: "We want no plaques in memory of mercenaries. We'd have to do the same for Canadians who fought in the Falklands War or the '67 war in the Middle East, or for any Canadian mercenaries that go all over the world shooting people."[34] Critics of the Legion's decision argued that the Canadians were fighting communism and therefore fighting for Canadian values as part of the Cold War, in which Canada was undeniably engaged. The Legion refused to budge.

Finally, on October 1, 1994, the Legion relented. It drew the line at Canadians who fought in Vietnam but who later became American citizens. Its Resolution 322 stated that Canadians who served in Vietnam and then retained their citizenship could become Legion members.[35] Canadian Vietnam veterans were also allowed to lay wreaths at Remembrance Day services.

Another effort by the CVVA to win recognition for Vietnam War vets involved lobbying Ottawa's National Capital Commission and the federal government to have a monument erected to honour Canadians killed in the war. All efforts failed. However, in 1989, the CVVA affiliate Association québécoise des vétérans du Vietnam (AQVV) proudly unveiled the Canadian Vietnam Veterans Memorial in Côte-Sainte-Catherine, Quebec. One vertical stone depicts a map of Vietnam with the dates 1965–1975. Another bears the simple but poignant phrase: *Dedicated to those who served, those who died, and those who are missing in action.* In 1994 a municipal decision to repurpose the site led to the monument being moved to Melocheville, thirty-nine miles west of Montreal.

Ed Johnson of Detroit heard about the struggles of Canadian vets and recalled having served with a Canadian in Vietnam. He and American vet Ric Gidner founded the Canadian Vietnam Veterans' Welcome Home Committee. They put up their own money and raised some more to stage an event in Detroit honouring Canadian vets. In March 1993 they dedicated themselves to creating a monument to the Canadian fallen with the formation of the Michigan Association of Concerned Veterans. They worked with the CVVA to secure an Ottawa site.

Jean Chrétien had served in the Pearson and Trudeau cabinets and became prime minister in November 1993. His spokesperson, Marie-Christine Lilkoff, said that no public land would be used for a memorial because Canada did not officially participate in the Vietnam War, adding, "The people who chose to participate did so on their own."[36] But the usually staid and steady Senate surprised everyone when, in June 1994, it approved the creation of a memorial and urged the government to provide federal land for its home. Newfoundland senator Jack Marshall said, "It's time to accept that Canadian Vietnam War veterans are a part of our history. They cannot and should not be ignored or forgotten any longer."[37] Minister of Canadian Heritage Michel Dupuy was asked in Question Period if the government would follow the Senate's lead. He said no and explained cryptically: "We have our own way of celebrating. We are going to respect Canadian ways."[38]

By that point, Johnson and Gidner's Michigan organization had raised $180,000. Carey and his Ottawa group had both made donations. The memorial was constructed but lay in storage. Then, in January 1995, the mayor of Windsor, Ontario, responded positively to a letter Johnson and Gidner had sent to mayors in a number of cities close to the American border. In May the Windsor council approved locating the memorial in Assumption Park, near the Ambassador Bridge at the Canada–U.S. border. The only stipulation was that it include an inscription stating: "This memorial was placed here to commemorate Canadians who died in the Vietnam tragedy. It is not intended as a political statement concerning the merits of this or any other foreign conflict."

On Saturday, July 2, Johnson, Gidner and sixty-five Canadian Vietnam vets marched in a parade that ended with the dedication of the new memorial. Its vertical black granite is inscribed with the names of 147 Canadian soldiers and four ICC personnel killed in Vietnam. Behind the monument stand the Canadian, American, and POW/MIA flags. Many people call it the North Wall.

WELLNESS

While fighting for a way to remember those who had died, those who survived continued to wrestle demons. At the end of the First and Second World Wars and the Korean War, the men returned on ships, with time at sea to decompress and gather strength from the knowledge of shared experience. They were welcomed together, as victors, with bands, bunting, and hometown parades.

Vietnam vets returned on planes with mere hours separating hell and home. They arrived alone or in small groups. They were symbols of a shunned war. They were the defeated.

Graeme Webster attended Ottawa's Fisher Park High School and was a lifeguard at the Château Laurier pool. It was there that he met a lawyer from Chicago who encouraged him to attend the University of Chicago. After four years there studying history, he decided to become part of it, and so enlisted with the Marines. Webster served a 1966–67 tour in Vietnam.

Upon his discharge, Webster was given a fresh haircut, handed a plane ticket and a month's pay, and ordered not to discuss anything he had done or seen. A day later he was walking through the airport in El Toro, California, when a University of California demonstration descended upon the line of service men and women. Webster then experienced what many American and several Canadian vets did, and what some later claimed was merely apocryphal. Someone spat on him. The next day he was back in Ottawa—home, but not really.[39]

Doug Carey, for his part, had been treated well upon his return to Canada. He never forgot the RCMP officers helping him from the plane and through customs. It was a year before he recovered from encephalitis. His family did what they could, but physical convalescence was only part of his difficult journey. For a long time, he could speak with no one about what he had done or what had happened to him, for few would believe the stories. Others learned of his time in Vietnam and called him a baby killer. He felt disoriented, lost, and invisible. He learned to be quiet, to suppress his memories and emotions; there seemed to be no one who could remotely understand or truly empathize.

The Pentagon Papers had proved that the war had been sold and fought on a foundation of lies. Popular books, television documentaries, and Academy Award–winning movies such as *The Deer Hunter* (1978), *Coming Home* (1978), and *Apocalypse Now* (1979) helped establish the consensus that the whole exercise had been an amoral debacle. It is therefore little wonder that, like so many other Canadian and American vets, Carey struggled to understand the meaning of his sacrifice and suffering. Those who volunteered to fight had been true to their principles of service and the fight against communism. Yet to believe what was being said about the war was to admit to having been duped. Many vets held fast to the belief that they had served well in a just war that could have been won if the political leadership had allowed them to do so. That minority stance helped, but only a little, for that struggle was merely political. Infinitely harder was the psychological battle.

Carey was among those who suffered embarrassing and debilitating symptoms he couldn't understand or control. When he was out for a walk one pleasant afternoon, for example, a car backfired and he instinctively leapt under a hedge. He constantly struggled, and too often failed, to control his temper and tongue. He worked as a truck driver and then a sales professional but knew he was not a good employee, often smashing workplace niceties by speaking his mind with co-workers and superiors when polite discretion would have been more appropriate.

Carey had met Patricia at a 1964 dance in the Cobourg Pavilion by the city's magnificent Lake Ontario beach. During his time in Vietnam they corresponded through numerous letters and in January 1970 they were married. Four years later they moved to a comfortable Carleton Place home, where they welcomed and raised three children. From the outside, all looked fine. But the war still haunted Carey's dreams and affected his reactions to the simplest of things. While times were slowly changing, the dominant culture of the day still taught men to "man up," "suck it up," and, as silently as possible, carry on. Asking for help was admitting weakness. But Carey knew he needed more help than the occasional beer with other vets could provide.

A number of American studies attempted to determine what was so dramatically affecting so many Vietnam vets. It was not until 1976 that professor of psychiatry Mardi Horowitz of the Langley Porter Psychiatric Institute at the University of California identified symptoms common to people exposed to unusual stress. Carey experienced them all: fear of an event's repetition, rage, shame, guilt about aggressive impulses toward others, survivor guilt, and a fear of being identified.[40] The symptoms presented themselves in ways Carey knew too well: sleep disorders, nightmares, frighteningly real flashbacks, hypervigilance, and sudden fits of unexplainable terror, violence, rage, or tears.

In 1980, more than fifteen years after vets had begun returning from the jungle, Horowitz's work, along with that of others, led to the identification and acceptance of a diagnosis called post-traumatic stress disorder (PTSD). Sufferers were finally allowed the relief of knowing that their symptoms were not due to a weakness within them but as a result of what had been done to them.

Despite this progress in the United States, there were only a couple of brief mentions of PTSD, and no articles about it, in Canadian professional psychiatric or medical journals throughout the late 1970s and 1980s.[41] Finally, in 1990 and 1991, U.S. Army Major and psychologist Dr. Robert Stretch published three articles based on his study of Canadian Vietnam vets and PTSD. Stretch conducted his work with the help of the Canadian Vietnam Veterans Coalition. He found that 40.2 percent of American and 65.9 percent of Canadian vets suffered symptoms of PTSD during their service or after returning home.[42] Without trivializing the tremendous suffering of American vets, he found that the Canadian vets' experience with PTSD was not only more common but more profound. The reason, he wrote, was that, "while many Americans returned to the U.S. to face hostility and rejection for their role in the war, Canadians essentially returned home to a void."[43] Their support community was smaller, more scattered, or absent. Fewer Canadian doctors and psychologists were properly trained to diagnose or treat PTSD and there was no government funding for treatment.

The research showed that Carey was not alone. Art Diablo spent a year in a Brooklyn hospital recovering from the wound that nearly took his arm before he returned home to Kahnawake. He married, had a son, and worked as a police dispatcher for eight years—but then the war came for him again. Delayed chronic PTSD symptoms resulted in the loss of his health, job, home, and marriage. It was years before he was able to return to school and begin again to rebuild his life.[44]

It was only when articles about PTSD began appearing that Port Hope's David Dear, who had served in a MASH unit, realized that he had all the symptoms. At age forty-five, he still found that he would suddenly and for no reason break down in uncontrollable tears and be unable to go to work or face friends or family. His wife and children struggled to understand the frightening episodes that from time to time, and without warning, stole from them the man they loved.[45]

If nothing else, the acceptance of PTSD as a legitimate diagnosis finally offered sufferers a vocabulary with which to discuss their symptoms. Some Canadian vets, such as Diablo, travelled to the United States for PTSD treatment, and some were helped by Canadian psychiatrists such as Toronto's Dr. Klaus Kuch and others who were ahead of their national professional organization in accepting the legitimacy of PTSD.

Through his work with the Ottawa branch of the CVCC, Carey found out about psychiatrist Dr. Frederick Lundell, who was associated with Montreal General Hospital. Lundell was a Second World War veteran who had flown missions during the Atlantic campaign and so had a unique understanding of the difficulties vets were experiencing. He had been treating Canadian Vietnam vets since 1973. Carey joined others who travelled to Montreal to consult with Dr. Lundell. For several years, Carey met with the doctor alone or as part of small groups. He later called Lundell the smartest man he had ever met. The doctor charged Carey and the other vets nothing for his services.

In 1956 the Canadian and American governments had signed an agreement whereby the American Department of Veterans Affairs would provide funds to help soldiers discharged from its armed forces who were living in Canada. The Canadian government gave nothing to help the Canadian Vietnam vets, but the Americans respected the old agreement. Diablo's trips to the United States and his treatments were covered by the Americans. The American GI Bill allowed Rob Purvis to complete his college education. The first six of Carey's trips to Montreal were subsidized by the American Department of Veterans Affairs but after that, he and all the others in need of help were on their own.

Carey and other Canadian Vietnam vets eventually better understood what had happened to them, the factors that continued to shape their behaviours and perceptions, and how best to control their attitudes and reactions. But a PTSD victim never really recovers. Life does not become easy, just easier. Carey knew that for the rest of his life, in the middle of a family dinner, a walk in the woods behind his home, or enjoying a drink with friends, the jungle could return. Treaties are signed. Monuments are built. But wars never truly end.

CHAPTER 6

REBECCA TRINH: DESPERATION MEETS COMPASSION

President Nixon lied in his January 1973 television address when he announced the end of the Vietnam War. At the very least, he told the politician's lie: shading the truth to put himself and the situation in the best possible light, while telling people what they longed to hear. The Vietnam War was not over. It was not over for Canada when a few months later the Canadians left the International Commission for Control and Supervision. It was far from over for the people of what was inaccurately but conveniently still called Indochina.

As Michel Gauvin and his ICCS staff had observed, the North Vietnamese government saw the Paris Peace Accords as simply another step toward attaining its long-established goals. In March 1973, the last

American military unit departed. North Vietnamese divisions stepped up their operations to conquer the South and unify the country, as American military and financial aid continued to bolster South Vietnam's increasingly shaky government, economy, and army. Congress began reasserting its constitutional power by passing a measure that blocked the reintroduction of direct American military activity in Vietnam. It then passed the War Powers Act, which curtailed the president's ability to wage war without Congressional approval.

When the Watergate scandal led to Nixon's resignation in August 1974, Vice-President Gerald Ford became president. With North Vietnamese forces enjoying more success, Ford urged Congress to allow increased American help for South Vietnam. Instead, it cut aid by 30 percent. The South Vietnamese government was in tatters, its economy was collapsing, and its soldiers were deserting in droves. Northern forces took major cities, the countryside, and town after town until, in April 1975, more than 100,000 troops prepared to attack Saigon from five directions.

As the people of Saigon trembled, the government of Laos crumbled. Laos was dismissed by some as a Vietnam War sideshow. But from 1964 to 1973, the United States had dropped 2 million tons of bombs on Laos, killing more than 200,000 people, nearly all of them civilians.[1] When America and Thailand withdrew support from the barely functioning government and the guerilla forces battling rebels from the communist organization Pathet Lao, a coalition of backstabbing groups took control of the country. In June 1975, the Pathet Lao seized power. By December, the monarchy was abolished and the Lao People's Democratic Republic was declared. Bedlam ensued.

The new government began a ruthless program of reprisals against former enemies. Army officers, senior bureaucrats, and business leaders were banished to re-education camps—places of torture, hard labour, and brutal ideological indoctrination. Many died in the camps and others survived for months or even years on a daily handful of rice.

The rule of law was gone, the economy lay in ruins, and tens of thousands were hopeless, homeless, and hungry.

Cambodia had been another so-called sideshow, even though throughout the war, the United States had dropped over 500,000 tons of bombs on the country. An estimated half million civilians had been killed, with many more left homeless.[2] In April 1975 what was left of the government fell to Pol Pot's communist movement, the Khmer Rouge. In an attempt to create a classless utopia, his regime renamed the country Kampuchea, established a new calendar, had artists and musicians killed as counter-revolutionaries, shuttered places of worship, banned education past elementary school, and instituted haphazard land reforms. The capital city of Phnom Penh went from a population of over 2 million to just 270,000. Up to 3 million of the country's 7.5 million people were uprooted and relocated, sent to re-education camps, pressed into forced labour, or executed. A genocide based on class, ethnicity, and ideology saw bodies pushed into mass graves or piled and left to rot in what a shocked world came to know as the Killing Fields. To save expensive bullets, children were killed by smashing their heads against tree trunks.

With North Vietnamese forces moving into Saigon, the 5,000 Americans remaining in the city and 140,000 Vietnamese who had worked with or supported them during the war began boarding planes and then helicopters to evacuate. Not everyone could get out in time. Southern soldiers vowed to turn their weapons on those attempting to flee. Amid the panic, desperate measures were taken. One example was a Vietnamese economist employed at the American embassy who offered an American $10,000 to marry his pregnant wife so she could qualify for one of the seats out of the country.[3]

Except for the French and Belgian, all Western embassies were abandoned. A Canadian military transport plane was loaded with embassy staff and files. Vietnamese who had worked for the Canadians and knew their lives would soon be worthless begged for spots on the plane, but none could obtain the necessary passports or exit permits. They were enraged when it was reported that the plane left the tarmac with some seats empty and that the ambassador's car had been loaded aboard, taking space that could have saved a few more of those begging for mercy.[4] On April 30 North Vietnamese tanks rumbled freely through Saigon. In a shuffle that had seen the president and vice-president flee the country, General Duong Van Minh had become the leader of South Vietnam's government. He welcomed the North's Colonel Bui Tin to the presidential palace and said, "I have been waiting since early this morning to transfer power to you." The colonel replied: "Your power has crumbled. You cannot give up what you do not have."[5] With that anticlimactic non-ceremony, two years after Nixon declared the war over, the war was over. But even then, not really.

Saigon was renamed Ho Chi Minh City. South Vietnamese soldiers, government officials, entrepreneurs and teachers, those who had worked with Westerners, and others were rounded up and placed in rural re-education camps to cleanse them of capitalist ways through hard labour and indoctrination. Businesses, possessions, bank accounts, and land were confiscated. As in Laos and Cambodia, the new government broke what remained of an already teetering economy and civil society. People whose homes and lives had been destroyed by the war found themselves, unbelievably, even worse off than before. Those who had managed to eke out relatively stable lives found everything they believed they could rely on suddenly gone. Bankers went broke. Farmers starved.

Many of the professional class and military leaders of Laos, Cambodia, and Vietnam transferred their suddenly worthless money to gold to buy and bribe their way out. Fifteen thousand of them were accepted by the United States.

The growing number of Indochinese refugees fleeing the aftermath of the war, in which Canada had been involved for over two decades, presented the Trudeau government with a dilemma. Canada's birth rate was declining, and the country needed more people. From the 1950s to the mid-1970s, Canada had admitted about 150,000 immigrants a year, of whom only about 3 percent were Asian.[6] To accept an influx of Indochinese people had the potential of altering both those numbers in ways the economy might be unable to handle and some Canadians unwilling to accept.

The United Nations High Commissioner for Refugees (UNHCR) had been formed in 1950 to address the post–Second World War refugee crisis. It defined a refugee as anyone who, prior to January 1, 1951, was living outside their country and had a well-founded belief that if they returned they would be persecuted due to their race, religion, political opinion, or membership in a social group. These people became known as Convention Refugees. Until 1969 successive Canadian governments refused to sign the agreement, fearing it would impede their ability to deport those from elsewhere who were deemed threats to national security.[7] But the government nonetheless applied the United Nation's definition when accepting 37,000 Hungarian refugees in 1956, 12,000 Czechoslovakians in 1968, 228 Tibetans in 1970, and then 8,000 Ugandan refugees in 1972–73.[8] The experiences demonstrated that certainly not all, but enough, Canadians, at least those in support of the political and academic elite, were sympathetic to the plight of refugees and willing to accept newcomers into their communities.

In April 1975, before Saigon's fall but with thousands already fleeing Vietnam, Cambodia, and Laos, the Trudeau government decided that Canada would step up again. The Canadian embassy issued letters promising visas to those who had indicated an interest in joining family members already in Canada. It announced that, of the 1,300 Vietnamese students currently studying in Canada, those who wished to remain would be granted permanent residency status.

Canada also supported an American initiative whereby over 2,500 orphaned children, many of them babies, were transported on military aircraft to the Clark Airforce Base in the Philippines. With the United

States, Australia, and other countries acting to save the children, Canada's federal government partnered with the governments of Ontario and Quebec to quickly arrange adoptive parents, and 131 babies were flown to Canada. Canadians Naomi Bronstein and Eloise and Anna Charet were instrumental in rescuing Cambodian orphans from certain death by spiriting them to Saigon on one of the last American planes to leave Phnom Penh. An extensive effort led by Victoria Leach from Ontario's Ministry of Community Health and Social Services determined that all were truly orphans. A Canadian RCAF Hercules was turned into a nursery and sixty-two babies were flown to Hong Kong and then on a commercial flight to Vancouver. A few days later, a second baby-flight rescued another sixty-nine orphaned babies.[9]

Federal Minister of Manpower and Immigration Robert Andras announced that Canada would accept another five thousand refugees from those who had fled their homes and were currently in Guam, Hong Kong, and at a number of American military bases. Immigration officers were quickly sent to act as gatekeepers with the power to decide who would be allowed in. They were instructed to forget the point system used for immigrants and instead to consider a prospective refugee's employment skills and ability to speak French or English, whether they were fleeing as a family or had family already in Canada, and whether they appeared able to adjust to life in Canada.[10]

In the course of addressing the Indochinese refugee crisis, Pierre Trudeau's government had been developing a new immigration law. It was passed in 1976 and came into effect two years later. It marked the first time that the goals of immigration were specifically expressed. Immigration quotas would now be based building Canada's economy; promoting family reunion; fulfilling international and humanitarian obligations; and addressing demographic challenges. The law differentiated immigrants from refugees. It declared that Canada would uphold its humanitarian traditions and obligations by applying the

United Nation's definition of Convention Refugees and would accept them on compassionate grounds. It allowed for the creation of a Designated Class of refugees; that is, rather than judging whether individuals fit the Convention definition, membership in an identified group, such as those in a particular war zone, would qualify all as Designated Refugees. The law stated that, after consultation with the provinces, Cabinet would establish how many refugees would be accepted in a particular year. It also allowed for private sponsors to partner with the government to support refugees.

By the end of 1976, a number of countries had accepted Indochinese refugees and Canada had admitted 150 Laotians, 250 Cambodians, and 7,800 Vietnamese. Many settled in Ontario, some in Alberta, and 65 percent in Quebec.[11] Nearly all the newcomers had been middle class in their home country and spoke at least passable English or French. It appeared that the humanitarian crisis was over—but it was not.

COURAGE IN THE FACE OF CHAOS

In the spring of 1978, tensions regarding a number of issues led Vietnam to end its strategic alliance with China. It joined the Soviet-dominated Council for Mutual Economic Assistance and signed a twenty-five-year friendship and cooperation treaty with the Soviet Union. China withdrew its advisors from Vietnam and ended its annual $300 million of economic aid. Then, after a number of border skirmishes, in December 1978 troops from Vietnam poured into Cambodia and within a month had sunk its navy, destroyed its air power, and taken its capital. Pol Pot was overthrown. China was enraged at the destruction of its client-state and in February launched a retaliatory attack against Vietnam. Both sides suffered heavy losses in a month of intense battle until a ceasefire was declared.

When the conflict with China began, Rebecca (Gai-Zhi) Trinh knew her family was in trouble. She was born in 1949, to a family with Chinese roots, in a village near Hanoi. As a child, she moved with her family to Macau, China, across the Pearl River Delta from Hong Kong, where her father ran an American goods importing business. When the political situation spurred economic turmoil, the family moved back to Vietnam, where her father started a similar company in Saigon.

It was love at first sight for Rebecca and Sam (Chi-Dung) when they met at a Chinese Alliance Church youth conference. They were married in 1973. Sam worked at a textile manufacturing company, where he was responsible for the dyes used to design patterns for mass-produced cloth. Rebecca had earned a college accounting diploma and became an accountant for a small business while freelancing as a reporter for a local Chinese-language newspaper. Soon their daughter Judy (Ai-Di) was born and then, two years later, Helen (Gai-Di) came along. Like most people in Saigon, they lived in a neighbourhood far from the violent areas within the city and the war raging in distant jungles. Like Canadians and Americans, every evening after dinner they watched the war on TV. But the war was now coming for them.

The ethnic Chinese of Vietnam had been discriminated against for years and now, with the increase in Sino-Vietnamese tensions, the government declared all those with a Chinese background disloyal and dangerous. Beginning in the spring of 1978, actions taken against ethnic Chinese included children being removed from schools and adults from their jobs; business licences being rescinded, refused, and confiscated; and the denial of food ration cards.[12] Many ethnic Chinese were imprisoned without charges, and many were assassinated. Trinh saw neighbours and friends disappearing, spirited off to new economic zones where they were fed little, housed in prison-like barracks, and worked from sun-up to sun-down clearing land and doing other types of back-breaking manual labour.

One night, with the children asleep, Rebecca and Sam talked and cried and talked some more until their decision was made. There was nothing left to do but get out of Vietnam by any means available.

The first step was to seek help from family. Sam's sisters Esther and Jenny were both in Canada and had studied at Prairie Bible Institute in Three Hills, Alberta. Esther had accepted the government's offer of landed status as a route to Canadian citizenship. After graduation she worked with the Chinese Alliance Church in Lethbridge. When Esther and her husband, James, accepted a mission assignment seeding Christian churches in Taiwan, Jenny took over her sister's work at the Lethbridge church. Esther provided a letter to Sam that would allow his family to obtain Canadian visas.

The problem was that, with the Canadian embassy closed and Vietnam's civic society in shambles, a visa was all but useless. Sam converted all the money and valuables that had not been taken by corrupt government officials into one-ounce gold squares. Gold was the only currency that mattered anymore, and the small bars could be discreetly slipped into the hands of whoever needed to be bribed. Sam talked to "a guy who knew a guy," who accepted the equivalent of $3,000 Canadian in gold for exit permits.[13] He was told the date, time, and place where a boat would be waiting. They packed and repacked, deciding what was absolutely essential.

The family was about to join the 1978 to mid-1980s second wave of Indochinese emigration that saw 160,000 Vietnamese flee the latest madness to grip their country. Between 60 and 80 percent were ethnic Chinese, determined not to be among the 1.5 million who would be physically abused, brainwashed, or killed.[14]

It was four in the morning on December 20, 1978. Cradling her sleepy children in her arms, Rebecca clambered up to join five others on the hood of an old and overcrowded truck. Sam stuffed himself into the back, clutching a large backpack that contained all they now owned. The truck joined a convoy that was soon bouncing along in the dark on bumpy dirt sideroads.

As the trucks approached a checkpoint, Sam and a few other men slipped off and ran across a field and into the trees. They couldn't risk being discovered by guards looking for men now deemed "collaborationists"—anyone who had served in the South's army. Sam had done military training, but the war had ended before he was called to serve. He was certain that distinction would matter little to the young men with automatic weapons at the checkpoint. The guards stopped the truck and slowly inspected everyone and everything aboard. For three hours the inspection and intimidation dragged on until they were finally told to repack their ransacked bags and move along. Rebecca scanned the scared faces of young men imprisoned in the scorching sun behind a barbed wire enclosure and was relieved not to see Sam among them.

The truck rumbled on with twenty-month-old Helen squirming in Rebecca's arms and four-year-old Judy asking where her daddy was. A mile or so along the rough road they came to a large bush protruding close by, and Rebecca breathed a sigh of relief as Sam and the others leapt out and back onto the truck.

It took ten hours to travel the 250 miles to Rach Gia, a small fishing town in Vietnam's southwest corner, on the Gulf of Thailand. It had been dark when they left and it was dark when they arrived. They were tired, famished, and anxiously hoping that the ship upon which they had all paid for passage would show up. They were taken to rooms in an abandoned building once owned by a Chinese business tycoon. Everyone scattered to find food in markets or restaurants. It was while they were having a modest dinner that Rebecca told Judy this was not merely an adventure, as she had framed it before, and that they would never be going back home. Judy burst into tears and baby Helen joined in with her own anguished wailing.

For five days they waited in a small, cold, tiled room until they were told they would be taken to the small island of Con, where the ship transporting them to freedom would meet them. Three hundred and sixteen people crammed onto a tiny vessel for the two-hour journey.

But no ship awaited them. Con was home to eighty families who lived in stilt homes along the shore and made a comfortable living fishing and harvesting pineapples, bananas, and coconuts. The locals had not asked for this invasion and chose to ignore the strangers thrust upon them. Like the other refugees, Rebecca and her family made camp using blankets and whatever they could scrounge. As the waiting dragged on, they were forced to sell jewellery and other goods hidden or sewn into clothing to buy food. More small boatloads of refugees arrived and soon there were 1,700 abandoned and cheated people surviving in a makeshift camp.

Days and then weeks went by. Many children fell ill, including Helen. Fortunately, among the group was a Dr. Cuong, who dedicated himself to managing Helen's fever and infections. But she grew thin and weak and wouldn't eat.

After three months of frustration, boredom, and efforts to maintain health and dignity, news came that their ship would arrive that evening. On the afternoon of March 22, 1979, a cheer rose up from the camp as three small ships approached the docks. Families were reminded that they would be allowed only one bag each, and so all again donned several layers of clothes and filled their pockets.

Rebecca carried the still quite ill Helen in her arms and took Judy's hand as they and 312 others clambered aboard the old and dangerously overfilled thirty-nine-foot boat, registered as KG-0016. Rebecca and Sam tucked their crossed legs beneath them to make room for passengers crammed shoulder to shoulder on the rough wooden deck. They held the girls close on their laps. In the crushingly hot and humid air, children cried and the elderly and sick moaned. The smells were terrible and only got worse.

For three days the ship moved slowly through the azure sea. People had brought a little food, but everyone was soon hungry and thirsty. Nothing could console a young woman behind Rebecca whose sick baby died in her arms.

On the third day, ships were spotted on the horizon and the captain raised the SOS flag. He soon realized that the dark sails belonged to pirates. One ship kept its distance while two others sandwiched the defenceless vessel and shouting pirates leapt aboard.

During the Indochinese diaspora, Thai pirates robbed thousands, raped over 2,400 women and girls, and kidnapped another thousand.[15] Many women and girls were taken to the Ko Kra islets, where they were repeatedly raped for weeks or months before being killed and dumped in the sea. Others were sold to Thai brothels.[16] It is estimated that thirty to forty thousand so-called boat people were lost to pirates, disease, and the sinking of derelict ships that had no business being at sea.[17]

Rebecca and Sam clutched each other and held their children tight. Ten pirates armed with axes, machetes, knives, and handguns shouted that all were to board the pirate ships now lashed to the gunnels. The pirates roughly groped their screaming victims and took anything of value. Rebecca's and Sam's wedding rings were ripped from their fingers. The boat was ransacked; bags were torn apart, secret compartments slit, and gold and personal mementos stolen. Finally, after three harrowing hours, the terrified passengers were shoved back on board and the pirates sailed toward the horizon.

That night, the captain spotted the approach of another pirate ship. He tried to outrun it but was soon overtaken. Pirates again came aboard but, while they trampled some passengers and struck others, they quickly realized there was nothing left to steal. Miraculously, this second crew of pirates spared the shuddering women and girls, leaving them unmolested.

At first light the next morning the now leaking KG-0016 entered Malaysian territory. The sight of coconut trees on a distant shore offered salvation. But a Malaysian naval vessel approached and announced through loudspeakers that they would not be allowed landfall. A chain was thrown and attached, and the boat overflowing with pleading refugees was towed back out to international waters. Like all ships under tow, it listed to and fro, with waves and spray drenching all aboard. Twice it almost capsized. After two hours of perilous hauling, the chain was released, and the Malaysian captain shouted over the waves that they were to sail straight ahead for two or three days to where they would find Indonesia.

Towing was a common occurrence. By the middle of 1978, the Malaysian government had decided that it had accepted enough Vietnamese refugees and could handle no more. Over the next couple of years about forty thousand desperate people were towed away. Thailand's government had made the same decision and posted its army on the Cambodian border. At one point, Thai soldiers aimed their weapons at thousands of starving people who had walked for weeks to escape their country's madness. They were turned around and forced down a mountain trail. Several hundred were killed and others mutilated as they walked through a minefield that the soldiers must have known was there.[18]

The KG-0016 captain knew no one had enough food or water for another three days at sea. People were falling ill and more children had died. He wanted to save his passengers and crew as well as his own family members who were on board. Conjuring a plan, he sailed northward to avoid naval vessels and then tacked back along the Malaysian coast. Picking his spot under the cover of a moonless night, the captain manoeuvred as close to shore as possible. Shouts rang out and everyone scrambled to their feet. They were told to grab their possessions and yank boards from decks or walls and salvage anything that could float. They were abandoning and scuttling the ship.

Rebecca stood at the rail, holding her two crying girls, as others leapt into the dark waters several feet below. Sam shouted that he would go first and that she should then throw Judy to him. She watched him jump and for a terrifying moment he disappeared. Sputtering and waving, he finally resurfaced and yelled up to her. Rebecca sat Helen on the deck and held her with one foot while she picked Judy up with both hands and with all her might threw the screaming child out into the darkness. Judy plunged into the water just in front of Sam, and in seconds he had her. Rebecca then picked up Helen and planned her move. She tossed her crying baby high into the air and at the same moment jumped. Smacking into the water, she frantically scrambled up to the surface, plunged her hands into a splash beside her and, astonishingly, caught her howling daughter. Treading water with one arm and pulling Helen close with the other, she thanked God for saving them all.

Sam was quickly beside them and they turned toward the shore, several hundred yards away. Screams for help pierced the night, but they had to keep swimming. Rebecca praised God again as she crawled, exhausted, onto the sand. The children had become too cold and wet and scared to cry. But now, safe on the huge, desolate beach, their mother sobbed.

The sun rose over three hundred exhausted and dehydrated souls who were starving but felt lucky to be alive. Sam and several other young men swam out to the boat to retrieve any belongings and pull the wreckage apart so that it could not be rebuilt. A group of women went exploring and returned with the happy news that they had found a clean freshwater lake nearby. The group drank heartily, fashioned cookstoves from rocks, and boiled salty rice salvaged from the ship.

Judy was soon romping with other children, but Helen was thin and pale, with lifeless eyes and no appetite. She could no longer summon the energy to cry. Diarrhea brought dehydration and, as a result of having been covered in urine and diesel-infected seawater, her skin had broken out in a pus-filled rash. Dr. Cuong warned Rebecca to expect the worst. While scrounging for food in the heap of salvaged boxes and bags, she spotted a smashed first aid kit and a bottle of intravenous saline solution. The doctor administered it and within a day Helen began to recover. She screeched when her bare bottom was dipped into the salt water, but it slowly cleared her rash.

The hardy group gathered wood and leaves to fashion crude huts, and foraged for food. Within a week, they were spotted and then rescued by the International Red Cross. With no boat to load them back onto and Red Cross officials applying pressure, Malaysian authorities finally relented and transported the castaways to the Cherating refugee camp.

CANADA STEPS UP

By the summer of 1979, nearly 300,000 refugees had fled their homes, and most were languishing in refugee camps in Hong Kong, Malaysia, Indonesia, and the Philippines.[19] The plight of those fleeing, sometimes drowning or surviving only to land in camps, touched many Canadian hearts. But those same stories stiffened the resolve of others intent on stopping the refugees from entering Canada. Newspaper editorials generally encouraged the government to step up its support for those in such obvious need, but a February 1979 poll revealed that 50 percent of Canadians were opposed to accepting more refugees.[20] By March, only seventy-three sponsors had registered to support those of the second wave. Clearly aware of the political risks, the Trudeau government nonetheless maintained its stated goal of bringing five thousand more Indochinese people to Canada by the end of the year as a Designated Class of refugees.

In July the UNHCR convened a conference in Geneva chaired by UN Secretary-General Dr. Kurt Waldheim. It was attended by representatives from sixty-five countries, including Canada and the United States. Trudeau's Liberals had lost the federal election two months before and so Secretary of State for External Affairs Flora MacDonald represented Prime Minister Joe Clark's new Progressive Conservative government.

Canada was on the UNHCR executive and played an important role in the conference. MacDonald delivered a dramatic speech in which she slammed the Vietnamese government for its human rights abuses. Already having won the support of Clark, Employment and Immigration Minister Ron Atkey, and the rest of Cabinet, MacDonald astonished many in attendance by stating that by the end of 1980, Canada would accept 50,000 Indochinese refugees. Given its relatively small population, Canada was clearly taking a stunningly large number of refugees, partly in an attempt to push other countries to do the same. MacDonald was blunt: "We urge other countries to find the humanity in the souls of their nations to make similar efforts."[21]

The conference ended with an agreement that many Western countries would send financial and other aid to the asylum countries to address some of the worst camp conditions. They would also accept refugees. The United States agreed to take up to 40,000, and the attendees raised their aggregate total from 125,000 to 260,000.[22]

Media around the world had been devoting a great deal of airtime and print space to the refugee crisis. In Canada, during the ten-week period in 1980 from mid-June to the end of August, 255 newspaper stories addressed the crisis. The *Toronto Star*, with twenty-seven front-page articles, took the lead, and many others published at least twenty.[23] What's more, televised footage of crowded boats and refugee camps vividly brought home the refugees' plight.

Ron Atkey had read Harold Troper and Irving Abella's *None Is Too Many*, the moving account of Canada's refusal to adequately respond to asylum-seeking European Jews during the Holocaust. The book title came from a response by the deputy immigration minister of the day to a question about how many Jews would be allowed into Canada: "None is too many," he said. Atkey took the book to Cabinet and to a meeting of senior staff and said that this time Canada would do better.²⁴ Atkey announced that, to reach its target of fifty thousand, the government would sponsor one refugee for each one who was privately sponsored.

The Cherating refugee camp was near the city of Kuantan, Malaysia. The camp's roughly seven thousand people were shoehorned together, riddled with sand fleas, and suffering from inadequate shelter, food, and water. After a child died of infectious meningitis, the camp was medically quarantined but, as more people arrived and were packed into spaces where there was already no room, the designation meant nothing.²⁵

Upon their arrival, Rebecca, Sam, and their girls were shoved into a line by shouting guards, told to wait, then yelled at to hurry into another line, only to wait again. Eventually they were shown to a small, dirty tent.

Overwhelmed Malaysian Red Crescent workers did their utmost to provide rice and water. Days became a relentless routine of lineups and boredom. Rebecca and the others could gaze longingly at the white sand beach and refreshing blue ocean, but they were kept from it by armed guards and a tall barbed wire fence. Helen slowly recovered her strength and energy, and Judy invented games to amuse herself, made friends with other children, and, by living in the moment as kids so magically do, adjusted to camp life.

Malaysia had established several camps on islands along its east coast; Cherating was the only one on the mainland. All were squalid, and Cherating was the worst.²⁶ At the outset of the Indochinese diaspora's second wave, Thailand, Indonesia, Hong Kong, and the Philippines had also set up additional camps they believed would offer temporary solutions to a temporary problem. By the time the Trinh family arrived at Cherating, all camps had taken on a semblance of sad permanence. While not all camp guards were corrupt or evil, many openly participated in beatings, robbery, and rape. The worst part of the camps was what they did to dignity and the human spirit. Idleness crushed hope. Trinh and her family did the best they could to hold on.

The identification documents that Sam had so carefully packed had disappeared. All that remained was a letter from Esther explaining "to whom it may concern" that she was Sam's sister, living and working in Lethbridge, with landed immigrant status. After nearly three months of barely surviving Cherating's degrading conditions, Sam finally secured a meeting with a Canadian immigration representative.

Immigration officers were the unsung heroes of the Canadian humanitarian effort. Most were men and all were young, dedicated, and passionate about their work. Civil servant Michael Molloy, the senior coordinator with the immigration department, ensured that selection, transportation, reception, and settlement all, somehow, meshed. It was a bureaucratic and logistical nightmare. But, as Molloy later observed: "The clarity of the direction from the top, and the commitment of the people at the top, was amazingly empowering. It allowed us to innovate. It allowed us to figure out new ways of doing things. It allowed us never to break the law, but to stretch it as far as it could be reasonably stretched to deal with what we actually saw as opposed to what the policy-makers might have imagined we'd see."[27]

Canada's primary domestic political concern in the 1960s and 1970s was whether Quebec's ethnic nationalism would lead the province out of the country. The fear became acute with the 1976 election of the Parti Québécois, whose raison d'être was to make separation happen. This dynamic led to two agreements between the federal and Quebec governments that resulted in Quebec immigration officials travelling and working with their federal counterparts to address the Indochinese refugee crisis. If prospective new Canadians were fluent in French, had family in Quebec, or indicated a desire to live in the province, they were handled by Quebec immigration officials. The arrangement allowed Quebec to position itself on the world stage and the federal government to demonstrate that federalism was flexible enough to accommodate Quebec nationalism within a united Canada.[28]

The men and women working for the federal and Quebec governments left political agendas at home and, despite—or perhaps because of—good-natured teasing, they cooperated well. They suffered the same hardships and felt the same satisfaction in knowing that they were helping to save lives. Quebec immigration officer Florent Fortin later reflected, "This period of work with Indochinese refugees, which lasted from 1978 to 1982, was the most exciting and satisfying of my career."[29]

Simply getting to the various camps often involved harrowing experiences. To do their work, the officers needed typewriters, multi-page carbon-paper forms, telexes, and expensive, unreliable, and often unavailable long-distance phone lines. Not until September 1979 was a single computer—the size of a washing machine—allocated to Molloy in Ottawa and used to match approved refugees with flights and sponsors.[30] Meanwhile, front-line officers worked in tents or out in the open, at little folding tables. Belligerent armed guards watched their every move, while before them stood thousands of desperate people who might choose to cooperate or riot. The officers often worked twelve-hour days and seven-day weeks. Most endured crude sleeping arrangements, with worktables as beds, beneath which scurried large, ravenous rats. They interviewed dozens of prospects a day in the knowledge that there would always be more people in need than could be liberated.

The Trinh family interview went well. The letter from Esther helped, for it meant they would be supported by a family member and so had a greater likelihood of adjusting relatively easily to life in Canada. They were quickly approved for visas and a government sponsorship. After three months at Cherating they were transported, with others who had been approved, to a transit camp in a suburb of the Malaysian capital of Kuala Lumpur.

Their new camp was on the football field belonging to the Convent of the Holy Infant Jesus. The mother superior, Sister Monica, worked tirelessly to ensure that camp conditions were the best they could be. She made daily visits to refugees and met regularly with immigration officers, arranging a daily supply of cold beer.

Trinh and her family were processed, assigned numbers, and then shown the tent where they would stay awaiting a flight to Canada; no one knew for how long. Once again, days turned to weeks, and then to months.

Ron Atkey said in September that the government expected eighteen thousand sponsorship applications.[31] Groups such as the YMCA, churches, and faith-based or grassroots community organizations, or groups of five or more citizens, could apply to become private refugee sponsors. Sponsors could ask for specific people—individual refugees or families. They had to commit for a year to help with such things as finding clothing, housing, language lessons, schools, and jobs, and learning how to open a bank account, use public transportation, and fill out tax and other government forms.

The first group to apply to become a sponsor was the Mennonite Central Committee. It negotiated an eleven-page Master Agreement, whereby it would support refugees and the government would pay for language lessons. The Mennonites' March 1979 agreement became a model for others and inspired more faith-based groups to come forward. The Presbyterian Church signed a similar agreement four days later, the Christian Reformed Churches of Canada in April, and then, in May, the Canadian Lutheran World Relief Organization. In July, the Canadian Jewish Congress met in Montreal and pledged to sponsor a thousand refugees by providing help and encouragement to individual Jewish groups and synagogues.

A number of ethnic-based organizations also answered the call. Perhaps not surprisingly, Chinese organizations were among the first. On July 15, 1979, Vancouver's Chinese Canadians Mutual Advancement

(CCMA), in coordination with the New York Chinese community, held rallies to generate support for refugees. In Vancouver a number of politicians spoke, and representatives from thirty other ethnic-based organizations were introduced. The rally's slogan was "No More Genocide." The CCMA, and other Chinese-Canadian organizations under its umbrella, lobbied the government to increase the refugee quota while they raised money and helped with settlement.

Established political groups such as the Voice of Women also played significant roles in organizing communities to sponsor refugees. Other groups were created specifically to meet the crisis. Among the first and most influential was the Toronto-based Operation Lifeline, which was established in June 1979 at a meeting in the living room of York University professor Howard Adelman. It grew with lightning speed, raising money and awareness. Its success led to the creation of chapters in sixty-two Ontario communities and similar groups in other provinces. Many circles of friends and neighbours who chose to sponsor a refugee or refugee family did so by linking with churches or one of these community-based organizations.

The mayors of several cities, including Vancouver, Winnipeg, and Windsor, also led calls to action. Many set up committees to promote private sponsorship. Ottawa's charismatic activist mayor Marion Dewar, for instance, organized Project 4000 to sponsor four thousand refugees. At the Lansdowne Park rally to launch the project, organizers put out six hundred chairs and three thousand people showed up.[32]

Within four months, 21,000 churches, organizations, and citizens' groups had exceeded Atkey's call for 18,000 sponsors. By the end of 1979 there were 35,000. But success created a problem. Atkey's promise that the government would match private sponsorships one-to-one would now mean increasing Canada's intake to over 70,000. After consulting with his provincial counterparts, Atkey knew difficulties would arise if the originally stated figure of 50,000 was surpassed. To boost the overall quota would also be fiscally untenable—money was already being shifted from other departments to meet the rising costs of the program. Also, many Canadians thought the number of refugees being brought to Canada was already too high.[33] It was decided that sponsors could take on more refugees and the government would take on fewer, thereby keeping the total at 50,000. The money saved would be diverted to other refugee needs.

After three months in the transit camp, the Trinh family's turn finally came. The immigration officer was soft-spoken, polite, and efficient, in keeping with the modus operandi of the department. As Molloy put it: "We had the ability to focus on a group of people that just needed to be moved and resettled. We also had the power to cut the crap—to cut through the red tape. . . . The procedures were new, and we realized that if we don't keep them simple, if we don't keep the paperwork to a minimum—both for the sponsors and particularly for the officers out there doing the work—we're going to drown and they're going to drown."[34]

By the time Trinh and her family met with the transit camp immigration officer, the paperwork approving each refugee had been simplified to a single form that also served as a visa. Each officer knew the number of seats on a particular plane for an upcoming departure day and reserved each one with a refugee linked to a Canadian sponsor. They couldn't overbook but also wanted no plane to leave with even a single seat empty. Air Canada, Wardair, and other Canadian airlines coordinated with the Canadian Employment and Immigration Commission to schedule flights. No one flew free. Interest-free loans were extended to refugees for travel: $750 per adult, $375 per child, and $75 per infant. Costs above those amounts were covered by the commission.

Before being cleared to fly, all refugees had to undergo medical examinations. Camp conditions were such that even people who arrived healthy often became sick, so that 20 percent usually had trouble passing exams.[35] There were not enough doctors to do the examinations or technicians to do x-rays and blood and urine tests. Not until 1981 were

mobile medical facilities arranged for most camps. Local bureaucra-
cies made medical tests more difficult than necessary. Malaysia, for
instance, insisted that only Malaysian doctors do all the tests, but could
not provide enough doctors. Rules were often ignored; Norwegian
doctors did many of the examinations in Malaysian refugee camps.

The RCMP reviewed every approved refugee to determine security
risks. Very few were declined. The Trinh family, having passed their
medical exams and review, were given the final stamp of approval.
They were heading home to a home they'd never seen before.

HOME

The morning of departure was a typical hurry-up-and-wait affair, but
they didn't mind. Buses transported the lucky ones to the airport,
where they filled every seat of the Air Canada plane. A spontaneous
cheer arose as they left the ground. The passengers enjoyed an over-
night stay in Hong Kong; having spent six months in refugee camps,
they found the airport hotel's clean sheets, comfortable beds, and
warm showers lavishly exquisite. The next day there was another cheer
as the plane set down in Vancouver and Canada's distinctive flag was
seen catching a warm July breeze.

The next leg of the flight took them to Canadian Forces Base Griesbach
in Edmonton. It and Montreal's Canadian Forces Base at Longue-Pointe
acted as refugee reception centres. Renovated barracks housed the
newcomers for a few days as final arrangements were made to connect
them with their sponsors. Refugees got a first taste of Canadian donuts
and hamburgers. Among the clothing the Trinh family received was a
Montreal Canadiens jersey. They knew nothing about hockey and Sam
guessed that the bold CH stood for Canada Home.

Finally, the family touched down in Lethbridge. Canadian officials
all along the line had clearly done their jobs; a gentleman from the local

Canada Manpower office picked them up at the airport and drove them to the Chinese Alliance Church on 6th Avenue South. When the car stopped and they saw Sam's sister Jenny, they rejoiced in an emotional reunion.

As a government-sponsored refugee family, and with Jenny and the church helping, everything was prepared. Their small, sparsely furnished two-bedroom apartment had food on the shelves and in the old refrigerator, and clothes hung in the closets. An information packet contained a city map, bus routes, the location of stores, laundromats, parks, schools, and more. It was all exciting and new—and a little overwhelming.

The Trinh family was among 1,281 Indochinese refugees who came to Canada in July 1979.[36] They were settled in provinces according to population and wealth, with Ontario taking the most, then Quebec, and then Alberta. Fifteen percent were children under five and 25 percent were between six and seventeen. Only 2 percent were older than sixty.[37] Most arrived healthy and ready to adjust to new lives. Some, however, needed medical attention. By the end of 1980, 224 were diagnosed with TB or other disabling diseases, and the federal government coordinated with sponsors and provincial governments to offer necessary help.

Unaccompanied minors were another group in need of special assistance. Many Indochinese parents had only enough money for one or two in their family to escape, and so had to make the heartbreaking decision to save their children by sending them away. While conditions for all were deplorable, children under the age of eighteen who were not tucked beneath the protective wings of responsible, compassionate adults suffered a special brand of hell. They were often underfed, ill, poorly clothed, and riddled with lice. Many were rejected by families doing all they could to cope with their own children. Physical and sexual abuse were common.

Immigration officers suspected that some unaccompanied minors were being sent ahead as "anchor children" who, once in Canada, could bring the rest of their family to safety. It was hard to determine whether children were telling the truth about being under eighteen and whether documentation, if available at all, was authentic. Canadian officers did their best and followed their hearts as well as the rules. Even if some mistakes were made, they decided, saving children was a worthwhile endeavour.[38] Between 1975 and 1991, about sixty thousand unaccompanied minors fled Cambodia, Laos, and Vietnam.[39]

In 1979 a Montreal group called Families for Children led the effort to find adoptive families. The Unaccompanied Minors Program was created, whereby adopting groups worked through a cooperative effort between the provinces and federal government to match children with families. Ontario, British Columbia, Newfoundland, Quebec, and Alberta established programs that by the summer of 1981 arranged adoptions for 418 unaccompanied minors.[40] More than 50 percent went to Quebec.[41]

One of the primary obstacles to adjusting to Canadian life was language. Only 12 percent of second-wave Indochinese refugees could speak English or French. Language classes were set up and funded by federal and provincial governments. Many operated as night schools so that refugees could attend school or work during the day and attend classes in the evenings. Rebecca took night classes and learned slowly. She was surprised and pleased by how quickly Judy picked up the language, and little Helen's first words were in English. Judy began kindergarten only two months after arriving in Lethbridge and had very few problems communicating with classmates.

Refugees who needed language classes risked having federal support cut off if they didn't attend, but truancy was rare. Because Asian languages are so unlike English and French, with their different alphabets, phrasing, and cultural assumptions, language acquisition was often difficult. In 1981 only 16 percent of refugees were fluent in English or French, but by 1983 that percentage had risen to 25. By 1991 all could at least get by, with 91 percent considered fluent.[42]

Another key to adjustment was employment. Sam immediately found work as an interpreter at the courthouse and for several social agencies, translating Cantonese, Mandarin, and Vietnamese to English. Having learned that there was good money to be made as a trades-man, he moonlighted as a carpenter while also taking evening classes in welding. His hard work and natural skills allowed him to make a respectable living as a welder, a job offering the important bonus of a pension and health benefits. Rebecca, meanwhile, put aside her college degree and skills as an accountant and writer and took work as a dish-washer at the Peking Garden restaurant. When her English improved, she became a waitress. After only three years of hard work and scrimp-ing, they had saved enough to purchase a house.

Like the vast majority of Indochinese refugees, the Trinhs were doing everything right. But for many Canadians, it was not enough.

BACKLASH

After months of media coverage telling stories of courage and heart-break, and stressing the need for humanitarian compassion for those in dire need, a national poll published in August 1979 indicated that only 38 percent of Canadians agreed that accepting fifty thousand refu-gees was a good idea. The majority believed the number was too high or felt none should be brought to Canada at all.[43]

Those opposing the refugee program found a lot of support. A December 1978 article in the *Regina Leader-Post* stated: "Modern peoples are not prepared to see their national characters altered through the presence of large, destabilizing ethnic groups different in background from themselves."[44] In June 1979, thirty prominent Quebecers signed a letter that appeared as a full-page ad in the English-language *Montreal Star* demanding that arrivals of Vietnamese boat people be curtailed.[45] Newspapers across the country printed scathing letters to the editor complaining about refugees, arguing they should not have been allowed into the country, and demanding that the door be slammed shut to keep out more. A May 1980 national poll found that two-thirds of respondents held negative views about incoming refugees.[46]

Influential Toronto radio host and television personality Gordon Sinclair was a vocal opponent of accepting Indochinese refugees. On one of many programs dedicated to the issue, he stated in July 1979 that Indochinese refugees would be as dependent on Canadian social programs ten years down the road as they were at that moment.[47] Future statisticians would prove him wrong, but at the time his views found a receptive audience.

Beginning in August 1979, a group called the National Citizens Coalition (NCC) placed a series of ads in prominent newspapers, predicting that each Indochinese refugee would soon sponsor fifteen relatives so that the government was really greenlighting an influx of 750,000 people. In fact, statistics showed that most immigrants and refugees from the 1960s onward sponsored the arrival of fewer than one family member.[48]

Other NCC ads betrayed the fact that their opposition was based less on fact than on racist attitudes. Before 1961, 90 percent of immigrants and refugees had been white, Christian, and European, and only 3 percent were Asian. By the early 1980s, mostly due to the Vietnam War's aftermath, half were Asian.[49] The NCC mentioned this racial shift, while claiming that the large numbers of Black and Asian people coming to Canada reduced the number of white Europeans who could be admitted.

The assertion was misleading, ignoring as it did that the number of Europeans seeking emigration to Canada had been declining for more than a decade. Plus, those shouting the loudest failed to recall or refused to acknowledge, the difference between the types of new Canadians: immigrants are brought in primarily to help the country, but refugees are welcomed to help them. The Indochinese refugees did not jump a queue—they were in a separate queue altogether.

Not all who opposed the presence of the refugees were racist, but all racists opposed the presence of the refugees. Rebecca and Sam both learned to turn away and pretend not to notice the looks and unkind words directed toward them and their children. When Judy was in grade two, she accidently rode her bike onto a man's lawn, and he yelled at her, calling her a *gook*. She was harassed by strangers and called a *slant*. Only later, when watching the Vietnam War movie *Platoon*, did she understand the hatred underlying the epithets and feel embarrassed rage. Twenty-five percent of Indochinese refugees reported experiencing some type of racial discrimination, whether it involved being turned down for a job or an apartment or being verbally assaulted. The actual numbers were probably much higher.[50]

Some of the criticism of the Indochinese refugee program involved legitimate concerns about Canada's capacity to absorb so many newcomers. Critics questioned the additional costs to federal and provincial social services. It was pointed out that increases in budgets meant increases in deficits and debt, and passing costs to future generations.

The program's price was indeed high. The federal government spent $120 million for immigration officers to go abroad to select refugees, and then for settlement assistance. Provincial governments paid another $50 million, and private organizations spent an additional $40 million. It was estimated, however, that if refugees worked and paid taxes, the investment would be repaid in about two years.[51] The national conversation broke down to fears versus facts.

The Clark minority government fell after only nine months, and Canadians were plunged into a winter election. Despite the media attention and growing backlash, the Indochinese refugee program played no substantive role in the campaign. In February 1980, the Trudeau Liberals were back in office.

The new minister of employment and immigration, Lloyd Axworthy, was told by department officials that over 100,000 refugees were in

Southeast Asia awaiting resettlement, that the applications for private sponsorships were still pouring in, and that Quebec was upset at having received only 3,200 of the 10,000 refugees it had been promised. Despite these facts, polls indicated that most Canadians did not want more Asian refugees.[52] With Trudeau's support, Axworthy demonstrated the same political courage as his predecessors and announced the allocation of more money to settlement services. By the end of 1980 Canada would welcome not 50,000 but 60,000 Indochinese refugees.

They continued to come to Canada, although in decreasing numbers, throughout the 1980s. By the time the political and economic situations in Cambodia, Laos, and Vietnam had stabilized and the camps began closing in the 1990s, over 2.5 million refugees had found new homes in over twenty countries. In terms of refugees per capita, Canada accepted more than any other country. The new Canadians found homes from coast to coast: 38% in Ontario, 24% in the Prairies, 22% in Quebec, 11% in British Columbia, and 5% in the Maritimes.[53]

The UNHCR Nansen Refugee Award was established in 1954 and is bestowed each year to the group or person who provides outstanding service to the cause of refugees or stateless, displaced persons. In 1986 Canada received the prestigious award. It was the first time it had been given to a country.

ADJUSTMENT

Numerous longitudinal studies have demonstrated that refugees acclimatize quite well to Canada. They find work and contribute in business, finance, sports, arts, and politics. After a few years of adjustment, they use fewer support services than native-born Canadians. However, it is also clear that many of the Indochinese newcomers demonstrated the same PTSD symptoms as soldiers returning from war, due to the events that drove them from their homes, their journey, the camps, and then the shock of acculturation.[54] Like most vets, nearly all Indochinese refugees suffered in silence. Adults who didn't experience PTSD still carried burdens of their own: the guilt of having left others behind, the pressures of straddling two cultures, and the generational stresses caused by children learning a new language and adopting Canadian ways more quickly than them.[55]

It was not easy, but Trinh and her family adjusted quickly and well. While dealing with the same trials as other refugees, they also faced the same challenges as all other Canadians in raising kids, making a living, and running a household. In 1982, a year after they purchased their house, their son, Abraham (Wing-Xian), was born. Rebecca had left waitressing to work for more money with better hours at a manufacturing plant, but after her sixteen weeks of maternity leave, given the economic downturn that was throwing millions out of work across the country, the plant was unable to keep her on. Another setback came when it was time to renegotiate their mortgage. Interest rates had rocketed to over 19 percent, and they had to deal with a dramatic increase in their monthly payments. As with other Canadians facing the turbulence of an unstable economy, they cut back and hung on.

When Trinh and her family arrived, they were helped greatly by the already established Vietnamese community. It was reassuring to speak with others in their own language and about similar experiences. To varying degrees, all Indochinese refugees participated in cultural associations, while at the same time interacting with Canadian culture at work, at play, while shopping, and elsewhere.[56] Slowly, and without noticing, they became transnational. That is, they maintained cultural ties to their homeland through food, language, songs, and holidays, while adopting other traditions that typified Canada's diverse culture.

As happened with every large infusion of people, whether Irish in the 1830s, Ukrainians in the 1890s, or Europeans in the late 1940s, the entry of so many Indochinese refugees changed Canada's demography and its national conversation. Even more than the influx of American

war resisters in the 1960s, the next waves of Vietnam War refugees—
the Indochinese—coloured that conversation by pitting those who celebrated diversity against those who yearned for a less welcoming time.

In 1947 Prime Minister William Lyon Mackenzie King said, "The
people of Canada do not wish, as a result of mass immigration, to make
a fundamental alteration in the character of our population. . . . Any
considerable Oriental immigration would . . . be certain to give rise to
social and economic problems."[57] King's assertion reflected the consensus of his day and informed years of immigration laws and refugee
decisions. Changes to immigration laws and regulations beginning in
the 1960s and 1970s moved the country past the King model, but the
backlash against the Indochinese refugees indicated that many
Canadians still held firm to old beliefs. However, in cooperating to
accept the Indochinese refugees, thousands of Canadians promoted
the idea that community reaches beyond race and nationality and that,
in the final analysis, we are all human. The echo of the Vietnam War
had inspired and changed not all but enough Canadians to establish a
new national consensus. Revolutions never happen when times are
good. Ramparts are never breached by a majority.

Without trying, Indochinese refugees, along with American war
resisters, forced a consideration of the notion that compassion can
trump fear and politicians can demonstrate courageous leadership
that is worthy of those they represent. If nothing else, it was shown that
Canada is worthy of people like Rebecca Trinh.

CONCLUSION

THE WHISTLING DOG

A man once told a friend he had taught his dog to whistle. "Wow," said his buddy, "let's hear a tune." But our guy replied: "Sorry, he can't whistle a note. I said I taught him; I didn't say he learned anything." Lessons are like that. But worse than learning nothing is learning the wrong thing. As the nineteenth-century French diplomat and historian Alexis de Tocqueville once counselled, "Misapplied lessons of history may be more dangerous than ignorance of the past."[1] Our tuneless dog and French warning are reminders that we are still arguing about the lessons of the Vietnam War.

In the United States, many vets who fought the war, and the brass who led it, agreed with the lessons drawn by President Reagan's secretary of defense Caspar Weinberger. In a November 1984 speech that laid out what became the Weinberger Doctrine, he argued that the United States should never fight a war unless its vital interests are at stake. It should never again creep into war but strike with overwhelming force, with clearly stated objectives, and then only with the backing of Congress and the people. The military must be allowed to do what it takes to win.[2]

Lieutenant General Phillip B. Davidson, who served as chief military intelligence officer in Vietnam, was among those who contended that another of Vietnam's lessons was that the media turned Americans against the war and must not be allowed to do that again.[3] Media access, he asserted, needed to be curtailed and controlled through pool reporting or by embedding journalists with handpicked units.

For his part, scholar, U.S. Army general, and CIA director David Petraeus determined that the Vietnam War offered three lessons: the American people will not support a protracted war; civilian leaders will make decisions based on more than just objective battlefield conditions; and some problems cannot be solved through military means.[4]

Clearly, the lessons gleaned did not suggest that America should no longer wreak havoc on innocent civilians by involving itself in civil wars for imperialist or geopolitical reasons. Rather, they offered ways to win those wars despite the presence of what was called the Vietnam syndrome—a faintheartedness restraining leaders and the people from wanting to fight.

In 1991 all of Vietnam's lessons were expertly applied in the quick and decisive Gulf War victory. With triumphant troops heading home, President George H.W. Bush euphorically told a group of congressmen: "The specter of Vietnam has been buried forever in the desert sands of the Arabian Peninsula. . . . By God, we've kicked the Vietnam syndrome once and for all."[5] America was back to winning wars again with the help of old-fashioned media complicity and public enthusiasm. It was as if Vietnam had never happened. However, with his attacks on Afghanistan following 9/11, the second president Bush forgot every Vietnam lesson and repeated every Vietnam mistake. A not-so-funny joke has it that the Russian word for *Afghanistan* is *Vietnam*.

For Canadians, the Vietnam War's first lesson was about their national soul. Canadian journalist and author Peter C. Newman wrote in 1972, "It's one of the more curious ironies of our history that it was the Vietnamization of the United States that finally brought about the Canadianization of Canada."[6] Along with assassinations and race riots, the war suggested that the United States might not have been the aspirational example it believed itself to be. For a good many Canadians, it had become a negative model, reeking of violence, amorality, and arrogance.[7] The presence of war resisters, the anti-war protests, and the relentless brutality at home and abroad, all viewed on the nightly news, seemed to hammer the point home. It became more acceptable, and for some even fashionable, to be openly anti-American just as a new Canadian civic nationalism was emerging in the glow of the 1967 centennial year.

The new nationalism did not resonate with Indigenous nations and Quebec sovereigntists, but it became a powerful force in English Canada. It lay in the imagery, metaphors, and symbols that informed the burgeoning of writing by and for Canadians. George Ryga, Margaret Atwood, Al Purdy, Margaret Laurence, George Grant, and others drew from anti-war sentiments and the antipathy to Canada's involvement in the war. Their stories informed Canada's national story by giving voice to the anti-American sentiments lurking beneath pro-Canadian sensibilities. Canadian songwriters weighed in as well. With reference to the 1970 Kent State killings, Neil Young's "Ohio" spoke of "tin soldiers and Nixon coming," while the Guess Who's "American Woman" dismissed a need for "ghetto scenes" and "war machines."

Canadian political scientist Gad Horowitz observed in 1967 that "Canadian nationalism . . . leads away from Vietnam."[8] Forty-five years later, historian Stephen Azzi agreed, noting: "The most important factor in spurring nationalism in English Canada was the American War in Vietnam, which one activist described as 'the backdrop against which everything else happened.'"[9] Writing in 2017, University of Toronto's Robert McGill argued: "Even today, ideas about what being Canadian means, or should mean, show the Vietnam War's influence. . . . The relationship between the war and Canadian writing is extraordinary."[10]

As Canadian songs and literature and the new civic nationalism evolved together, harsh anti-Americanism slowly receded, allowing pro-Canadian feelings to stand on their own. But the war was still there. It figured heavily in Johanna Skibsrud's Giller Prize–winning novel *The Sentimentalists*, published in 2009, and Kim Thúy's *Ru*, first published in 2009 in Quebec and whose translation went on to win CBC's Canada Reads. The images and metaphors have become a little gentler, a little more understanding, and more forgiving of the lies and mistakes of the past.

Vietnam still hums in the background as an example of what can go wrong and be made right as Canadians have learned to take pride in their unique culture while still enjoying America's. The more mature civic nationalism allows that societal problems can be addressed in a Canadian way without the poison of tribal politics, gun culture, and religious chauvinism. Canadian civic nationalism is based on decisions, not blood. It rests not on rejecting or merely tolerating diversity, but on encouraging and accepting it. As noted by historian Robert Bothwell, the border can still offer "psychological reassurance" while allowing a celebration of differences with an acknowledgement of similarities.[11]

The war's second lesson was about Canadian power. During the war, Canadian diplomats and political leaders acted as if Canada was still in its Golden Age of diplomacy: a helpful fixer, punching above its weight and influencing big-power decisions, or at least, as Pearson said, helping shape the environment in which they were made. The Vietnam War taught Canadians that without real power, hard work and good intentions don't matter.

Political philosopher Charles Taylor argued: "Our Vietnam record [shows that] on any issue which the United States regards as vital to its own interests, Canada has scarcely more clout than Luxembourg or Afghanistan."[12] Political scientist Joel Solosky put it even more bluntly: "How Canadians operated in the context of the ICC and ICCS, what messages Canadians conveyed in secret to their American counterparts, and how carefully Ottawa crafted statements about the war had absolutely no bearing on American decision-making with regard to Vietnam."[13]

Vietnam buried what remained of Canada's Golden Age. It forced the white, Oxford-educated, Protestant, Laurentian elite who had ruled

Canadian diplomacy from the mid-1940s, with Pearson as their hero, to accept a new reality: leaders and diplomats must have more limited goals based on more realistic assessments of Canada's power. Within that lesson was that Canadians would no longer simply shut up and blindly trust the diplomats and politicians to lead as they had in the past.[14] As Bothwell notes of the Vietnam era: "Diplomats recall the period with a shudder, remembering when diplomacy came up against public opinion and lost."[15]

Related to that lesson was that, while the best diplomacy is quiet, quiet diplomacy sometimes does a disservice to Canada and Canadians. Pearson and Trudeau demonstrated that a government appears to be either deaf to citizens' opinions or possibly even betraying them if it refuses to speak out in support of Canadian interests and values and against the actions or pronouncements of those who contradict them. The few times when Canadian leaders did speak out demonstrated that to publicly criticize American policies that run counter to Canadian interests or values is more than good leadership; it is good politics. It also precipitates no significant repercussions from Washington.

The internalization of these lessons was revealed in 2003 when the Bush administration, Canadian media, business leaders, and opposition leader Stephen Harper all urged Prime Minister Jean Chrétien to join America's coalition of the willing and send troops to Iraq. Instead, on February 13, he declared to the Chicago Council on Foreign Relations: "Great strength is not always perceived by others as benign. Not everyone around the world is willing to take the word of the United States on faith."[16] It was a much bolder statement than the one Pearson offered in Philadelphia in 1965, which led to his presidential tongue-lashing from Lyndon Johnson. But this time there was both public and private silence from the White House.

Citizens had learned something too. Vietnam taught them not just to trust less but also to protest sooner. On February 15, 2003, unconvinced by Bush's talk of weapons of mass destruction, anti-war protesters rocked cities around the world. In Canada many of those who had marched against the Vietnam War in the 1960s were on the streets again, but this time with their children and grandchildren. Forty-five Canadian cities saw marches, with 5,000 protesters in Toronto, 10,000 in Vancouver, and 150,000 braving the frigid cold in Montreal.[17] The politically savvy Chrétien could not ignore so many voices on the street, especially in Montreal, with a Quebec election coming in April.

On March 17 Chrétien stood in the House of Commons and declared that, like the United Nations Security Council, Canada was unconvinced by the evidence Americans were presenting as a justification for war. Canada would not fight. Then, just as Johnson did nothing when Pearson refused to send troops to Vietnam and Nixon did nothing when Trudeau passed his anti-bombing resolution, repercussions were minimal. The American ambassador made a few harsh comments, Canadian diplomats were shut out of a few meetings—but otherwise, Washington was silent.

Polls indicated that 71 percent of Canadians backed Chrétien's decision.[18] His communications director, Peter Donolo, called it the Chrétien Doctrine: "Every subsequent prime minister can rely on that doctrine with the confidence that Canada could take a path that was independent of the economic giant to our south without fear of reprisal."[19] Vietnam had taught and Iraq had reminded Canadians that it was all right to speak up and stand alone because Canada was big enough to be independent and small enough to be ignored.

Another of the war's lessons was economic. Vietnam taught Canadians about the hypocrisy of working for peace while profiting from war. As Vietnam-era diplomat John Holmes observed, "You hang on to your principles but find a way around it."[20] In November 2017 the Standing Committee on Foreign Affairs and International Development was considering changes to laws regulating arms production and sales to foreign customers. Christyn Cianfarani, president and CEO of the Canadian Association of Defence and Security Industries, appeared before the committee and stated that she represented 800 Canadian defence and security companies that generated $10 billion in annual revenues and employed 63,000 Canadians who earned wages 60 percent higher than average manufacturing wages.[21] Her point was the same and as clear as Jean Marchand's in his argument with Claire Culhane on Parliament Hill a generation before: jobs matter.

The committee ended up recommending no changes that would threaten Cianfarani's impressive numbers. In 2017 Canada exported $1.03 billion in arms, with the United States its best customer. Second was Saudi Arabia, which had just been tagged by Amnesty International for violating human rights at home and in its dirty war in Yemen.[22] Perhaps Vietnam's economic lesson was that money does more than talk, it swears.

Vietnam also taught Canadians about their hearts. In 2015, after years of civil war complicated by big-power involvement, Syria was a smoking ruin. As in Indochina forty years earlier, thousands of Syrian people had no choice but to escape. It was their turn to endure the inhumanity of boats, pirates, and refugee camps. Canadian prime minister Stephen Harper agreed to accept ten thousand Syrian refugees over the upcoming three years. There was an outcry among Canadians—including Joe Clark, who had been prime minister during a critical phase in the Indochinese refugee rescue effort—demanding that more be done. Ron Atkey, Clark's immigration minister, made specific recommendations regarding how it could be done.[23]

Liberal leader Justin Trudeau pledged during the 2015 federal election campaign that his government would welcome 25,000 Syrian refugees. Once in office, Trudeau's immigration minister John McCallum used the Vietnam-era model to employ the combination of government and private sponsorships that had worked so well in the 1970s and 1980s. Again, people and groups seeking to be sponsors overwhelmed the government. Canada's sponsorship system became the envy of the world. McCallum worked with the United Nations High Commissioner on Refugees (UNHCR) and influential billionaire George Soros's Open Society Foundation to help other countries adopt the Canadian system.

In 1977 61 percent of Canadians said Canada was accepting too many immigrants and refugees, but in 2015 that number had shrunk to 38 percent.[24] The Indochinese experience had proven that Canada had the absorptive capacity to accept a large number of refugees. The Syrian refugees reminded Canadians of another of Vietnam's lessons: resistance to refugees rested largely upon the contradictory fears that "others" are dangerous either because they might not blend in to Canada's culture or because they might blend in too well and thereby change the culture. But the forty-year trend was clear. The still significant minority driven by fear was being overtaken by those moved by love and the belief that Canada's evolving story should rest upon compassion and include many voices. Among the Canadians who sponsored Syrian refugee families were Helen Trinh in Calgary and Judy Trinh in Ottawa.

The Vietnam War is still playing a part in the writing of national stories, for it is still affecting people's lives. When the Americans finally quit the war and went home, they left behind approximately three million land mines, cluster bombs, and unexploded ordinance. Over the next forty years, the orphaned weapons killed over forty thousand people and injured over sixty thousand. Every month, children die while innocently playing in fields and yards.[25]

In Quang Tri province, north of Hue, 80 percent of the once fertile land remains unusable due to the long-term effects of Agent Orange. Meanwhile, the Agent Orange used during the war is responsible for the birth every year of thousands of babies with horribly disfiguring birth defects.[26]

It took until November 2013 for Veterans Affairs Canada to issue a policy stating that it "accepts that Veterans who served in Vietnam between January 9, 1962 and May 7, 1975 were exposed to Agent Orange.

A disability claim will be paid if the applicant proves that he or she has an illness directly associated with exposure."[27]

Agent Orange was not banned by the Canadian government until 1985. Nearly twenty years later, it was revealed that Ontario's Ministry of Natural Resources had used Agent Orange to clear "weed trees" from twenty thousand acres of Crown land in Northern Ontario, where, throughout the 1960s and 1970s, it was sprayed over forest rangers and junior rangers.[28] In 2013 an Ontario government investigation reported on the liberal use of Agent Orange, apologized, and promised to compensate those suffering long-term effects.[29] The people of Elmira, where Uniroyal made the stuff for Vietnam and then continued to produce it for domestic use, are still waiting for fair compensation for the damage done to them and their community.

Meanwhile, Basil McAllister was among those who lived in New Brunswick in the 1960s and saw American war planes dropping the mist that covered people's houses, fields, crops, and gardens. He fought for years to obtain compensation for the cancer he claimed to have contracted due to exposure. In December 2010, the Canadian government issued over three thousand tax-free $20,000 compensation payments to those who lived near the Gagetown base at the time of the American testing if they were diagnosed with one of twelve related diseases. In June 2013, a federal court decided that McAllister had indeed proven that the prostate cancer that had metastasized to his bones was a direct result of his exposure. In November 2017, Canada's Veterans Review and Appeal Board officially admitted what had been done illegally decades before.[30] Unfortunately, McAllister died the year before and didn't get to witness the final vindication.

The State Department's George Ball was among the few Kennedy and Johnson advisors who consistently advocated pulling out of Vietnam. He later wrote that among the problems faced in the war was that "South Vietnam was never a nation but an improvisation—a geographical designation."[31] Ball was right. But he could have said the same thing about the United States or Canada. Every country is an imagined community resting primarily upon the stories its people agree to believe.

The Vietnam War changed the United States and Canada by changing their stories. The war was so tragic, revealed so many lies, touched so many lives, challenged and changed so many assumptions, and offered so many contradictory lessons that arguments about the war will never be resolved. The dog may never whistle. And so, the lies and lessons of the Vietnam War will forever colour our national story. They will be among the sparks igniting our perpetual desire to more clearly understand who we are and to somehow, hopefully with grace, make ourselves a little better tomorrow than we are today.

POSTSCRIPT: OUR GUIDES

Not long after his return from Vietnam, Sherwood Lett was appointed chief justice of the Supreme Court of British Columbia. He earned a reputation for being quick and fair while adjudicating on a wide range of cases. In July 1963 Lett was appointed chief justice of the Court of Appeal, the province's most important judicial office. Every Christmas he received cards from Ho Chi Minh and General Giap.

In January 1964 Lett was with other justices observing the opening of a new session of the B.C. legislature when he felt ill but quietly suffered through his pain and nausea, not wanting to interrupt the ceremony. Doctors determined he had suffered a heart attack; subsequently, they found he had cancer. He died at his home in July. All of the province's public buildings lowered their flags to half-staff. His funeral was attended by 1,800 people, and tributes came from across the country. Lester Pearson wrote, "I know of no Canadian who has served his country in war and peace with greater distinction and more unselfishly."[32]

Blair Seaborn returned to Ottawa and continued his storied career in public service. He was the assistant deputy minister of consumer and corporate affairs from 1970 to 1974 and then deputy minister of Environment Canada from 1975 to 1982. From 1982 to 1985 he was the Canadian chairman of the International Joint Commission, and led the negotiation of tricky bilateral agreements. He was Prime Minister Brian Mulroney's intelligence and security co-ordinator at the Privy Council Office. After his retirement, he served eight years as chairman of the Environmental Assessment Panel, Nuclear Fuel Waste. In 2001, to commemorate forty years of public service, Seaborn was made a Member of the Order of Canada.

In February 2003, Seaborn was interviewed on CBC Radio about his secret missions to Hanoi. He sounded somewhat annoyed when asked if he'd acted as an American spy. He explained: "We have to get our definitions straight. I was doing what any diplomat would be asked to do. I was asked to say, what's the mood of the country . . . how are they feeling about the possibility of war . . . that's not espionage or spying. Spying involves using secret agents and taping messages, intercepting messages and that type of thing."[33] The question and curt response indicated that the controversy regarding his missions had not abated. Well into his nineties, Seaborn remained engaged in the Ottawa community. In September 2019 he reflected on his Vietnam mission and observed, "We knew the odds of obtaining a peaceful settlement were slim, but we had to try." He died just two months later, on November 11.

Nine months after the signing of the January 1973 Paris Peace Accords, Claire Culhane returned to Vietnam for a short visit. She was shocked by how four more years of war had destroyed the country and spiritually damaged its citizens. She spoke with many people she had worked with during her time at the hospital and found them rake-thin, morose, and broken.[34] Mortar and rocket-fire still echoed in the distance. Many of the people of Quang Ngai were reduced to eating tree bark.

Back home, Culhane became appalled at the conditions in British Columbia's prisons, especially the mistreatment of those in solitary confinement. She became one of Canada's premier advocates for prison reform, while also working on behalf of the wrongly convicted. By writing letters to editors, appearing on television, publishing a book, and lobbying wardens and politicians, she became instrumental in bringing about important reforms. She was made a Member of the Order of Canada in 1995. A year later the fearless fighter nicknamed the "One Woman Army" died peacefully in her sleep.

On his second day in office, in January 1977, President Jimmy Carter offered an unconditional amnesty to all draft dodgers living in Canada. Carter did not exonerate deserters. The American media rushed to border crossings to film the crowds streaming back home. They were disappointed. Certainly many did return, but most, like Joe Erickson, were already home.

Erickson has sold his horses but remains involved with the horse community, occasionally driving a team for school and community events. He is retired and living in Hastings, Ontario, where he regularly meets with friends to discuss politics, ethics, and morality. He helped organize a group called the Ibsen Obsession, which meets to read and discuss plays by the man called the "father of realism." He takes pride in the accomplishments of his son, Karl, now a professor of education at Michigan State. Erickson remains awed by the character and strength of the women who bore such enormous burdens in the Vietnam era and believes their stories are yet to be fully told. Meanwhile, he continues to enjoy classical music, occasionally at a volume that annoys the neighbours.

———

Doug Carey never expected to see his twenty-second birthday. He feels lucky to have met his wife, Patricia, and to have been granted the chance for them to raise their sons, Sean and Ryan, and daughter, Kathryn. All three were talented athletes and attended university. He was worried but proud when Ryan enlisted in the Canadian army and did a tour in Afghanistan. Carey is now retired and a doting grandfather to eight. He enjoys golf but finds that he can't stop his gaze from darting into the woods looking for danger or scanning the turf for booby traps. If anything, anywhere, looks out of place, he still feels a rush of adrenaline and can't help planning a response to an impending ambush.

Carey stays in touch with some Canadian vets and men with whom he served. Shortly after his return home from Vietnam, his Alpha Company platoon leader, Lieutenant Black, told him that someone had visited the mother of his good friend Ricky Lee Doye and told her that the NVA had thrown her son into a well and dropped a grenade on top of him. Carey found her address and wrote a letter to relieve her of the anguish of thinking her son had died that way. He told her the real story of the listening-post firefight and assured her that Ricky had died bravely, fighting hard, doing his duty. Every Christmas, a card arrives in Carleton Place from Mrs. Doye. When in 2019 it became time for Mrs. Doye to leave her home for a retirement residence, Carey flew to the United States to help, and spent a moment of reflection at his friend's grave.

When the 1980s recession hit the Trinh family, they left Lethbridge for Calgary. Rebecca became a financial planner and Sam a restaurant owner. Both are now happily retired. Judy, Helen, and Abraham all graduated from university and pursued ambitious careers. Judy is a broadcast journalist, Helen a pharmacist, and Abraham an engineer. All remain profoundly grateful for the chance Canada gave their family and consciously strive to give back.

When Judy wrote a brief story of her family's escape from Vietnam, it caught the attention of Historica Canada. The story became the basis for a Heritage Minute, one of the short films portraying pivotal moments in Canada's history. Many of the details were changed, but at its heart was the reminder of the Vietnam War's most fundamental lesson: that beyond the politics of power, horror of war, and superficiality of race and nationality lie our shared humanity and love for our children.

NOTES

INTRODUCTION

1. Brocheux, *Ho Chi Minh*, 17.
2. Lawrence, *Vietnam War*, 27.
3. Lawrence, 31.
4. Moss, *Vietnam*, 22.
5. Moss, 26.
6. John Prodos, "Assessing Dien Bien Phu," in Lawrence and Logevall, *First Vietnam War*, 218.
7. Lawrence, *Vietnam War*, 48.
8. Lawrence, 46.

CHAPTER ONE

1. Holmes, "Geneva 1954," 464.
2. Ray, "The Politics of Conference," 401.
3. Watt, "The Geneva Agreements," 11.
4. Holmes, "Geneva 1954," 467.
5. Pearson to St. Laurent, May 6, 1954, Pearson Papers, LAC, RG 25, 50273-40 (3).
6. House of Commons, *Debates*, May 28, 1954.
7. Eden, *Memoirs of Sir Anthony Eden*, 141.
8. Levant, *Quiet Complicity*, 113.
9. Paul Heinbecker, "On the World Stage: Projecting Our Values and Advancing Peace," in Joyal and Seidman, *Reflecting on Our Past*, 70.
10. Pearson, *Mike* Vol. 2, 35.
11. Pearson, 180.
12. Thakur, *Peacekeeping in Vietnam*, 4, 15.
13. Department of External Affairs, *External Affairs Bulletin*, July 1948, 7.

14. House of Commons, *Debates*, February 2, 1951.

15. Eayrs, *In Defence of Canada* Vol. 4, 150–53.

16. Holmes, "Geneva 1954," 472.

17. J.L. Granatstein, "Peacekeeping: Did Canada Make a Difference? And What Difference Did Peacekeeping Make in Canada?" in English and Hillmer, *Making a Difference?*, 226.

18. Cited in Eayrs, *In Defence of Canada* Vol. 5, 61.

19. Eayrs, 61.

20. Thakur, *Peacekeeping in Vietnam*, 48.

21. *The Pentagon Papers*, Gravel Edition, Vol. 1 (Boston: Beacon Press, 1971), 604.

22. Ross, *In the Interests of Peace*, 7–9.

23. Thakur, *Peacekeeping in Vietnam*, 53.

24. Herring, *America's Longest War*, 41.

25. Pearson to Lett, "Letter of Instruction," August 22, 1954, DEA Files, LAC, 4629/50052-A-40 (1).

26. Pearson to Lett, August 22, 1954.

27. Pearson to Lett, "Letter of Instruction," August 22, 1954.

28. Department of External Affairs, "Canadians in Indochina," *External Affairs* 7, no. 2 (February 1955): 34–37.

29. "Mission to Indochina Diary," October 15, 1954, Sherwood Lett Papers, LAC, Box 1, R 219.

30. "Mission to Indochina Diary," October 20, 1954, Sherwood Lett Papers, LAC, Box 1, R 219.

31. Hoang, "Early South Vietnamese Critique," 17–32.

32. Lett to SSEA, "Re: Future of the International Commission," no. 67, February 7, 1955, DEA Files, LAC, 50052-A-40, Vol. 10, 1.

33. Jacobs, *America's Miracle Man*, 12, 29.

34. Sheehan, *Bright Shining Lie*, 170.

35. Boot, *Road Not Taken*, 220, 225, 228.

36. Hansen, "Bắc Di Cư," 180.

37. Jacobs, *Cold War Mandarin*, 52.

38. Letter from Sherwood Lett to Evelyn Lett, October 15, 1954, cited in Roy, *Sherwood Lett*, 140.

39. Kahin and Lewis, *United States in Vietnam*, 74.

40. Ross, *In the Interests of Peace*, 89; Thakur, *Peacekeeping in Vietnam*, 63.

41. Brosnan, "International Control Commission," 52.

42. *First and Second Interim Reports of the International Commission for Supervision and Control in Vietnam, 11 August 1954–10 February 1955*, Cmd. 9461 (London: H.M. Stationery Office, 1955), 21.

43. Lett to SSEA, "Re: Elections," no. 183, December 2, 1954, DEA Files, LAC, 50052-A-40, Vol. 10, 1.
44. Roy, *Sherwood Lett*, 140.
45. SarDesai, *Indian Foreign Policy*, 87.
46. Lett to SSEA, "Re: Future of the International Commission," no. 67, February 7, 1955, DEA Files, LAC, 50052-A-40, Vol. 10, 6.
47. Levant, *Quiet Complicity*, 137.
48. Moise, "Land Reform," 78.
49. Roy, *Sherwood Lett*, 146.
50. Lett to SSEA, "Re: The International Commission and the Implementation of the Geneva Agreement," no. 110, October 10, 1954, 1955, DEA Files, LAC, 50052-A-40, Vol. 10, 1.
51. *Third Interim Report of the International Commission for Supervision and Control in Vietnam, 11 February to 10 April, 1955*, Cmd. 9499 (London: H.M. Stationery Office, 1955), 17.
52. Ross, *In the Interests of Peace*, 109.
53. Thayer, *War By Other Means*, 116–17.
54. *Toronto Star*, April 7, 1955.
55. *Globe and Mail*, April 21, 1955.
56. House of Commons, *Debates*, March 24, 1955.
57. "Radio Broadcast for Mr. Lett on the Record of the Indochina Commissions, April 5, 1955," Sherwood Lett Papers, LAC, Box 1, R 219.
58. Lett to SSEA, "Re: Elections," no. 156, March 18, 1955, DEA Files, LAC, 50052-A-40, Vol. 10, 6.
59. Lett to SSEA, "Re: Elections in Vietnam," no. 178, November 11, 1954, DEA Files, LAC, 50052-A-40, Vol. 10, 2.
60. Lett to SSEA, "Re: Elections," no. 156, March 18, 1955, DEA Files, LAC, 50052-A-40, Vol. 10, 6.
61. Lett to SSEA, "Re: Elections."
62. Lett to SSEA, "Re: Elections."
63. Ross, *In the Interests of Peace*, 146.
64. Lett to SSEA, "Re: Current Problems" No. 70, February 9, 1955: DEA Files, LAC, 50052-A-40, Vol. 10., 3.
65. Ross, *In the Interests of Peace*, 152.
66. Ross, 153.
67. Chapnik, *Canada's Voice*, 84.
68. Holmes, *Better Part of Valour*, 226.
69. Preston, "Balancing War and Peace," 79.

70. Eayrs, *In Defence of Canada* Vol. 5, 175.

71. Eayrs, 175.

72. Roy, *Sherwood Lett*, 154.

73. *Fourth Interim Report of the International Commission for Supervision and Control in Vietnam, 11 April to 10 August, 1955*, Cmd. 9654 (London: H.M. Stationery Office, 1955), 16.

74. Roy, *Sherwood Lett*, 155.

75. Ross, "Middlepowers," 187. For an alternative view, see Granatstein, "Canada and Peacekeeping," 14–19.

76. Lawrence, *Vietnam War*, 53.

77. *Fourth Interim Report of the ICSC*, Appendix IV, 30.

78. Roy, *Sherwood Lett*, 140.

CHAPTER TWO

1. John F. Kennedy, "The Terrain of Today's Statecraft," *Saturday Review*, August 1, 1959. See also Pearson, *Mike* Vol. 3, 100.

2. Martin, *Presidents and Prime Ministers*, 222.

3. Brosnan, "International Control Commission," 94.

4. Levant, *Quiet Complicity*, 106.

5. Holmes, *Better Part of Valour*, 226.

6. Bothwell, "Further Shore," 98.

7. Thakur, "Peacekeeping and Foreign Policy," 135.

8. "Trends in Canadian Foreign Policy," May 2, 1961, JFKLM, POF, Countries File: Canada–Kennedy Trip to Ottawa 5/61, Box 113, File 3.

9. Merchant to State Department, June 2, 1961, JFKLM, Kennedy Papers, NSF, Box 18. File: Canada.

10. *Globe and Mail*, February 16, 1966.

11. Maclear, *Vietnam*, 106.

12. Dallek, *An Unfinished Life*, 444.

13. McNamara, *In Retrospect*, 29.

14. Gareth Porter, "Coercive Diplomacy in Vietnam," 13.

15. Moise, "Mirage of Negotiations," 74.

16. Moise, 74.

17. Lerner, "Four Years and a World of Difference," 81.

18. Laurie and Vaart, *CIA and the Wars in Southeast Asia*, 8.

19. Preston, "Balancing War and Peace," 94.

20. Minutes of Rusk, SSEA Meeting, April 30, 1964, LAC, RG 25, Vol. 10113, File 20-22-Viet.S-2-1.

21. Minutes of Rusk, April 30, 1964.

22. J. Blair Seaborn, interview with author, August 30, 2019.

23. Taylor, *Snow Job*, 59.

24. Memorandum of Conversation, May 28, 1964, FRUS Files, Johnson Administration, 1964–1968, Vol. 1, 281–86.

25. Memcon, Washington to Ottawa, May 30, 1964, LAC, 1980-81/22, Box 50, File 20-22-Viet.S-2-1, 4.

26. Memcon, Washington to Ottawa, May 30, 1964, 4.

27. Record of Conversation, Visit of Messrs Sullivan and Cooper to the Department, June 3, 1964, LAC, RG 25, Vol. 10113, File 20-22-Viet.S-2-1.

28. Summary Record of Conversation, Sullivan and Martin, May 29, 1964, LAC, Record Group 25, Vol. 3092, No. 29-39-1-2-A, North Vietnam-USA Relations— Special Project (BACON).

29. J. Blair Seaborn, "Mission to Hanoi: The Canadian Channel, May 1964–November 1965," in Blanchette, *Canadian Peacekeepers in Indochina*, 87.

30. Summary Record of Conversation, Sullivan and Martin, May 29, 1964.

31. Logevall, *Choosing War*, 159–60.

32. Seaborn, "Mission to Hanoi," 86.

33. Roy, *Sherwood Lett*, 147.

34. Seaborn to Ottawa, June 22, 1964, LAC, RG 25, Vol. 10113, File 20-22-Viet.S-2-1.

35. Seaborn to Ottawa, June 22, 1964.

36. Logevall, *Choosing War*, 163.

37. Seaborn to Ottawa, June 22, 1964.

38. Seaborn to Ottawa, June 22, 1964.

39. Seaborn to Ottawa, June 22, 1964.

40. Seaborn to Ottawa, June 22, 1964.

41. "Report of the Liaison Team on Its Visit to the Canadian Delegations to the Commissions for International Supervision and Control in Indo-China," September 1964, LAC, RG 25, Vol. 10123, File 21-13-Viet-ICSC-4, 3.

42. Seaborn to Ottawa, June 22, 1964.

43. Seaborn to Ottawa, June 22, 1964.

44. Washington to Ottawa, June 24, 1964, LAC, RG 25, Vol. 10113, File 20-22-Viet.S-2-1.

45. Seaborn to Ottawa, June 22, 1964.

46. RG 25, Vol. 10113, File 28-29-Viet.S-2-1.

47. Seaborn to Ottawa, June 22, 1964.

48. Bothwell, "The Further Shore," 101.

49. Lyndon Johnson, Speech to the Nation, August 4, 1964, https://www.youtube.com/watch?v=3Sfj_7n6H4A (accessed September 4, 2018).

50. Telegram from the Department of State to the Embassy in Canada, Washington, August 8, 1964, 4:41 p.m., FRUS Files, Johnson Administration, 1964–1968, Vol. 1, Vietnam, 1964, Doc. 304.

51. Logevall, *Choosing War*, 210.

52. Logevall, 211.

53. Logevall, 211.

54. J. Blair Seaborn, interview with author, August 30, 2019.

55. Blair Seaborn to SSEA, Dispatch No. 332, September 1, 1964, LAC, RG 25, Vol. 8795, File 21-31-Viet-ICC-11.

56. Donaghy, *Grit*, 230.

57. Telegram-Y-830, "Visit to North Vietnam," from DEA Ottawa to the Canadian Embassy in Washington DC, November 20, 1964, LAC, RG 25, Vol. 10113, Red Registry, File 20-22-Viet.S-2-1.

58. Telegram-4313, "Seaborn's Visit to North Vietnam," from the Canadian Embassy in Washington DC to DEA Ottawa, December 12, 1964, LAC, RG 25, Vol. 10113, Red Registry, File 20-22-Viet.S-2-l.

59. Telegram-4313, December 12, 1964.

60. Lodge to Rusk, October 7, 1963, JFKLM, Box 204, NSF DF.

61. McNamara, *In Retrospect*, 106–07.

62. Message from the Ambassador in Vietnam (Lodge) to the President/1/Saigon, May 15, 1964, 4 p.m., /1/Source: Department of State, Central Files, JFKLM, POL 27 VIET S, Top Secret.

63. Memorandum from the Joint Chiefs of Staff to the Secretary of Defense (McNamara)/1/JCSM-426-64 Washington, May 19, 1964, /1/Source: Washington National Records Center, RG 300, OASD/ISA Files: FRC 69 A 926, 092 North Vietnam, Top Secret; Sensitive. A summary version is printed in *The Pentagon Papers*, Gravel Edition, Vol. 3 (Boston: Beacon Press, 1971), 511–12.

64. Draft Congressional Resolution Prepared in the Department of State/1/ Washington, May 24, 1964, /1/Source: Department of State, S/S-NSC Files: Lot 70 D 265, NSC Meeting, May 5, 1964, Top Secret.

65. Harrison. "Johnson, The Wise Men," 55.

66. See Sokolsky "'Lessons' of Vietnam for Canada," 444–51.

67. Donaghy, *Tolerant Allies*, 148.

68. Ross, *In the Interests of Peace*, 23.

69. Bothwell, "Further Shore," 111.

70. J. Blair Seaborn, interview with author, August 30, 2019.

71. J. Blair Seaborn, interview with author, August 30, 2019.

72. Maclear, *Vietnam*, 173.

73. Seaborn, "Mission to Hanoi," 107.

74. Robertson, "Our Man in Saigon," 14.

75. Robertson, 13.

76. Mahant and Mount, *Invisible and Inaudible*, 58.

77. Donaghy, "Minding the Minister," 140.

CHAPTER THREE

1. *Weekend Magazine*, May 27, 1967.

2. "Memorandum of Conversation, Trip to Ottawa, May 17, 1961," JFKLM, NSF, Box 18, File: Canada—General—Ottawa Trip.

3. Ellis, *Britain, America*, 6.

4. Thompson, *Pacific Basin*, 99.

5. From President Johnson to Prime Minister Pearson, Sept. 5, 1965, LAC, NSF/CF/Canada, Box 165, Vol. II, Cables, 8/64–2/65, LBJL, 22a.

6. Melakopides, *Pragmatic Idealism*, 78.

7. Levant, *Quiet Complicity*, 118.

8. Claire Culhane, "Behead and Cure: The Truth Behind Canada's Medical Aid to Vietnam," *Canadian Dimension* (December 1968): 21. Claire Culhane Papers, MUA, Published Articles, Box 32, File: December 1968.

9. Letter to Ann Hartley from Culhane, November 3, 1967, Claire Culhane Papers, MUA, Correspondence, Box 1, Feb. 1956–Dec. 1968, File: November 1967.

10. David Van Praagh, "Canadian Doctor Bitter Over Vietnam Casualties," *Winnipeg Free Press*, August 26, 1967.

11. Mick Lowe, *One Woman Army: The Life of Claire Culhane*, 128.

12. Van Praagh, "Canadian Doctor Bitter."

13. Culhane, *Why Is Canada in Vietnam?*, 36.

14. Letter to Ann Hartley from Culhane. December 28, 1967, Claire Culhane Papers, MUA, Correspondence, Box 1, Feb. 1956–Dec. 1968, File: December 1967.

15. Culhane, *Why Is Canada in Vietnam?*, 57.

16. Lowe, *One Woman Army*, 151.

17. Hutchins, *Swimmers Among the Trees*, 210.

18. Culhane, *Why Is Canada in Vietnam?*, 61–63.

19. Culhane, 66.

20. Letter to Ann Hartley from Culhane. February 1, 1968, Claire Culhane Papers, MUA, Correspondence, Box 1, Feb. 1956–Dec. 1968, File: February 1968.

21. Culhane to Vennema, March 4, 1968. Claire Culhane Papers, MUA, Correspondence, Box 1, Feb. 1956–Dec. 1968, File: March 1968.

22. Culhane to Martin, April 3, 1968, Claire Culhane Papers. MUA, Correspondence, Box 1, Feb. 1956–Dec. 1968, File: April 1968.

23. Culhane, *Why Is Canada in Vietnam?*, 89.

24. Culhane, 92.

25. Culhane, 92–93.

26. Pearson, *Mike* Vol. 2, 138.

27. English, *Worldly Years*, 364.

28. Gordon, *Political Memoir*, 281.

29. Gordon, 283.

30. Donaghy, *Tolerant Allies*, 41.

31. English, *Worldly Years*, 360.

32. "Reciprocity and World War I," in Mahant and Mount, *Introduction to Canadian-American Relations*, 100–101.

33. Cuff and Granatstein, *Ties That Bind*, 7.

34. Robinson and Ibbott, "Canadian Military Spending."

35. *Le Devoir*, January 24, 1975.

36. Levant, *Quiet Complicity*, 34.

37. *Cabinet Minutes*, February 9, 1965.

38. *Cabinet Minutes*, September 8, 1965.

39. Paul Martin, Statements and Speeches, No. 64/36. 2, LAC.

40. *Cabinet Minutes*, September 8, 1965.

41. *Globe and Mail*, January 8, 1966.

42. *Toronto Star*, March 28, 1967.

43. *Financial Post*, February 4, 1967.

44. Levant, *Quiet Complicity*, 54.

45. *Toronto Star*, May 29, 1967.

46. Levant, *Quiet Complicity*, 22.

47. CBC, *The Way It Is*, November 12, 1967, ISN. 16437.

48. Regehr, *Arms Canada*, 49.

49. *Ottawa Citizen*, December 15, 1965.

50. *Ottawa Citizen*, March 2, 1968.

51. Levant, *Quiet Complicity*, 61.

52. Claire Culhane, "Report on Project of Anti-tuberculosis Hospital Quảng Ngãi, Vietnam, Canadian Colombo Plan," prepared for Department of External Aid, Government of Canada, April 18, 1968, 15–16. Claire Culhane Papers, MUA, File: April 1968.

53. Arsenault to Culhane, May 6, 1968, Claire Culhane Papers, MUA, Correspondence, Box 1, Feb. 1956–Dec. 1968, File: May 1968.

54. Strong to Culhane, May 9, 1968, Claire Culhane Papers, MUA, Correspondence, Box 1, Feb. 1956–Dec. 1968, File: May 1968.

55. Frazier, *Women's Antiwar Diplomacy*, 5.

56. Unsigned to Culhane, June 28, 1968, Claire Culhane Papers, MUA, Correspondence, Box 1, Feb. 1956–Dec. 1968, File: June 1968.

57. Culhane to *Montreal Gazette*, April 24, 1969, Claire Culhane Papers, MUA, Correspondence, Box 1, Feb. 1956–Dec. 1968, File: April 1969.

58. Sharp to Culhane, July 18, 1968, Claire Culhane Papers, MUA, Correspondence, Box 1, Feb. 1956–Dec. 1968, File: July 1968.

59. Strong to Culhane, September 6, 1968, Claire Culhane Papers, MUA, Correspondence, Box 1, Feb. 1956–Dec. 1968, File: September 1968.

60. Lowe, *One Woman Army*, 181.

61. Lowe, 182.

62. Levitt, *Children of Privilege*, 47.

63. "Ottawa's Complicity in Vietnam," Radical Organizations Archive, MUA, Box 7, File: "Student Association to End the War in Vietnam Pamphlet," [n.d.], 9–13; Canadian Student Social and Political Organizations (1968–1977).

64. Culhane, "Behead and Cure."

65. VOW Press Release, September 30, 1968, Claire Culhane Papers, MUA, Correspondence, Box 1, Feb. 1956–Dec. 1968, File: September 1968.

66. Svahnström to Culhane, October 4, 1968, Radical Organizations Archive, MUA, Correspondence, Box 1, Feb. 1956–Dec. 1968, File: October 1968.

67. *Globe and Mail*, October 4, 1968; *Ottawa Citizen*, October 2, 1968.

68. Lowe, *One Woman Army*, 190.

69. Lowe, 191.

70. Lowe, 191.

71. Head and Trudeau, *The Canadian Way*, 181.

72. Lowe, *One Woman Army*, 193.

73. Presented to the International Press Conference, Paris, France, December 19, 1969, Claire Culhane Papers, Correspondence, Box 2, Feb. 1956–Dec. 1968, File: December 1969.

74. "Church Says Canada Must Cut War Strings," *Montreal Gazette*, December 2, 1969.

75. "Yule Vigil to Stress We've Had Enough War," *Edmonton Journal*, December 24, 1969.

76. Transcript of tape recording by *CBC 6 o'Clock News*, Ottawa, January 12, 1970, Claire Culhane Papers, MUA, Correspondence, Box 2, Feb. 1956–Dec. 1968, File: January 1970.

77. *Globe and Mail*, January 13, 1969.

78. Culhane to Trudeau, January 13, 1970, Claire Culhane Papers, MUA, Correspondence, Box 3, Feb. 1956–Dec. 1968, File: January 1970.

79. Lawless to Culhane, January 30, 1970, Claire Culhane Papers, MUA, Correspondence, Box 3, Feb. 1956–Dec. 1968, File: January 1970.

52. See Hagan, *Northern Passage*, 241; Jones, *Contending Statistics*, 34; and Surrey, *Choice of Conscience*, 5.

53. By 2019, Erickson's records were back in the historical archives with no explanation as to who had them expunged or replaced.

CHAPTER FIVE

1. Gould, *Investigations in the Military*, 59.

2. Gaffen, *Cross-Border Warriors*, 14.

3. Rachel Lea Heide, "The Clayton Knight Committee: Clandestine Recruiting of Americans for the Royal Canadian Air Force, 1940–1941," in Behiels and Stuart, *Transnationalism*, 225–27.

4. Kolb, "We are Fighting Evil," 24.

5. Levant, *Quiet Complicity*, 210.

6. House of Commons, *Debates*, February 16, 1966.

7. Gaffen, *Unknown Soldiers*, 36–37.

8. Gaffen, 36.

9. Arial, *I Volunteered*, 10.

10. "1,500 March in Toronto Protest Against War in Vietnam," *Globe and Mail*, April 26, 1971.

11. Gaffen, *Unknown Soldiers*, 159.

12. Thorne, "Born on the First of July."

13. "Canadian Vietnam Vets Fight for Benefits," CBC Radio interview, June 18, 1986, https://www.cbc.ca/archives/entry/canadian-vietnam-vets-fight-for-benefits (accessed January 2, 2019).

14. Gaffen, *Unknown Soldiers*, 39.

15. Christopher S. Wren, "Vietnam War Also Haunts Canadians Who Volunteered," *New York Times*, January 24, 1985.

16. "Viet-Oakville Man Back from Battlefront," *Oakville Beaver*, June 30, 1967.

17. Gaffen, *Unknown Soldiers*, 81.

18. Arial, *I Volunteered*, 46.

19. English, *Just Watch Me*, 166, 169.

20. Trudeau, *Memoirs*, 216–17.

21. Bothwell, *Alliance and Illusion*, 328.

22. Sharp, *Which Reminds Me*, 213–15.

23. R.D. Jackson, ICCS for Vietnam, *Minutes, 770th Meeting*, March 13, 1973, DEA Files, LAC, 2-500052-A-12-40. See also Ross, *In the Interests of Peace*, 24.

24. Granatstein and Bothwell, *Pirouette*, 57.

25. Head and Trudeau, *The Canadian Way*, 182.

26. Trudeau, *Memoirs*, 218.

27. Government of Canada, "Operation GALLANT," https://www.canada.ca/en/
    department-national-defence/services/military-history/history-heritage/
    past-operations/asia-pacific/gallant.html (accessed March 8, 2019).

28. Head and Trudeau, *The Canadian Way*, 184.

29. Chambers, *Death in the A Shau Valley*, 143.

30. Linderer, *Six Silent Men*, 213.

31. Chris Corday, "Lost to History: The Canadians Who Fought in Vietnam," *CBC
    News*, November 10, 2015, https://www.cbc.ca/news/canada/british-columbia/
    lost-to-history-the-canadians-who-fought-in-vietnam-1.3304440 (accessed
    January 5, 2019).

32. Lowell Thomas, "A Vietnam veteran, and a daughter who understands,"
    Midland Daily News, November 10, 2004.

33. Chris Nelson ("The Unknown War: Military Museums to host Canadians and
    the Vietnam War Exhibition," *Calgary Herald*, September 28, 2018) established
    the number of Canadians on the wall at 160; Chris Corday ("Lost to History")
    at 134; and Fred Gaffen (*Unknown Soldiers*, 334–39) at 79. The Canadian Vietnam
    Veterans Memorial in Windsor, Ontario, lists 147 soldiers and 4 peacekeepers
    who died in Vietnam, while the Canadian Vietnam Veterans Memorial in
    Melocheville, Quebec, lists 128.

34. Gaffen, *Unknown Soldiers*, 295.

35. Thorne, "Born on the First of July."

36. Clyde H. Farnsworth, "Canada Rebuffs Veterans of U.S. Forces in Vietnam,"
    New York Times, June 19, 1994.

37. Farnsworth, "Canada Rebuffs Veterans."

38. House of Commons, *Debates*, June 15, 1994.

39. Gaffen, *Unknown Soldiers*, 101.

40. Montgomery, "Shocked, Exhausted, and Injured," 124–25.

41. Montgomery, 137.

42. Stretch, "Psychosocial Readjustment," 189.

43. Stretch, 189.

44. Arial, *I Volunteered*, 57–58, 69.

45. Gaffen, *Unknown Soldiers*, 267–68.

CHAPTER SIX

1. Fredrik Logevall, "Laos: America's Lesser Known Human and Political Disaster
   in Southeast Asia," *Washington Post*, February 2, 2017.

2. Lindsay Murdoch, "Fury in Cambodia as US Asks To Be Paid Back Hundreds of
   Millions in War Debts," *Sydney Morning Herald*, March 11, 2017.

3. Maclear, *Vietnam*, 454.

4. Maclear, 455.
5. Karnow, *Vietnam*, 669.
6. Beiser, *Strangers at the Gate*, 34–35.
7. Molloy et al., *Running on Empty*, 18.
8. Lanphier, "Canada's Response to Refugees," 115.
9. Molloy et al., *Running on Empty*, 42.
10. Molloy et al., 67.
11. Dorais, *Cambodians, Laotians, and Vietnamese*, 7.
12. W.E. Wilmott, "The Chinese in Indochina," in Tepper, *Southeast Asian Exodus*, 78.
13. Beiser, *Strangers at the Gate*, 57.
14. Lam, *From Being Uprooted to Surviving*, 6.
15. Beiser, *Strangers at the Gate*, 82.
16. Freeman and Nguyen, *Voices from the Camps*, 8.
17. Grant, *The Boat People*, 81.
18. Freeman and Nguyen, *Voices from the Camps*, 10.
19. Kelley and Trebilcock, *Making of the Mosaic*, 397.
20. *Toronto Star*, March 21, 1979.
21. Molloy et al., *Running on Empty*, 120.
22. Molloy et al., 121.
23. Adelman, *Canada and the Indochinese Refugees*, 23.
24. Beiser, *Strangers at the Gate*, 42.
25. Molloy et al., *Running on Empty*, 237.
26. Molloy et al., 257.
27. Michael Friscolanti, "Mike Molloy, the Man Who Delivered the 'Boat People,'" *Maclean's*, September 12, 2015.
28. Kelley and Trebilcock, *Making of the Mosaic*, 387.
29. Molloy et al., *Running on Empty*, 353.
30. Axworthy, *Indochinese Refugees*, 12.
31. *Globe and Mail*, September 19, 1979.
32. Molloy et al., *Running on Empty*, 117.
33. Adelman, *Canada and the Indochinese Refugees*, 42.
34. Friscolanti, "Mike Molloy, the man who delivered the 'boat people'."
35. Adelman, *Canada and the Indochinese Refugees*, 48.
36. Molloy et al., *Running on Empty*, 152.
37. Lanphier, "Canada's Response to Refugees," 121.
38. Lanphier, 205, 241–42.
39. Freeman and Nguyen, *Voices from the Camps*, 3.
40. Axworthy, *Indochinese Refugees*, 15.
41. Adelman, *Canada and the Indochinese Refugees*, 58.

42. Beiser, *Strangers at the Gate*, 150, 154.
43. *Toronto Star*, August 8, 1979.
44. *Regina Leader-Post*, December 21, 1978.
45. *Montreal Star*, June 22, 1979.
46. *Toronto Star*, May 21, 1980.
47. Gordon Sinclair, CFRB Radio, July 31, 1979.
48. Adelman, *Canada and the Indochinese Refugees*, 143.
49. Kelley and Trebilcock, *Making of the Mosaic*, 381.
50. Beiser, *Strangers at the Gate*, 108.
51. Adelman, *Canada and the Indochinese Refugees*, 146.
52. Privy Council Office, Memorandum to Cabinet, "Indochinese Refugee Program 1979–1980," March 12, 1980, LAC, PCO 270-80MC.
53. Dorais, *Cambodians, Laotians, and Vietnamese*, 8.
54. Beiser, *Strangers at the Gate*, 120.
55. Gilad, "Refugees in Newfoundland," 379.
56. Chan and Dorais, "Family, Identity," 288.
57. Kelley and Trebilcock, *Making of the Mosaic*, 377.

CONCLUSION

1. Cited in Petraeus, "Lessons of History," 49.
2. Kinross, *Clausewitz and America*, 111.
3. Davidson, *Vietnam at War*, 810.
4. Petraeus, "Lessons of History," 50–51.
5. William Schneider, "The Vietnam Syndrome Mutates: An 'Iraq Syndrome' May Be Emerging as Disillusionment with the Iraq War Intensifies," *The Atlantic*, April 2006.
6. Peter C. Newman, "Our American Godfather and How the Vietnamization of the U.S. Made Us Canadians," *Maclean's*, November 1, 1972.
7. Harrison and Friesen, *Canadian Society*, 143.
8. Horowitz, "On the Fear of Nationalism," 7–9.
9. Azzi, "Nationalist Movement," 216.
10. McGill, *War Is Here*, 4, 6.
11. Bothwell, *Your Country, My Country*, 344.
12. Taylor, *Snow Job*, iii.
13. Sokolsky, "'Lessons' of Vietnam for Canada," 449.
14. Adam Chapnick, "The Golden Age: A Canadian Foreign Policy Paradox," 219.
15. Bothwell, *Alliance and Illusion*, 195.
16. Chrétien, *My Years as Prime Minister*, 311.
17. "Antiwar Protests Held Worldwide," *Globe and Mail*, March 16, 2003.

18. Tim Harper, "Canadians Back Chrétien on War, Poll Finds," *Toronto Star*, March 22, 2003.

19. Plamondon, *Shawinigan Fox*, 121.

20. Stursberg, *Lester Pearson*, 125.

21. House of Commons Canada, Standing Committee on Foreign Affairs and International Development, "Minutes of Proceedings," November 7, 2017, http://www.ourcommons.ca/DocumentViewer/en/42-1/FAAE/meeting-79/minutes (accessed March 15, 2019).

22. Global Affairs Canada, "Report on Exports of Military Goods from Canada—2017," https://www.international.gc.ca/controls-controles/report-rapports/mil-2017.aspx?lang=eng (accessed March 15, 2019).

23. Michael Tutton, "Canada Can Use Lessons of Vietnam Airlifts in Syrian Refugee Crisis: Joe Clark," *Ottawa Citizen*, September 4, 2015.

24. Les Perreaux, "Canadian Attitudes Toward Immigrants, Refugees Remain Positive: Study," *Globe and Mail*, March 22, 2018.

25. Ariel Garfinkel, "The Vietnam War Is Over—The Bombs Remain," *New York Times*, March 20, 2018.

26. Jennifer Newton, "Four Decades after Agent Orange—Heartbreaking Pictures Show Even Now Babies in Vietnam Are Being Born with Horrific Defects," *Daily Mail*, April 25, 2014.

27. Director General, Veterans Affairs, "Exposure to Agent Orange and Other Unregistered US Military Herbicides," Document ID: 1190, November 28, 2013, http://www.veterans.gc.ca/eng/about-us/policy/document/1190 (accessed January 3, 2019).

28. "Agent Orange Once Sprayed Across Northern Ontario, Drenching Teen Workers," *Waterloo Region Record*, February 16, 2011.

29. Maria Babbage, "Agent Orange Used Widely in Ontario over Decades, Minister Says," *Globe and Mail*, February 28, 2011.

30. Thomas Jarmyn, "Letter to the Minister of Veterans Affairs Regarding Agent Orange Claims," November 29, 2017; http://www.vrab-tacra.gc.ca/Documents/Agent-Orange-letter-Agent-Orange-lettre-eng.cfm (accessed March 26, 2019).

31. George W. Ball, "The Lessons of Vietnam," *New York Times*, April 1, 1973.

32. Roy, *Sherwood Lett*, 167.

33. "Top Secret Mission to Hanoi During Vietnam Conflict," *CBC Radio Archives*, February 17, 2003, https://www.cbc.ca/player/play/1631530778 (accessed March 12, 2019).

34. Lowe, *One Woman Army*, 229.

BIBLIOGRAPHY

INTERVIEWS AND CORRESPONDENCE

Gary Birdsong

Doug Carey

Dick Crawford

Joe Erickson

Beth Jansen

Blair Seaborn

Roisin Sheehy-Culhane

Gary Townsend

Judy Trinh

Rebecca Trinh

NEWSPAPERS AND PERIODICALS

The Atlantic

Canadian Forum

Daily Mail

Edmonton Journal

Globe and Mail

Hamilton Spectator

Legion Magazine

Maclean's

Midland Daily News

Montreal Star

New York Times

Newsweek

Oakville Beaver

Ottawa Citizen

Peterborough Examiner

Regina Leader-Post

Saturday Night

Time

Toronto Star

Vancouver Sun

The Varsity

Washington Post

Waterloo Region Record

Weekend

Zoomer Magazine

PRIMARY SOURCES

John F. Kennedy Library and Museum, Boston (JFKLM)
    Foreign Relations of the United States (FRUS) Files
    National Security Files

President's Office Files
Robert McNamara Papers

Library and Archives Canada, Ottawa (LAC)
Department of External Affairs (DEA) Files
Holmes Papers
Pearson Papers
St. Laurent Papers
Sherwood Lett Papers
Cabinet Minutes
Hansard

McMaster University Archives, Hamilton (MUA)
Claire Culhane Papers
Radical Organizations Archive

SECONDARY SOURCES

Adelman, Howard. *Canada and the Indochinese Refugees* (Regina: L.A. Weigl
   Educational Associates, 1982).
Arial, Tracey. *I Volunteered: Canadian Vietnam Vets Remember* (Winnipeg: Watson and
   Dyer, 1996).
Axworthy, Lloyd. *Indochinese Refugees: The Canadian Response, 1979–1980* (Ottawa:
   Immigration and Employment Canada, 1980).
Azzi, Stephen. "The Nationalist Movement in English Canada." In Lara Campbell,
   Dominique Clément, and Gregory S. Kealy (eds.), *Debating Dissent: Canada and
   the Sixties* (Toronto: University of Toronto Press, 2012), 213–28.
Baritz, Loren. *Backfire: Vietnam—The Myths That Made Us Fight, the Illusions that
   Helped Us Lose, the Legacy that Haunts Us Today* (New York: Ballantine Books,
   1985).
Baskir, Lawrence M., and William A. Strauss. *Chance and Circumstance: The Draft, the
   War, and the Vietnam Generation* (New York: Alfred A. Knopf, 1978).
Behiels, Michael, and Reginald C. Stuart (eds.). *Transnationalism: Canada-United
   States* (Montreal & Kingston: McGill-Queen's University Press, 2010).
Beiser, Morton. *Strangers at the Gate: The 'Boat People's' First Ten Years in Canada*
   (Toronto: University of Toronto Press, 1999).
Blanchette, Arthur E. (ed.). *Canadian Peacekeepers in Indochina, 1954–1973: Recollections,*
   Rideau Series, no. 2 (Ottawa: Golden Dog Press, 2002).
Boot, Max. *The Road Not Taken: Edward Lansdale and the American Tragedy in Vietnam*
   (New York: Liveright, 2018).

Bothwell, Robert. *Alliance and Illusion: Canada and the World, 1945–1984* (Vancouver: University of British Columbia Press, 2007).

———. "The Further Shore: Canada and Vietnam." *International Journal* 56, no. 1 (Winter 2000/2001): 89–114.

———. *Your Country, My Country: A Unified History of the United States and Canada* (New York: Oxford University Press, 2016).

Brewster, Hugh. "Remembering the Draft Evaders." *Zoomer Magazine*, January 21, 2013.

Brocheux, Pierre. *Ho Chi Minh: A Biography* (Cambridge: Cambridge University Press, 2003).

Brosnan, Vivienne. "The International Control Commission for Vietnam: The Diplomatic and Military Context" (master's thesis, University of British Columbia, 1975).

Cameron, David. "The Making of a Polluter: A Social History of Uniroyal Chemical in Elmira." In Michael D. Mehta and Éric Ouellet (eds.), *Environmental Sociology: Theory and Practice* (North York, ON: Captus Press, 1995), 297–320.

Chambers, Larry. *Death in the A Shau Valley: L Company LRRPs in Vietnam, 1969–70* (New York: Ballantine, 1995).

Chan, Kwok Bun, and Louis-Jacques Dorais. "Family, Identity, and the Vietnamese Diaspora: The Quebec Experience." *Sojourn: Journal of Social Issues in Southeast Asia* 13, no. 2 (October 1998): 285–308.

Chapnick, Adam. *Canada's Voice: The Public Life of John Wendell Holmes* (Vancouver: University of British Columbia Press, 2009).

———. "The Golden Age: A Canadian Foreign Policy Paradox." *International Journal* 64, no. 1 (2008/2009): 205–22.

Chomsky, Noam. *Necessary Illusions: Thought Control in Democratic Societies* (Toronto: CBC Enterprises, 1989).

Chrétien, Jean. *My Years as Prime Minister* (Toronto: Vintage Canada, 2008).

Churchill, David. "When Home Becomes Away: American Expatriates and New Social Movements in Toronto" (PhD dissertation, Chicago: University of Chicago Press, 2001).

Clarkson, Stephen (ed.). *An Independent Foreign Policy for Canada?* (Toronto: McClelland & Stewart, 1968).

Cormier, Jeffrey J. "The Canadianization Movement in Context." *Canadian Journal of Sociology/Cahiers canadiens de sociologie* 30, no. 3 (Summer 2005): 351–70.

Cuff, R.D., and J.L. Granatstein. *Ties That Bind: Canadian-American Relations*, 2nd ed. (Toronto: Samuel Stevens Hakkert, 1977).

Culhane, Claire. *Why Is Canada in Vietnam? The Truth about Our Foreign Aid* (Toronto: NC Press, 1972).

Dallek, Robert. *An Unfinished Life: John F. Kennedy, 1917–1963* (Boston: Little, Brown, 2003).

Davidson, Phillip B. *Vietnam at War: The History, 1946–1975* (New York: Oxford University Press, 1988).

Dickerson, James. *North to Canada: Men and Women Against the Vietnam War* (Westport, CT: Praeger, 1999).

Doan. *Escape from Vietnam: The Story of Doan* (Montreal: Optimum, 1984).

Donaghy, Greg. *Grit: The Life and Politics of Paul Martin, Sr.* (Vancouver: University of British Columbia Press, 2015).

———. "Minding the Minister: Pearson, Martin and American Policy in Asia, 1963–1967." In Norman Hillmer, *Pearson: The Unlikely Gladiator* (Montreal & Kingston: McGill-Queen's University Press, 1999), 131–149.

———. "The Rise and Fall of Canadian Military Assistance in the Developing World, 1952–1971." *Canadian Military History* 4, no. 1, article 7 (1995), 83–93.

———. *Tolerant Allies: Canada and the United States, 1963–1968* (Montreal & Kingston: McGill-Queen's University Press, 2002).

Dorais, Louis-Jacques. *The Cambodians, Laotians, and Vietnamese in Canada* (Ottawa: Canadian Historical Association, 2000).

Dorais, Louis-Jacques, Kwok B. Chan, and Doreen M. Indra (eds.). *Ten Years Later: Indochinese Communities in Canada* (Montreal: Canadian Asian Studies Association, 1988).

Duiker, William J. *Ho Chi Minh: A Life* (New York: Hachette, 2001).

Dumbrell, John (ed.). *Vietnam and the Antiwar Movement: An International Perspective* (Aldershot: Avebury, 1989).

Eayrs, James. *In Defence of Canada* Vol. 4, *Growing Up Allied* (Toronto: University of Toronto Press, 1980).

———. *In Defence of Canada* Vol. 5, *Indochina: The Roots of Complicity* (Toronto: University of Toronto Press, 1983).

Eden, Anthony. *The Memoirs of Sir Anthony Eden: Full Circle* (London: Cassell, 1960).

Eisenhower, Dwight D. *Mandate to Change, 1953–1956* (New York: Doubleday, 1963).

Ellis, Sylvia. *Britain, America, and the Vietnam War* (Westport: Praeger, 2004).

Emerick, Kenneth Fred. *War Resisters Canada: The World of the American Military-Political Refugees* (Knox: Pennsylvania Free Press, 1972).

English, John. *Just Watch Me: The Life of Pierre Elliott Trudeau, 1968–2000* (Toronto: Vintage Canada, 2010).

———. *The Worldly Years: The Life of Lester Pearson* (Toronto: Knopf Canada, 1992).

English, John, and Norman Hillmer (eds.). *Making a Difference? Canada's Foreign Policy in a Changing World Order* (Toronto: Lester, 1992).

Fantina, Robert. *Desertion and the American Soldier, 1776–2006* (New York: Algora, 2006).

Foley, Michael S. *Confronting the War Machine: Draft Resistance During the Vietnam War* (Chapel Hill & London: University of North Carolina Press, 2003).

Foner, Eric. *Gateway to Freedom: The Hidden History of America's Fugitive Slaves* (London: Oxford University Press, 2015).

Frazier, Jessica M. *Women's Antiwar Diplomacy during the Vietnam War Era* (Chapel Hill: University of North Carolina Press, 2017).

Freeman, James M., and Nguyen Dinh Huu. *Voices from the Camps: Vietnamese Children Seeking Asylum* (Seattle & London: University of Washington Press, 2003).

Gaffen, Fred. *Cross-Border Warriors: Canadians in American Forces, Americans in Canadian Forces: From the Civil War to the Gulf* (Toronto: Dundurn Press, 1995).

———. *Unknown Soldiers: Canadians in the Vietnam War* (Toronto: Dundurn Press, 1990).

Gilad, Lisa. "Refugees in Newfoundland: Families after Flight." *Journal of Comparative Family Studies* 21, no. 3 (Autumn 1990): 379–96.

Goldsworthy, Ryan. "The Canadian Way: The Case of Canadian Vietnam War Veterans." *Canadian Military Journal* 15, no. 3 (Summer 2015): 48–53.

Gordon, Walter. *A Political Memoir* (Toronto: McClelland & Stewart, 1977).

Gould, Benjamin. *Investigations in the Military and Anthropological Statistics of American Soldiers.* (New York: Arno Press, 1979).

Granatstein, J.L. "Canada and Peacekeeping: Image and Reality." *Canadian Forum* 54, no. 643 (August 1974): 14–19.

———. *Yankee Go Home? Canadians and Anti-Americanism* (Toronto: HarperCollins, 1996).

Granatstein, J.L., and Robert Bothwell. *Pirouette: Pierre Trudeau and Canadian Foreign Policy* (Toronto: University of Toronto Press, 1990).

Grant, Bruce. *The Boat People: An "Age" Investigation* (Harmondsworth: Penguin Books, 1979).

Hagan, John. *Northern Passage: American Vietnam War Resisters in Canada* (Cambridge, MA: Harvard University Press, 2001).

Haig-Brown, Alan. *Hell No, We Won't Go: Vietnam Draft Resisters in Canada* (Vancouver: Raincoast Books, 1996).

Hansen, Peter. "Bắc Di Cư: Catholic Refugees from the North of Vietnam, and Their Role in the Southern Republic, 1954–1959." *Journal of Vietnamese Studies* 4, no. 3 (Fall 2009): 173–211.

Harrison, Benjamin T. "Johnson, The Wise Men and Vietnam 'Peace' Publicity." *Peace Research* 32, no. 2 (May 2000): 53–71.

Harrison, Trevor, and John W. Friesen. *Canadian Society in the Twenty-First Century: An Historical Sociological Approach* (Toronto: Women's Press, 2010).

Head, Ivan, and Pierre Trudeau. *The Canadian Way: Shaping Canada's Foreign Policy, 1968–1984* (Toronto: McClelland & Stewart, 1995).

Heineman, Kenneth J. *Campus Wars: The Peace Movement at American State Universities in the Vietnam Era* (New York: New York University Press, 1993).

Herring, George C. *America's Longest War: The United States and Vietnam, 1950–1975* (New York: Wiley, 1979).

Hewitt, Steve. *Spying 101: The RCMP's Secret Activities at Canadian Universities, 1917–1997* (Toronto: University of Toronto Press, 2002).

Hoang, Tuan. "The Early South Vietnamese Critique of Communism." In Tuong Vu and Wasana Wongsurawat (eds.), *Dynamics of the Cold War in Asia* (New York: Palgrave Macmillan, 2009), 17–32.

Holmes, John W. *The Better Part of Valour: Essays on Canadian Diplomacy* (Toronto: McClelland & Stewart, 1970).

———. "Geneva, 1954." *International Journal* 22, no. 3 (Summer 1967): 470–71.

———. *The Shaping of Peace: Canada and the Search for World Order, 1943–1957* Vol. 2 (Toronto: University of Toronto Press, 1982).

Horowitz, Gad. "On the Fear of Nationalism—Nationalism and Socialism: A Sermon to the Moderates." *Canadian Dimension* 4, no. 4 (May–June 1967): 1–9.

Hutchins, Joel M. *Swimmers Among the Trees: SEAL Operations in the Vietnam War* (New York: Presido Press, 1996).

Jacobs, Seth. *America's Miracle Man in Vietnam, Ngo Dinh Diem: Religion, Race and U.S. Intervention in Southeast Asia* (Durham, NC: Duke University Press, 2004).

———. *Cold War Mandarin: Ngo Dinh Diem and the Origins of America's War in Vietnam* (Lanham, MD: Rowman and Littlefield, 2006).

John, Henry Richard Lawrence. "Resisting the War in 'Little Brother Country': Vietnam War Exiles, Identity Crisis and Canadianization" (master's thesis: Durham University, 2001).

Jones, Joseph. *Contending Statistics: The Numbers for U.S. Vietnam War Resisters in Canada* (Vancouver: Quarter Sheaf, 2005).

Joyal, Serge, and Judith Seidman (eds.). *Reflecting on Our Past and Embracing Our Future: A Senate Initiative for Canada* (Montreal & Kingston: McGill-Queen's University Press, 2017).

Kahin, George McTurnan, and John W. Lewis. *The United States in Vietnam: An Analysis in Depth of the History of America's Involvement in Vietnam* (New York: Dial Press, 1969).

Karnow, Stanley. *Vietnam: A History* (New York: Viking Press, 1983).

Kasinsky, Renée Goldsmith. *Refugees from Militarism: Draft-Age Americans in Canada* (Fredericton, NB: Transaction Books, 1976).

Kelley, Ninette, and Michael Trebilcock. *The Making of the Mosaic: A History of Canadian Immigration Policy*, 2nd ed. (Toronto: University of Toronto Press, 2010).

Kinross, Stuart. *Clausewitz and America: Strategic Thought and Practice from Vietnam to Iraq* (London & New York: Routledge, Taylor & Francis Group, 2008).

Kolb, Richard. "We are Fighting Evil: Canadians in Afghanistan." *Veterans of Foreign Wars* (March 2007).

Kusch, Frank. *All American Boys: Draft Dodgers in Canada from the Vietnam War* (Westport, CT: Praeger, 2001).

Lam, L. *From Being Uprooted to Surviving: Resettlement of the Vietnamese-Chinese "Boat People"* (Toronto: York Lanes Press, 1996).

Lanphier, C. Michael. "Canada's Response to Refugees." *International Migration Review* 15, no. 1–2 (Spring–Summer 1981): 113–30.

Laurie, Clayton D., and Andres Vaart. *CIA and the Wars in Southeast Asia, 1947–75: A Studies in Intelligence Anthology* (Washington, DC: Center for the Study of Intelligence, 2016).

Lawrence, Mark Atwood. *The Vietnam War: A Concise International History* (New York: Oxford University Press, 2008).

Lawrence, Mark Atwood, and Fredrik Logevall (eds.). *The First Vietnam War: Colonial Conflict and Cold War Crisis* (Cambridge, MA: Harvard University Press, 2007).

Lerner, Mitchell. "Four Years and a World of Difference: The Evolution of Lyndon Johnson and American Foreign Policy." *Southwestern Historical Quarterly* 107, no. 1 (July 2003): 68–95.

Levant, Victor. *Quiet Complicity: Canadian Involvement in the Vietnam War* (Toronto: Between the Lines, 1986).

Levitt, Cyril. *Children of Privilege: Student Revolt in the Sixties; A Study of Student Movements in Canada, the United States, and West Germany* (Toronto: University of Toronto Press, 1984).

Linderer, Gary A. *Six Silent Men* (New York: Ballantine, 1997).

Logevall, Fredrik. *Choosing War: The Lost Chance for Peace and the Escalation of War in Vietnam* (Berkeley: University of California Press, 1999).

Long, Ngo Vinh. *Before the Revolution: The Vietnamese Peasants Under the French* (New York: Columbia University Press, 1991).

Lowe, Mick. *One Woman Army: The Life of Claire Culhane* (Toronto: Macmillan Canada,1992).

Maclear, Michael. *Vietnam: The Ten Thousand Day War* (London: Thames Mandarin, 1981).

Mahant, Edelgard E., and Graeme S. Mount. *An Introduction to Canadian-American Relations* (Toronto: Methuen, 1984).

————. *Invisible and Inaudible in Washington: American Policies towards Canada during the Cold War* (Vancouver: UBC Press, 1999).

Maneli, Miecczyslaw. *War of the Vanquished.* (New York: Harper and Row, 1971).

Martin, Lawrence. *The Presidents and the Prime Ministers: Washington and Ottawa Face to Face; The Myth of Bilateral Bliss, 1867–1982* (Toronto: Doubleday Canada, 1982).

Martin, Paul. *A Very Public Life: So Many Worlds* Vol. 2 (Toronto: Deneau, 1985).

Mattilla, J. Peter. "G.I. Bill Benefits and Enrollments: How Did Vietnam Veterans Fare?" *Social Science Quarterly* 59, no. 3 (December 1978): 535–45.

Maxwell, Donald W. "Religion and Politics at the Border: Canadian Church Support for American Vietnam War Resisters." *Journal of Church and State* 48, no. 4 (Autumn 2006): 807–29.

McGill, Robert. *War Is Here: The Vietnam War and Canadian Literature* (Montreal & Kingston: McGill-Queen's University Press, 2017).

McMaster, H.R. *Dereliction of Duty: Johnson, McNamara, the Joint Chiefs of Staff, and the Lies That Led to Vietnam* (New York: HarperCollins, 1998).

McNamara, Robert. *In Retrospect: The Tragedy and Lessons of Vietnam* (New York: Vintage, 1995).

Melakopides, Costas. *Pragmatic Idealism: Canadian Foreign Policy, 1945–1995* (Montreal & Kingston: McGill-Queen's University Press, 1998).

Moise, Edwin E. "Land Reform and Land Reform Errors in North Vietnam." *Pacific Affairs* 49 (Spring 1976): 70–92.

————. "The Mirage of Negotiations." In Lloyd C. Gardner and Ted Gittinger (eds.), *The Search for Peace in Vietnam, 1964–1968* (College Station: Texas A and M University Press, 2004), 73–82.

Molloy, Michael, Peter Duschinsky, Kurt F. Jensen, and Robert J Shalka. *Running on Empty: Canada and the Indochinese Refugees, 1975–1980* (Montreal & Kingston: McGill-Queen's University Press, 2017)

Montgomery, Adam. "Shocked, Exhausted, and Injured: The Canadian Military and Veterans' Experience of Trauma from 1914 to 2014" (PhD dissertation, University of Saskatchewan, 2015).

Moss, George Donelson. *Vietnam: An American Ordeal*, 6th ed. (London: Routledge, Taylor & Francis Group, 2010).

Mount, Graeme Stewart. *Canada's Enemies: Spies and Spying in the Peaceable Kingdom* (Toronto: Dundurn Press, 1993).

Murphy, Aisling. "Journeys to the North Country Fair: Exploring the Vietnam War Migration to Vancouver" (PhD dissertation, University of Alberta, 2001).

Newman, John M. *JFK and Vietnam: Deception, Intrigue, and the Struggle for Power* (New York: Warner Books, 1992).

Owram, Doug. *Born at the Right Time: A History of the Baby Boom Generation* (Toronto: University of Toronto Press, 1997).

Palmer, Bryan D. *Canada's 1960s: The Ironies of Identity in a Rebellious Era* (Toronto: University of Toronto Press, 2009).

Pearson, Lester. *Mike: The Memoirs of the Rt. Honourable Lester B. Pearson* Vol. 2, *1948–1957* (Toronto: University of Toronto Press, 1973).

———. *Mike: The Memoirs of the Rt. Honourable Lester B. Pearson* Vol. 3, *1957–1968* (Toronto: University of Toronto Press, 1975).

Petraeus, David H. "Lessons of History and Lessons of Vietnam." *Parameters* (Winter 2010–11): 50–51.

Plamondon, Bob. *The Shawinigan Fox: How Jean Chrétien Defied the Elites and Reshaped Canada* (Ottawa: Great River Media, 2017).

Porter, Gareth. "Coercive Diplomacy in Vietnam: The Tonkin Gulf Crisis Reconsidered." In Jayne Susan Werner and David Hunt (eds.), *The American War in Vietnam* (Ithaca, NY: Southeast Asia Program, 1993).

Preston, Andrew. "Balancing War and Peace: Canadian Foreign Policy and the Vietnam War, 1961–1965." *Diplomatic History* 27, no. 1 (January 2003): 73–111.

Ray, J.Y. "The Politics of Conference: The Political Conference on Korea in Geneva, 26 April–15 June 1954." *Journal of Contemporary History* 34, no. 3 (July 1999): 399–416.

Regehr, Ernie. *Arms Canada: The Deadly Business of Military Exports* (Toronto: James Lorimer, 1987).

Robertson, Terence. "Our Man in Saigon." *Maclean's*, November 15, 1965, 11–13, 42–44.

Robinson, Bill, and Peter Ibbott. "Canadian Military Spending: How Does the Current Level Compare to Historical Levels?" Project Ploughshares, December 1, 2003.

Ross, Douglas A. *In the Interests of Peace: Canada and Vietnam, 1954–1973* (Toronto: University of Toronto Press, 1984).

———. "Middlepowers as Extra-Regional Balancer Powers: Canada, India, and Indochina, 1954–62." *Pacific Affairs* 55, no. 2 (Summer 1982): 185–209.

Roy, Reginald H. *Sherwood Lett: His Life and Times* (Vancouver: University of British Columbia Alumni Association, 1991).

SarDesai, D.R. *Indian Foreign Policy in Cambodia, Laos, and Vietnam, 1947–1964* (Berkeley: University of California Press, 1968).

Satin, Mark (ed.). *Manual for Draft-Age Immigrants to Canada* (Toronto: Anansi, 1968).

Sharp, Mitchell. *Which Reminds Me . . .: A Political Memoir* (Toronto: University of Toronto Press, 1995).

Sheehan, Neil. *A Bright Shining Lie: John Paul Vann and America in Vietnam* (New York: Random House, 1988).

Smith, Miriam. *A Civil Society? Collective Actors in Canadian Political Life* (Peterborough, ON: Broadview Press, 2005).

Sokolsky, Joel. "The 'Lessons' of Vietnam for Canada: Complicity, Irrelevance, Earnestness, or Realism?" *International Journal* 69, no. 3 (September 2014): 444–51.

Squires, Jessica. *Building Sanctuary: The Movement to Support Vietnam War Resisters in Canada, 1965–1973* (Vancouver: University of British Columbia Press, 2013).

Stretch, R.H. "Psychosocial Readjustment of Canadian Vietnam Veterans." *Journal of Consulting and Clinical Psychology* 59, no. 1 (February 1991): 188–89.

Stursberg, Peter. *Lester Pearson and the American Dilemma* (Toronto: Doubleday, 1980).

Surrey, David S. *Choice of Conscience: Vietnam Era Military and Draft Resisters in Canada* (Westport, CT: Praeger, 1982).

Taylor, Charles. *Snow Job: Canada, the United States and Vietnam (1954–1973)* (Toronto: Anansi, 1974).

Tepper, Elliot L. (ed). *Southeast Asian Exodus: From Tradition to Resettlement* (Ottawa: Canadian Asian Studies Association, 1980).

Thakur, Ramesh. "Peacekeeping and Foreign Policy: Canada, India and the International Commission in Vietnam, 1954–1965." *British Journal of International Studies* 6, no. 2 (July 1980): 125–53.

———. *Peacekeeping in Vietnam: Canada, India, Poland, and the International Commission* (Edmonton: University of Alberta Press, 1984).

Thayer, Carlyle A. *War By Other Means: National Liberation and Revolution in Viet-Nam, 1954–60* (Sydney: Allen & Unwin, 1989).

Thompson, Roger C. *The Pacific Basin Since 1945: An International History*, 2nd ed. (London: Routledge, Taylor & Francis Group, 2001).

Thorne, Stephen J. "Born on the First of July." *Legion Magazine*, January 19, 2018.

Todd, Jack. *A Taste of Metal: A Deserter's Story* (Toronto: HarperCollins, 2001).

Tran, Quan Tue. "Remembering the Boat People Exodus: A Tale of Two Memorials." *Journal of Vietnamese Studies* 7, no. 3 (Fall 2012): 80–121.

Trudeau, Pierre Elliott. *Conversations with Canadians* (Toronto: University of Toronto Press, 1972).

———. *Memoirs* (Toronto: McClelland & Stewart, 1993).

Vallero, Daniel A. *Biomedical Ethics for Engineers: Ethics and Decision Making in Biomedical and Biosystem Engineering* (Burlington, VT: Academic Press, 2011).

Warner, Geoffrey. "Lyndon Johnson's War? Part I: Escalation." *International Affairs* 79, no. 4 (July 2003): 829–53.

Watt, Alan. "The Geneva Agreements in 1954 in Relation to Vietnam." *Australian Quarterly* 39, no. 2 (June 1967): 7–23.

Williams, Roger Neville. *The New Exiles: War Resisters in Canada* (New York: Liveright Publishers, 1971).

ACKNOWLEDGEMENTS

I am indebted to Blair Seaborn, Joe Erickson, Doug Carey, and Rebecca Trinh for speaking with me about their experiences. Reliving some memories was difficult but they remained dedicated to allowing their stories to be told as a way to help tell a greater story. Joe Erickson's sister Beth Jansen, Claire Culhane's daughter Roisin Sheehy-Culhane, and Rebecca Trinh's daughter Judy Trinh helped me with facts and ensured that I captured the right spirit. Dick Crawford, Gary Townsend, and Gary Birdsong added to my understanding of the time, people, and sacrifices.

The good people at Trent University's Bata Library, Library and Archives Canada, McMaster University's Mills Library and Archives, the University of British Columbia's Archives, and the John F. Kennedy Presidential Library and Museum could not have been more enthusiastic in providing help and support.

My literary agent, Jackie Kaiser of Westwood Creative Artists, offered unwavering faith and support, as did Craig Pyette at Knopf Random Canada. I am also indebted to KRC Publisher Anne Collins and Lynn Henry, the publishing director of Knopf Canada. The talented and patient Pamela Murray did an exceptional job editing the manuscript and then shepherding it through the publishing process. Jane McWhinney deserves praise and thanks for her skills as a copy editor, and I am grateful as well to proofreader Sue Sumeraj. Thank you once again to the hard-working Shona Cook for her energy and skills as publicist.

Sue Boyko reads and improves everything I write while affording the support and allowing me the freedom needed to dedicate endless hours to research and writing. To Sue I owe everything.

INDEX

JOHN BOYKO is the author of seven previous books, including *Cold Fire: Kennedy's Northern Front*, which was shortlisted for the Dafoe Literary Award for non-fiction, and *Blood and Daring: How Canada Fought the American Civil War and Forged a Nation*, which was shortlisted for a Governor General's Literary Award for its English-to-French translation, *Voisins et ennemis. La guerre de Sécession et l'invention du Canada*. Boyko is an op-ed contributor to the *Globe and Mail*, *Calgary Herald*, *Ottawa Citizen*, *Montreal Gazette*, *Maclean's*, and more. He also writes entries for the Canadian Encyclopedia.

He has addressed audiences across Canada and appeared on radio and television discussing his books and various historical and current political issues. *The Globe and Mail* has called Boyko "a distinguished scholar of Canadian political history" and the *Winnipeg Free Press* has praised his "encyclopaedic knowledge of Canadian history."

Boyko has earned degrees from Trent, Queen's, and McMaster universities, served on and chaired many boards, and been elected to municipal office. He lives in Lakefield, Ontario.

www.johnbokyo.com
Twitter: @johnwboyko